# Government in the Federal Republic of Germany

## THE EXECUTIVE AT WORK

BY

NEVIL JOHNSON

PERGAMON PRESS

Oxford · New York · Toronto
Sydney · Braunschweig

Pergamon Press Ltd., Headington Hill Hall, Oxford

Pergamon Press Inc., Maxwell House, Fairview Park, Elmsford,
New York 10523

Pergamon of Canada Ltd., 207 Queen's Quay West, Toronto 1

Pergamon Press (Aust.) Pty. Ltd., 19a Boundary Street,
Rushcutters Bay, N.S.W. 2011, Australia

Vieweg & Sohn GmbH, Burgplatz 1, Braunschweig

Copyright © 1973 Pergamon Press Ltd.

First edition 1973

**Library of Congress Cataloging in Publication Data**

Johnson, Nevil.
Government in the Federal Republic of Germany.

Bibliography: p.
1. Germany (Federal Republic, 1949–   )—
Executive departments. 2. Federal government—
Germany (Federal Republic, 1949–   ).      I. Title.
JN3971.A55 1973a       354'.43'04       73–12759
ISBN 0–08–017699–2

*Printed in Great Britain by The Anchor Press Ltd., Tiptree, Essex*

*To Ulla*

9

# Contents

PREFACE      ix

## 1. The Inheritance of the State      1

*The Absence of a Unitary State*      2
*German Constitutionalism and the Rechtsstaat*      7
*The Separation between State and Society*      16

## 2. The Political Framework of the Federal Republic      21

*The Revolution of Destruction and Its Aftermath*      21
*The Reconstruction of Political Institutions*      24
*The Reshaping of the Party System*      30
*The Social and Economic Context of Political Reconstruction*      39

## 3. Federal Executive Leadership      44

*The Federal Government*      45
*The Federal Chancellor*      49
*Federal Ministers*      60
*Ministers and Their Departments*      64
*The Social Character of West German Governments*      69
*Executive Stability and Continuity*      71

## 4. The Federal Administration      74

*The Federal Ministries*      74
    *Allocation of Functions*      74
    *Scale and Structure*      76
*The Federal Departments and Their External Relations*      81
*Relations between the Federal Departments*      91
*A Pluralist Executive*      96

vii

**5.** **Federalism and Decentralisation in West German Government** 98

*The Main Features of German Federalism* 99
*The Länder and Federal Legislation* 106
*The Länder within the Framework of German Administration* 110
*The Financial Basis of Federalism* 120
*Other Aspects of Decentralisation within the Federal Structure* 126
*Trends in German Federalism* 131

**6.** **The Bureaucracy in the Federal Republic** 138

*The Historical Heritage* 138
*The Organisation of the Public Services* 144
*Officials—Beamte* 149
*Politics, Policy-making and Patronage* 153

**7.** **Controlling the Executive** 164

*The Judicial Modes of Control* 164
*The Internal Control of Financial Performance* 172
*Political Controls over the Activities of Government* 176

**8.** **The Challenge of Expanding Government** 185

*Co-operation and Co-ordination* 186
*Planning the Use of Resources* 193
*The European Community Dimension* 200
*Political Change and the Rule of Law* 204

BIBLIOGRAPHY 211

INDEX 213

# *Preface*

THE Federal Republic of Germany is one of two successor states of a single German national state which, under differing political régimes, endured for only seventy-four years. The immediate cause of the collapse of modern Germany was, of course, defeat in the Second World War. Its subsequent political division was an inevitable consequence of the hostility between the two super-powers, the U.S.A. and the Soviet Union, and of the determination of the latter to ensure that it and its satellites should fill the power vacuum created by the destruction of the German position in Eastern Europe. In essentials this situation has persisted now for over a quarter of a century, and the existence of two German states has become an apparently permanent fact of the European political order.

The evolution of these two states has been markedly different. The smaller of the two, the German Democratic Republic, has had to develop within the narrow confines laid down by Soviet hegemony. The other, the Federal Republic, rapidly gained more or less complete sovereignty and became a major power both within the Western European context and within the wider North Atlantic defence system. But for reasons both practical and moral, the Federal Republic has had to use its sovereignty with care. For many years after 1949 its leaders were acutely aware of the extent to which the country's security depended on its commitment to the collective defence system led by the U.S.A. Even now, despite a climate of détente, this fundamental dependence persists. Similarly, in relation to its European neighbours the Federal Republic saw good reasons for accepting limitations on its autonomy both in defence and economic relations: only in this way could it successfully establish those ties of interdependence which were a support for its own exposed position. Nor were the moral reasons for accepting many restraints on its freedom of action unimportant. Those who built up the Federal Republic, some of whom are still in authority today, were highly sensitive to the need for a new start in relations with the outside world, for only on this basis could political trust in the Federal Republic grow and the painful memories of the past be effaced.

That the Federal Republic has regained the full confidence of her Western allies, and to some extent even softened the suspicions of her neighbours to the East, owes much to the successful construction of a stable democratic political system. Given the history of modern Germany and the condition of the country in 1945, this is an astonishing achievement. Indeed, it is one of the most striking examples known of the complete reshaping of the political habits and relationships of a society. Today political scientists take it for granted that the Federal Republic belongs to the still relatively small group of liberal democracies: it has a party system approximating to the two-party configuration, Governments are stable and effective, citizen awareness of politics is relatively keen, there is a broad plurality of interests with access to policy-making, and there are effective guarantees of rights granted by constitutional law. German political life has taken on qualities of sobriety and readiness to compromise which were often notably absent in the past. All in all, therefore, it is reasonable to put the Federal Republic alongside such countries as Sweden, Holland, Norway or Switzerland, countries in which political life usually proceeds at an even tempo and people are interested more in practical accommodation than in the accentuation of their conflicting interests.

This short study is not primarily concerned with an analysis of the reasons for this pervasive change in the style and content of German politics, though it may indirectly throw light on this evolution. The emphasis in this work is firmly on government as an executive activity, on the institutional framework which exists in the Federal Republic for the overall control and direction of public action. Perhaps it may be held that nowadays a specialisation of interest on these lines requires some justification. This is because so much of contemporary political science is, broadly speaking, behavioural. It sees the key to an understanding of political systems in the analysis of political behaviour and tends further to discount the significance of institutional structures as factors constraining political behaviour. In addition the bias of much political science is reductionist.

It tends to look for possibilities of explaining political activity and the institutions through and in which this takes place by reference to factors which are not in themselves political—social class, economic structure, the expression and organisation of interests, cultural traditions, to quote some leading examples of independent explanatory variables.

It is not the purpose of this book to come to grips with the theoretical difficulties of political explanation alluded to here. But it has to be said that the author is not convinced by the reductionist treatment of political categories, nor is he satisfied that political institutions can be adequately and exhaustively explained as functions of particular categories of social behaviour, structure and interest. In short, if this were a theoretical work, he would argue that political institutions have a certain autonomy as determinants of political behaviour and activity. It is on these grounds that there is justification for analysing how institutions have evolved, the principles on which they rest, and the manner in which they operate. And amongst the political institutions of a developed society, there can be little doubt that those which have executive powers are of major and perhaps primary importance.

There are three assumptions underlying the treatment of government in the Federal Republic in this work which ought to be made explicit. They too may help to explain its concentration on the executive area of government. The first of these is that it is important in the study of political systems to consider how government operates and the extent to which it performs effectively. In other words, a political system is instrumental, and its executive competence influences both its prospects of survival as well as the evolution of political habits in it. It hardly needs to be said that in an epoch in which the expectation of public action is unusually intense, it behoves us to pay particular attention to the institutions through which most of this action is determined and carried out.

The second assumption is that political institutions express in varying degrees ideas about political authority. Their structure is not haphazard, nor is it determined solely by crude considerations of efficiency. In a society which thinks seriously about the problems of political order, the institutions reflect in the relationships they establish, or seek to establish, the conditions on which power may be exercised. In other words they embody a continuing approach to resolving the issues which arise in the relations between citizens and government. Within this framework there is every reason for paying attention to the institutions which specialise in the taking of decisions on measures which will be backed by the authority of the political system, and in seeing to their implementation.

Finally, there is a third assumption, which has the air of a truism. This is that political institutions often show a great capacity for survival over time, and for this reason the procedural norms which they embody may continue to be influential, even though patterns of collaboration for political ends in the wider context of the whole society have greatly changed. This might usefully be put in another way as follows. It takes considerable time for a society to develop and consolidate political institutions embodying a considered view of how authority should be exercised. Once established, these institutions are hard to dislodge, if only because they express the dominant tradition in that society's thinking about political authority. However, a wide variety of circumstances may supervene to change radically the structure of interests in the society and the modes of behaviour in political life. Such changes will affect the institutions, probably modifying their shape and certainly altering the ways in which they are used. But in the absence of a deliberate attempt to destroy existing institutions in order to create a new political order (an event commonly described as revolution and rarer in occurrence than many are inclined to believe), it is likely that changes in the quality and direction of political life will take place within pre-existing institutional limits. As is argued in this book (though hardly in a systematic way), this seems to have happened in the Federal Republic. Powerful external and internal pressures brought about far-reaching changes in political behaviour and expectations, with the result that the party system was radically changed and a new style of politics became possible. But this was achieved within an institutional framework which reaches back into the past. This is particularly true of those parts of it which constitute the executive apparatus of the state: here there is a relatively high degree of historical continuity. It is worth stressing that these remarks are not intended to suggest that political change was achieved *despite* an inherited institutional structure. Indeed, it is far nearer the truth to say that the success of this process owes much to the fact that it did prove possible to adapt to the demands of recent political reconstruction institutional arrangements built up during the earlier stages of the emergence of the modern German state.

The terms of reference of this study are, as just indicated, limited. It does not claim to offer an overview of the whole political system, and it is assumed that the reader will have some familiarity with the main features of the post-1949 evolution of the Federal Republic. The development of the major political forces has been outlined only to the extent that this seems necessary for an understanding of the operations of government. Considerable attention is paid to major aspects of historical continuity, partly for the reasons already indicated, and partly to counteract the tendency of many to regard the Federal Republic as essentially "new", rather like the Veneerings whom Dickens described with such relish in the opening pages of *Our Mutual Friend*. But above all, an effort has been made to describe the different levels of government and to dispel the idea that, provided we know all about the Federal or central level of government, then we need do no more than direct a nod at the other, subordinate levels. Even centralised political systems are often analysed too narrowly and exclusively in terms of their central structures. But in the case of the Federal Republic neglect of the arms of government operating below the central level leads to a serious misunderstanding of the whole position. Western Germany is a decentralised state, and remains so despite the many pressures which are now at work to reinforce the central authorities. The fact that there is a decentralised structure of government has significant effects on the patterns of political activity, on the bureaucracy, and on the manner in which public services are provided. We pay some attention to the second and third of these points, and make reference to the first. To analyse in detail the effects of the decentralised structure on party behaviour and relationships would, however, call for a different kind of study than was intended here. Perhaps, however, the time will soon come when this crucial aspect of German politics will no longer be so much neglected as it has been up to the present. Finally, some effort has been made to indicate how important legal norms, constitutional and otherwise, still are for the work of government in the Federal Republic as well as for the shaping of political behaviour. In few western political systems is the language of law so pervasive as in the Federal Republic. Nor does this fact necessitate the conclusion that the Federal Republic suffers from some peculiar time-lag which will be overcome when informal behavioural conventions are seen to take precedence over the more formal relationships posited by inherited legal norms. To assume this smacks of Anglo-American parochialism. Surely it is more realistic to assume that there are different ways of regulating the authority relationships in a modern pluralist society, and that the German approach is valid within its own context, and probably capable of further development within the terms on which it rests.

The student of government and politics is nowadays peculiarly subject to the difficulty that what he is concerned to explain changes so quickly. Even though the main features of an institutional pattern may retain their contours, much of the detail about organisation and procedures suffers from a high rate of obsolescence. This is as true of the Federal Republic as of other Western European countries. Indeed this particular problem has been accentuated in recent years because, after a long period of relative stability, the governmental structures of the Federal Republic became more open to question in the later sixties: increasing demands were made on them in the pursuance of an ever-wider range of public services, whilst a more broadly-based political critique also began to have an effect. Without doubt this account has not seized all the nuances of change. The fact that work on it was begun some time ago may also have had the effect of putting too much emphasis on habits and methods already well established in the period of the Federal Republic's consolidation. Hopefully, however, the author can take comfort in the fact that even in the midst of what appears as a phase of critical reappraisal and reform, surprisingly many of the old landmarks still survive. Certainly there seems to be no conclusive reason for believing that major changes in the structure and style of German government are imminent.

In the course of several years I have been fortunate in being able to benefit from the advice of many members of the German public services, both at the level of the Federal Government and of Land North Rhine Westphalia. To all of them I am grateful. I am indebted too to the Library of the Bundestag in Bonn, and to my many friends there. To Herr Ministerialrat Werner Blischke of the Parliamentary Staff of the Bundestag I owe a special debt of gratitude, both for his patience in answering queries and his unfailing readiness to establish contacts with people in German public life who have been glad to advise me. I would like also to acknowledge help received from academic colleagues in the Federal Republic, amongst them Professor Kurt Sontheimer, Professor Wilhelm Hennis, Professor Frido Wagener, Professor Roman Schnur, Professor Prodromos Dagtoglou, and in particular the late Fritz Morstein Marx who never failed to offer perceptive encouragement. My thanks go too to Mr. W.

Paterson of the University of Warwick for his kindness in scrutinising the final draft, to my former colleague, Dr. Malcolm Anderson, and to Professor Christopher Hughes. I am deeply grateful to my secretary, Mrs. Lyn Yates, for her indispensable support, especially in the later stages of putting together this study. Finally I must record my appreciation of the help given by the Volkswagen Foundation which at the outset of my researches enabled me, with the kind support of the University of Warwick, to spend some time in the Federal Republic.

NEVIL JOHNSON

*Nuffield College, Oxford*

# CHAPTER 1

# *The Inheritance of the State*

THEORISING about the idea of the state has played an important part in the German political and legal tradition. Despite the abstract quality which much of this theorising has had, it has nevertheless had a powerful influence on the development of the system of government. At a more practical level, it must be remembered that Germany has had but limited experience of national unity, and practically none of a unitary state. To consider in more detail how important both these factors have been requires an historical discussion. Institutional structures and procedures evolve slowly, gradually giving firm shape to particular ideas about law, politics and government. Because the modes of government in a particular society embody beliefs about how government should be structured and the conditions under which it should operate, they often have a capacity for survival and even revival, which is greater than the ability of a specific constellation of political forces to recast them—or to do without them. This argument seems to be borne out by the West German experience where, despite all that has happened in the recent past, the inheritance of ideas about constitutional principles and the structure of governmental institutions derived from the experience of the nineteenth century has proved to be very enduring. In the language and behaviour of present-day government and politics we can still discern the influence and persuasive appeal of some of the major ideas and experiences of the past, and many aspects of the institutions and activity of government in the Federal Republic can be satisfactorily explained only if account is taken of this legacy.

1

## THE ABSENCE OF A UNITARY STATE

The first point to be discussed is the retention of a federal structure of government. *Prima facie* this is an unexpected state of affairs. The Federal Republic is no larger than Britain and more or less as densely populated. Socially the country is more homogeneous than at any time in the past. The economy is highly integrated on a nation-wide basis, and communications are very well developed. Culturally there are provincial variations, but these are probably less marked than in a number of other European countries of comparable size. Moreover, Western Germany now has no serious problem posed by the claims to special attention of ethnic, linguistic or religious minorities. Yet government is organised on a decentralised pattern which finds expression in the official title of the state, and which justifies the political scientist in describing it as a federal system.[1] How is this to be explained and how significant is it?

German national unity came late. Until a century ago Germany was a geographical and linguistic expression. For the purposes of political life and government it was still a collection of separate and independent states. Though the Napoleonic conquest had achieved a major simplification of the political map of Germany, there was in 1815 no basis for a national state. A shadowy confederation was established, the thirty-nine members of which ranged from the two major powers of Prussia and Austria through the middle layer of states like Bavaria and Saxony to minor principalities like Schaumburg-Lippe and Waldeck. Militarily and in other respects all the German states were weak in comparison with Austria and Prussia. But their continued existence was guaranteed by the competition for influence in Germany between these two major powers, and by the commitment of the governments of both of them to the maintenance of dynastic interests throughout Germany. Thus political unification could be achieved in only two ways. One would have been by a revolutionary process sweeping away the existing structure of political authority in all the states. Then the way would have been open to the construction of a new and probably unitary German state. This course was never followed: the memories of 1789 in France and of all that followed weighed too

---

[1]Some writers on federalism have questioned this, e.g. K. C. Wheare in his *Federal Government* (4th ed., OUP, 1963). He discusses federalism entirely in Anglo-American terms, paying relatively little attention to Western European federal experience.

heavily on the German liberals of the mid-nineteenth century for them to dare embark on a revolutionary adventure. Instead they indulged in constructing a liberal political order in the abstract, until swept away by the only effective powers in Germany, the governments of the major states. After 1848 it was more or less certain that only the other course offered hope of unification, that is to say extension of the authority of Prussia at the expense of Austria.

This, of course, is what happened. By 1866 the Prussian Government under Bismarck brought about the expulsion of Austria from internal German affairs. In 1867 a North German Confederation was established, and three years later the way was opened by the Franco-Prussian War for the entry of the four South German states of Bavaria, Baden, Württemberg and Hesse-Darmstadt into this confederation which, from 1871, constituted the revived German Reich or Empire.

But there was something essentially limited about the Bismarckian solution to the problem of political unification. Obviously it did not mean the establishment of a single national state for all Germans: the continuance of the Habsburg Empire was proof enough of that. Nor did it mean a radical reconstruction of the various structures of government which were brought together in the new federal system: there was no sign of a Prussian desire to establish a unitary state in the Empire. Both these facts are explained by the pragmatic and limited purposes pursued by Bismarck. His primary objective was to exclude Austria from the area covered by the old confederation of 1815. Only if this were done could Prussia establish a political order in Germany which would be extensive enough to satisfy *most* national aspirations and at the same time limited enough to avoid disrupting the Habsburg Empire with consequent dangers for the European state system. Moreover, unification on a somewhat restricted basis conveniently assisted in the preservation of Prussian hegemony.

Almost equally important, Bismarck wanted a "conservative" political order to emerge at the end of the unification struggle. Although prepared occasionally and, when it was convenient, to use radical weapons such as universal suffrage, Bismarck never once deviated from his determination to uphold something like the structure of monarchical authority with which he had grown up. True, the political systems of most of the German states[2] had been modified between 1815 and 1871 in the direction of

[2]The *ancien régime* survived almost unchanged in a few, e.g. the two Mecklenburgs.

constitutional government with limited representative institutions. Absolute monarchy of the *ancien régime* type was no longer tenable. But the progress towards representative and responsible government was modest, especially in Prussia, and the forces upholding the monarchical forms of government were nearly everywhere strong. Thus there was at the time nothing unrealistic in Bismarck's conviction that an authoritarian form of government tempered by constitutionalism could and should be maintained.

It is this political attitude which really explains why the Empire appeared in the guise of a federal state. To have destroyed or supplanted the existing patchwork of states would have been, even for Bismarck and still more for most of his contemporaries in the Prussian Government, a revolutionary act, subversive of the political order in Prussia itself. Thus, once Austria was out for good, the problem was simply to induce the other states to accept a constitutional structure which would formalise and confirm the predominance of Prussia in, and only in, those functions of government which are inseparable from the notion of a sovereign state, i.e. the control of foreign and defence affairs, the general framework of law and order, and certain areas of taxation. A federal structure was therefore maintained not only for the sake of political stability and in the interests of monarchical rule, but also because the Prussian Government had no interest in assuming more burdens than it needed to in order to ensure the survival of the new state.

The absorption into the Empire of the confederal traditions peculiar to the political coexistence of the German states had important consequences. Most obviously it facilitated the survival of particularism in both government and politics. The retention by the states of administrative autonomy which meant in some fields exclusive powers to legislate (e.g. in education), and in others the right to administer services on behalf of the central government, became the hallmark of German federalism. This control of administration (and a major influence over the allocation of revenue) was the element of "statehood" which the German states insisted on retaining. And, as we shall see later, it is roughly this conception of federalism which is embodied in the constitution of the Federal Republic.

It is difficult to assess exactly what influence the federal structure of the Empire exerted on the development of political parties, if only because so many other factors helped to shape them. Undoubtedly the style of Bismarck's leadership as Chancellor of the Reich and the absence of any serious prospect of parliamentary government at the Reich level had a more decisive effect on the parties than had the specifically federal characteristics of the political structure. Nevertheless, it is reasonable to hold that the retention of federalism assisted in the transfer to the parties of many of the particularist attitudes and interests of the states. In this way there was additional encouragement to the process of division and inter-party conflict which led to a multi-party system which was later to prove itself singularly unfitted to operate parliamentary government.

German federalism was, therefore, essentially a device which perpetuated into the era of a single national state the particularist habits and traditions of the dynasties and estates which were dominant in the separate states of Germany. It is surprising indeed that it should have shown so much capacity for survival. Originally the Imperial Reich Government had only limited powers and a very sketchy organisation.[3] Gradually it assumed a dominant role in social and economic legislation, and its administrative services expanded. Under the Weimar Republic these tendencies were more openly encouraged: the constitution limited considerably both the autonomy of the states or Länder (reduced in number to seventeen) and their ability to influence or reject legislative proposals put to the Reichstag by the central government. Moreover, the recurrent political and economic crises which beset the Weimar Republic underlined the need for a strong central authority to control the situation. The forces of particularism were to some extent strengthened by the sudden transition from a political system with many authoritarian characteristics to one based on a conscientious translation of all the principles of liberalism into constitutional law. In the short life of the Weimar Republic the central government had to face strong and sometimes violent opposition from political groups of the Left in Saxony and Thuringia, from those of the Right in Bavaria, and from quasi-secessionists in the Rhineland. For the whole period Prussia had a Social Democrat majority in its Landtag, and this led to constant friction between the Reich and the Prussian governments, leading finally to the suspension of the latter by Chancellor v. Papen in 1932. Indeed the

[3]The Imperial Government developed by an extension of the Imperial Chancellor's Office, from which functional offices were gradually split off, headed by state secretaries. A collegial ministry was never achieved. The position was enormously complicated by the fact that the Chancellor was nearly always Minister President of Prussia, so that eventually the Prussian Government constituted a kind of parallel government, assuming many of the functions of policy-making which properly belonged to the Imperial executive.

imbalance resulting from the preponderance of Prussia (roughly equivalent to two-thirds of the Reich in area and resources) was one of the basic weaknesses of the federal structure.[4] And often it was in the Länder parties that positions of power were built up which increased the disunity and the rate of disintegration in a party system which already, at the national level, lacked any basis for coherent governing majorities.

The events of the Nazi era effaced many of the memories of the disadvantages and artificialities of German federalism. The collapse of the Third Reich did, however, entail too the disappearance of what remained of the geographical and political bases of federalism. This was underlined by the decision of the allied powers in 1947 formally to decree the dissolution of Prussia.[5] Yet despite all this, in the reconstruction of government and political life which began in 1946, the old federal tradition reasserted itself. Though this was partly due to the influence of the Western occupying powers, it is doubtful whether allied influence alone explains the persistence of federal arrangements. Indigenous German preferences also worked in their favour.

Two factors were particularly important in bringing about a revival of a federal state organisation. First there was the fact that by 1949 the main political parties had been re-established and organised on a provincial basis. This was especially marked in the new Christian Democrat Party which was essentially a coalition of political groups having sufficient aims in common to make co-ordinated action at the national level a practical possibility, but each entrenched in positions of influence or control in different parts of the country.[6] Even within the Social Democratic Party there were powerful influences working in favour of a less centralised party organisation and which recognised the advantages of a federal system in terms of retaining political control in particular parts of the country. In short, a return to federalism offered the prospect of maintaining

[4]An interesting account of the problems of the federal structure shortly before the fall of the Weimar Republic can be found in Arnold Brecht, *Federalism and Regionalism in Germany*, OUP, 1945.

[5]Control Council, Law No. 46: *Abolition of the State of Prussia Documents on Germany under Occupation 194–254*, p. 210, Beate Ruhm von Oppen.

[6]It has to be remembered that it took some time for Adenauer to establish his own wing of the CDU in North Rhine Westphalia as the leading group in the new party: a less forceful politician might not have succeeded. See A. Heidenheimer, *Adenauer and the CDU*, Nijhoff, 1960; also K. Adenauer, *Memoirs*, Vol. I.

a dispersal of political power even within a simplified and more unified party system.

Second, the institutional traditions of the country reasserted themselves. The federalism which was retained in the national state of the late nineteenth century and onwards was a means of maintaining a high degree of administrative decentralisation: the states surrendered their pretensions to genuine sovereignty, but each retained its own governmental apparatus to administer national legislation and those services which remained within its competence. Yet decentralisation of this kind was not simply a mechanical device or an exercise in the division of labour in the state organisation. It placed restrictions on the discretion and freedom of manoeuvre of the central authority and inevitably encouraged some decentralisation of political power. With the experience of totalitarian centralisation just behind them, this way of thinking about the structure of government had a strong appeal to most of those who in the late forties were concerned with drafting a constitution for the western part of Germany. They saw the central government as having extensive, but nevertheless restricted, areas of competence. The actual execution of central policies would fall mainly to provincial Land authorities, which in turn would have exclusive competence in some fields, chiefly education and culture, police and the organisation of local government (all of which had been traditionally reserved to the states in Germany). By these means, it was considered, a central government strong enough to act on behalf of the whole political community could be established, but at the same time the restrictions on its competence and its lack of responsibility for the administration of many of its policies would help to ensure an acceptable level of dispersion of political authority throughout the country. In short, the device of federalism by administrative decentralisation was to function as a support for the dispersal of political power. And as we shall see when we turn to examine the operation of the present federal system, this is broadly what has happened.

## GERMAN CONSTITUTIONALISM AND THE RECHTSSTAAT

The second legacy of the past which is to be considered can be subsumed under the concept of the Rechtsstaat and the influence of the particular form of constitutional government, often referred to simply as "constitutionalism", which developed in Germany during the nineteenth century. Let us consider German notions of constitutionalism first, though as will be apparent these are closely linked with Rechtsstaat conceptions.

The Liberal reformers of the last century were, for reasons which cannot be elaborated here, concerned first to establish the rule of law, and only second to make governments responsible to elected representatives. German constitutionalism was essentially a solution to the first of these problems, but it failed to solve the second. Indeed had it been successful in tackling this issue too, it would have become a very different doctrine from that which appears in the legal textbooks of the last thirty years of the nineteenth century. After their defeat in the Prussian constitutional conflict of 1862–6, most Liberals reconciled themselves to a doctrine of constitutionalism which treated a constitution primarily as a formal and necessary instrument for restricting the area of arbitrary action by governments. Faced with a situation in which the dynasties and the landed aristocracy, the former backed by their armies and bureaucracies, were in effective control of governments, the Liberals' policy was to press for legal and institutional limitations on the executive rather than for participation in government and a redistribution of political authority. And despite the failures of 1848 and 1862–6—which meant that a radical shift in the pattern of political power was to be deferred until 1918—the Liberal programme for constitutional government as a means of ensuring the rule of law was for the most part realised. Within two years of 1848 Prussia was granted a constitution by Frederick William IV: in parts of south Germany some form of constitutional government had appeared even before 1848, and these developments were later confirmed and carried further. By the time the Empire was formed nearly all the member states had some kind of constitution, and these guaranteed much of what the liberal then (and now) understood by the term "rule of law". Thus the Prussian constitution contained a catalogue of basic rights, including equality before the law, free access to public office, no limitation of personal freedom except by the processes of law, freedom of religious practice, freedom to express opinions and so on. Admittedly most of these rights were subject to the possibility of restriction by positive legal enactment, which is indeed the logical consequence of almost any abstract statement of a right, and their exercise was frequently limited in the political interests of various governments. Nevertheless this species of constitutionalism did succeed in substantially modifying the *ancien régime*, substituting for it an order based on the legal recognition of individual rights. Respect for a specific statement of basic rights has endured in Germany, and indeed been reinforced by recent experience. This is an element in earlier constitutionalism which finds clear expression in the first nineteen articles of the Basic Law of the Federal Republic.

If constitutionalism had some strength as a means of establishing the rule of law as envisaged by liberal political philosophy, it was less clear and less successful in resolving the problems affecting the terms on which governments were to be made and unmade. Broadly speaking, constitutionalism recognised the independence of the executive, subject to limitations. The principal limitations were that there should be some kind of representative body to act as a legislature, and that in the making of laws the executive should be subject to its consent, though retaining substantial inherent powers for the conduct of government. Thus in the enactment of laws and in the establishment of the budget the executive in nearly all German states became subject to the need to secure the approval of a body of representatives. The concept of the responsibility of ministers to Parliament hardly struck root anywhere before 1918. Kings and princes—the formal executives—were generally subjected to the counter-signature requirement, which meant that once an executive decision had been countersigned by a minister, the latter assumed responsibility for it.[7] What this meant in terms of constitutional doctrine was never clear. In fact the term "responsibility" was in this context empty; all it could mean was that a minister had approved this or that executive act. It said nothing about "to whom" or "to what" the minister was responsible. It is curious that a similar kind of obscurity attaches to the meaning of the responsibility of ministers other than the Federal Chancellor under Article 65 of the present Basic Law, when it states that they conduct the affairs of their departments "on their own responsibility".

There is no need to labour the point that German constitutionalism failed to achieve "responsible" government in any rigorous sense of the

[7]For example, as in the Prussian Constitution of 1850, Titel III, Art. 44. Constitution for a German Empire 1849, Art. II, paras. 73 and 74, Constitution of the German Empire 1871, Art. 17.

term.[8] The forces behind the demand for constitutional government were not strong enough to bring about a redistribution of political power which would have displaced the aristocracy and its upper-middle-class allies from their dominant positions and subjected the dynasties, their armies and bureaucracies, to control by ministers dependent on parliamentary support. Some modern commentators on German constitutional development have, however, tried to present "constitutionalism" as a rational and well-thought-out attempt to achieve a balanced system of government. It was not, so their argument runs, merely a temporary resting-place on the road from absolutism to fully parliamentary (and, therefore, party) government, but a serious attempt to evolve principles for a balanced constitution, adapted to the distribution of interests in the society, attentive to the rights of individual citizens, responsive to popular demands by its acceptance of elected bodies, and productive of stable government by its respect for the monarchical principle and the need for a strong and independent executive authority.[9] Such arguments carry little conviction: the logic of the constitutional provisions enacted in most German states as well as in the North German Confederation and Empire pointed towards responsible parliamentary government. This was accepted by implication in the provisions which confirmed the legislative authority of the parliaments. Once the legitimacy of a non-parliamentary executive was challenged, there was no alternative to governments based on parliamentary majorities.

However, the argument about the status of constitutionalism as a doctrine need not detain us. What is important is to identify its enduring influence. This is to be found in two aspects of modern German government. First, there is the continuing acceptance of a certain degree of separation between legislature and executive which was part of the older constitutionalism. This has been reinforced by the failure of parliamentary

[8]It should not be thought that this general conclusion overlooks entirely the approximation to responsible parliamentary government which was achieved in some states, e.g. in Baden and in Bavaria (1912). But modest progress here and there did not present a serious challenge to the monarchical/constitutional system. For a devastating critique of nineteenth-century notions of ministerial responsibility in Germany see P. G. Hoffmann, *Monarchisches Prinzip und Ministerverantwortlichkeit*, 1911.

[9]See E. R. Huber, *Deutsche Verfassungsgeschichte seit 1789*, Vol. III (1963), for a monumental and, for this writer at least, unconvincing exposition of this point of view.

government under the Weimar Republic. The Federal Republic has returned to provisions which guarantee the rights and powers of Parliament, but at the same time are intended to protect the executive against divisions of opinion within Parliament. The powers of the Federal Government are carefully defined, parliamentary responsibility is concentrated on the Federal Chancellor, and there are elaborate provisions to ensure that the Bundestag cannot withdraw its confidence from a Chancellor without first agreeing on a successor. In some formal respects, therefore, the German Government today has been given back the stability and independence which constitutionalism wished to see the executive possess. Naturally, this point must not be exaggerated: the real powers of the Bundestag are immensely greater than those of the Imperial Reichstag, and the development of coherent parliamentary parties has radically changed the relationship between Government and legislature. Nevertheless the practice of government and the terms in which political argument is carried on in the Federal Republic do suggest that the Bundestag and the Federal Government are still perceived as separate, occasionally perhaps co-equal, entities. There is not that symbiosis of political leadership in Parliament and Government which the logic of a parliamentary régime demands.[10]

Another legacy of constitutionalism is the survival of a view of Parliament which sees the institution primarily as a legislative machine. Before 1918 the Reichstag and most state parliaments (Landtage) could raise no other claim: such powers as they had derived primarily from their rights in relation to the passage of laws. During the Empire the rights of the legislatures in this field were gradually extended: specialised committee systems began to take shape, procedures both in committees and in the plenary sessions were consolidated, lobbyists and pressure groups began to exert a powerful influence over members and party groups, and governments found it more and more necessary to negotiate with and manipulate the parties if legislative proposals were to come through safely to the statute book. The disorganised condition of parliamentary politics under the Weimar Republic made it virtually impossible for the Reichstag to exercise its legislative powers effectively: in the final stages of the régime there was no alternative to rule by decree. The reassertion of law

[10]This point is pressed by many contemporary German critics of the Bonn parliamentary system: yet their arguments seem to make little impact on political behaviour.

as the sheet-anchor of society has helped to give new life to the traditional view of Parliament as primarily a law-maker. And this is the role in which the Bundestag has excelled: it has through its committees provided a diligent, well-informed, and influential scrutiny of legislative proposals put to it by the Government, and has even succeeded in making rather more use of its own powers of legislative initiative than many other Parliaments in Western Europe. Furthermore, this emphasis on the legislative role of Parliament harmonises well with the separation between Parliament and executive which has just been discussed. Both reflect the continuing influence of the "resting-place" between absolutism and full parliamentary government which nineteenth-century constitutionalism sought to define.

We come now to the rather more perplexing concept of the Rechtsstaat. The doctrines of constitutionalism were concerned mainly with how powers in the state should be distributed so that their purposes and use would remain within lawful limits and assure respect for basic civil rights. The conception of the Rechtsstaat was at once wider and less sharply defined than the doctrines of constitutionalism, and yet also in its full elaboration more detailed and comprehensive.

It is by no means easy to translate "Rechtsstaat" into English. "A state based on the rule of law" is probably as near to the sense of the German term as one can get. "Rule of law" by itself will not do, with its strong overtones of Anglo-American Common Law pragmatism. But even "a state based on the rule of law" fails to convey the fusion of state and law (= Right) implied in the German expression.

There is no need in this context to trace the idea of the Rechtsstaat back to its origins in medieval natural law doctrines. In Germany it became an influential concept chiefly as a result of the late-eighteenth-century critique of the "Police State" (Polizeistaat).[11] That in turn was fed by Kant's philosophy. Kant's principal interest was to establish the form of moral reasoning, to define the conditions which any moral rule must satisfy if it is to be regarded as a moral rule at all. This resulted in a moral philosophy

---

[11]Polizeistaat is not to be confused with the modern police state. It was rather a species of socially conscious absolutism. "Polizei" had a wide sense extending to social and economic regulation as well as to the maintenance of law and order (*Polizei: politeia*). See H. Maier, *Die ältere deutsche Staats- und Verwaltungslehre (Polizeiwissenschaft)*, Luchterhand, 1966.

which was expressed in general and abstract rules. It was for the individual to act freely in such a way that the principles of his actions could be universalised. When this type of reasoning was applied to the nature of the state it led Kant and many of his successors to see the state as a means of subordinating public power to general legal norms. In other words the reality of the state consisted in the basic rules which it sanctioned, and to which all its acts should be subject. Even if the basic rules did not significantly extend the freedom of the individual, a state founded on them would still be a Rechtsstaat in virtue of treating all alike and of subjecting political power to law. And this, after all, was to be a key element in Liberal political thought.

These conceptions were developed further in the first half of the nineteenth century. We shall consider in a moment the way in which Hegel used them. But there were also Liberal thinkers who developed the idea of the Rechtsstaat, both for the extension of individual civil rights and for the purpose of justifying representative government. Notable amongst them was Robert von Mohl, one of the leading South German Liberals. He argued that the Rechtsstaat must be one in which the law was made by constitutional means, i.e. by representative bodies, and was anxious to see the area of legitimate state action restricted (here the *laissez-faire* influence was at work). Unfortunately Mohl had few successors: he is remembered as a gifted and serious exponent of South German liberalism, but his influence remained slight. Some traces of it are to be found in the thinking of Gneist, the great admirer of English local self-government, who argued that the Rechtsstaat must have genuine political support, and that this could be achieved by associating a lay element with the work of administration and of public law adjudication.[12]

However, the concept of the Rechtsstaat was destined to develop towards legal formalism, even though it was also to be significantly influenced by the value judgments involved in the metaphysical notion of the state propagated by Hegel and his successors. The chief reasons for the formal character retained by the Rechtsstaat idea lies in the failure of constitutionalism to achieve the second part of its programme, responsible parliamentary government. Attention was, therefore, shifted from the

---

[12]From 1857 onwards Rudolf von Gneist published numerous studies of English local government and of English administrative procedures, some of them drawing lessons for German experience.

problems of participation in politics and of the sharing of political power to the means by which the corpus of public law might be perfected so that all powers would be exactly specified and their use controlled and defined. The rule of law in the state and through the state became the ideal of liberal-minded jurists throughout Germany. In the period after 1870 there was a great blossoming of German jurisprudence. Today we are likely to be oppressed by the sheer weight of the learned volumes produced in these years, and tempted to dismiss them as containing little but legal formalism. In part the reproach is justified. In the work of some of the leading exponents of the Rechtsstaat conception—Otto Bähr, Jellinek, Laband, for example—the Rechtsstaat appears as a state in which all public action takes place within limits prescribed by a pattern of legal rules logically consistent with each other. But since nearly all these writers were legal positivists, the content of the legal rules remains immaterial. The Rechtsstaat idea as it finally emerged is defined in terms of the supremacy of law, the subordination of the administration to law, the liability of the state for the illegal acts of its agents, guarantees against unfair application of laws through appeal to administrative courts, and finally a continuous improvement in the system of public law to exclude from it those elements which reflect the capricious influence of political or administrative convenience. Whatever logical merits this approach may have had, it showed a naïve indifference to the specific objects of the law and to the relationship between law and society.

Despite the political weaknesses of the mode of thought just outlined, the Rechtsstaat conception as it was evolved during the Empire was accompanied by a substantial improvement in the machinery for protecting the citizen in his dealings with public authority. As in several other continental states a coherent system of public law and adjudication was built up. Administrative courts distinct from the executive administration were established, notably in Prussia, and as early as 1882 had successfully asserted the doctrine of *excès de pouvoir* as a ground for annulment of a public action. Although the opportunities for appeal against administrative action remained enumerated—no general clause was to be introduced until 1949—the citizen's scope for appeal was steadily widened as the functions of the state increased. Moreover, the higher levels of the bureaucracy, trained predominantly in law, were increasingly conscious of their duty to observe legal norms, and to base their actions on general rules which could be related to the principle of equality of treatment.[13]

Political experience from 1918 to 1945 showed often enough that the formal definitions of the Rechtsstaat offered no guarantee of political freedom and good government. Yet whilst the excesses of the Nazi régime underlined the need for a far more realistic appreciation of the political conditions necessary for a democratic system of government, at the same time they also strengthened the commitment to important aspects of the older conception of the Rechtsstaat. Here at least, so it seemed to many, was something in the German political tradition which was still worthy of respect. But if it was to be revived in order to provide a framework for the protection of human rights and dignity, then it was necessary to strengthen the moral content of the Rechtsstaat idea by an injection of natural rights doctrine. Thus we find that the Basic Law of the Federal Republic opens with a long catalogue of human rights, setting out what might be described as the ethical content of the Rechtsstaat.[14] In order to make these rights enforceable there is provision for judicial review of the constitutionality of a wide range of public acts and decisions,[15] and the scope for appeal to the courts against administrative action is extended by a clause stating that in no circumstances shall the aggrieved citizen be denied access to the courts.[16] And in particular the need for law as a basis for public action, law approved by Parliament, is reaffirmed. This whole-hearted return to a revitalised concept and practice of the Rechtsstaat has had important consequences for the style and content of German administration which will be examined in some detail later. Here the important point to be noted is that the emphasis on legal norms and on institutional devices for ensuring that public actions conform to them expresses a continued preference for the resolution of political disputes through authoritative judicial decisions rather than by resort to the more informal methods of political accommodation. The establishment of the Federal Constitutional Court and its subsequent activity has introduced a new dimension of essentially political decision-making into the theory and practice

[13]It should not be forgotten that in the early and mid-nineteenth century many of the most serious reformers were officials in the Prussian civil service who were anxious to see administration conducted within the limits of formal legal restraints.

[14]Articles 1 to 19, Basic Law.

[15]Art. 93, Basic Law.

[16]Art. 19 (4), Basic Law.

of the Rechtsstaat. There can be no return to the juridical positivism which characterised the classical exposition of the Rechtsstaat. For better or worse the Constitutional Court has to interpret the constitution and must, therefore, base many of its decisions on explicit political value judgments. The continued acceptability of this role depends not only on the sensitivity and skill of the Court's judges, but also on the maintenance of a political consensus favourable to this mode of resolving certain categories of disputes. In this sense the maintenance of the Rechtsstaat is now more explicitly related to the political conditions necessary to its survival.

## THE SEPARATION BETWEEN STATE AND SOCIETY

It is difficult to understand German political development and the role of government without paying some attention to the distinction drawn between state and society. This is deeply rooted in German political thought, is to be found in much of the theoretical discussion of society and its structure, and has decisively influenced German public law doctrines. In recent times the distinction has been taken less seriously, and has been sharply criticised or rejected by some political scientists and sociologists, especially by those who have come under the influence of Anglo-American empiricism. Nevertheless, the distinction remains influential enough to justify some comment on it.

The classic formulation of the separation between state and society is to be found in the writings of Hegel. He saw civil society as a complex pattern of interacting and often conflicting interests, much as it was conceived by the classical economists. In this condition the individual could have only a subjective freedom, definable in terms of his ability to pursue his own interests. As Hegel saw it, the state comes into existence when man is capable of conceiving rationally of an order in which private and public interests can be identified. Thus the state is an instrument for the attainment of a degree of freedom more rational and more complete than is possible in civil society.

We cannot in this context attempt a critique of Hegel's political philosophy.[17] It is enough to note that Hegel succeeded in imposing on future

[17]For a scrupulously fair-minded exposition of Hegel's political ideas see J. Plamenatz, *Man and Society*, Vol. II, chaps. 3 and 4, Longmans, 1963.

generations of political thinkers and jurists a dualism which it has been virtually impossible to overcome. Even those who have disagreed most violently with him have felt this influence, and nowhere more than in Hegel's own country. It is difficult in a short space to do justice to Hegel's influence. His arguments owed something to Plato (Socrates' final decision to obey the law of the polis had a Hegelian quality about it) and something to Rousseau (the General Will translates fairly easily into the Hegelian State). Undoubtedly in underlining the manner in which having a concept of the state can open up new perspectives for the enlargement of human freedom, Hegel was pin-pointing significant weaknesses in the philosophies of utilitarianism and individualist liberalism. On the other hand, there were obvious dangers and absurdities in Hegel's tendency to deify the state, to present it as *the* moral agent essential to the attainment of human freedom, and to attribute an inferior value to all forms of social activity which in the Hegelian dialectical process were placed at a lower point in human development towards rationality than the state itself.

Perhaps we are justified in summing up the Hegelian legacy in Germany in the following manner. First, the desire to draw a more or less sharp distinction between state and society has persisted. The state has been seen, and to a large extent is still seen, as a structure of both moral and legal order superimposed on society, something which gives to the society its political and constitutional shape. This is reflected in the large number of expressions employing the term *Staat* which can barely be translated into English: to mention only a few, *Staatlichkeit* (having the quality of the state), *Staatsgewalt* (state power or sovereignty), *Staatsrecht* (that part of public law dealing with the rights and duties of the state), and *Staatslehre* (the inquiry into the nature and *modus operandi* of the state). In all these cases it is difficult to convey into English the overtones of an order distinct from and superior to that found in social relationships not dependent on public regulation and approval.

Historically the most important political consequence of the separation between state and society was the tendency to view the state as a means of making authoritative decisions for the society in isolation from the political forces through which demands in the society are articulated. Thus on the one hand there were organised groups advancing claims, defending interests and seeking power, whilst on the other there was a sphere of objective, rational assessment—the state—of what is in the public interest. It is not

B

difficult to see that this view postulated a discontinuity in the political process which it is impossible to reconcile with the realities of political life in a pluralist society. What is more it is an encouragement to a mistaken analysis of the relationships between political activity and the functions of government. It demands of government a degree of objectivity, rationality and isolation from the political inputs of the society which it cannot have. It is a constant temptation to a Utopian view of the possibility of overcoming conflict and division in the political life of the society by shifting the responsibility for decisions to some level—the state level— which is supposedly above the battle.

There is no doubt that the effect on politics of the state–society dichotomy as just outlined has diminished greatly in the Federal Republic. The political history of the period since 1949 indicates that in many respects the gap between the area of political activity in society and that of the state acting on society has been closed. The state has been extensively demythologised and party politics legitimised. On the other hand, a lot of political argument is still carried on in terms of the state–society distinction (*Staat* and *Gesellschaft*) and when signs of an above-average intensity of political conflict have appeared, they have been accompanied by a tendency to reassert the separation under discussion. Instead of seeking solutions through the process of political conflict and conciliation, there can be a hankering for an arbitration from on high. In addition, as we shall notice when we examine more closely the functions of government, the style of administration, and the role of judicial interpretation, the traditional view of the state as the concrete embodiment of public order still retains some vitality.

Another effect of this separation is the extent to which it has supported an idea of the state as an agency for moral improvement. This, of course, is directly derived from Hegel's arguments about the state as a condition of rational freedom. The idea that the state has a moral purpose became an important component of political theorising in Germany. Indeed it has close links too with the concept of the Rechtsstaat. If it is assumed that the fundamental norms of the Rechtsstaat are intended to serve essentially moral ends—human dignity, freedom of the person, protection against the arbitrary infringement of human rights, etc.—it is a very short step to assimilate the idea of the Rechtsstaat with the metaphysical view of the state as an agent for moral good.

It is difficult to define satisfactorily the continuing influence of this attitude which sees the state as a necessary condition for achieving moral ends which are necessarily individual. It still maintains a predisposition to accept the desirability of public regulation on a consistent and equal basis of a wide range of activities which in some countries are left entirely unregulated. And despite an ideological commitment to private property rights and private economic enterprise since 1945, it is probably a continuing sense of the state's necessity for individual well-being which has prevented the emergence of sharp controversy about the relative size of the public and private sectors of the economy and of social service provision. There is a continuing preference for seeing public powers as a whole, vested in an entity which is a unity, not only in the straightforward juridical sense, but also in this vaguer, all-embracing form of a moral agent. This again provides a background favourable to acceptance of the idea that individuals ought to be able to pursue their own ends, but within a framework of public regulation. Finally, there have been occasions when this mode of thought has had a more dramatic influence. For example, it played a part in the reasoning of the Federal Constitutional Court in its famous decision in the Article 131 case.[18] Here the outcome of the claims made by former officials of the Third Reich turned in part on the Court's judgment of whether, at a certain point in time, the Third Reich ceased to be a state at all. And it was not just a question of whether it had ceased to be a state in the straightforward political sense, but whether it had lost those attributes of law and moral purpose which alone justify a state's claim on the loyalties of its members. It was because the German state had ceased to exist in this sense, that the Court held that its legal ties with former officials of the Third Reich were dissolved too.

Finally, and on a less speculative level, the separation between state and society implied that some person or group of persons constituted the state. Behind all the abstract argument, legal, moral, or political, there had to be some specific authority which was the state. This meant that in fact the state was the executive. Given the slow and frustrated development of representative government in Germany, it is not surprising that this identification of the state with the executive was accepted. Just as the monarch came to embody or represent an abstract idea of the state in eighteenth-century Prussia, so the bureaucracy and the army, which were

[18]This judgment is to be found in *B Verf GE*, Vol. 3, pp. 58 ff.

the monarch's instruments of government, came to represent in the nineteenth century the idea of the state. For the less sophisticated the state was nothing more than the bureaucracy, civil and military, which operated as the indispensable tools of government. In the Anglo-Saxon tradition the official is simply a clerk or a servant, someone who carries out particular tasks in virtue of lawful authority conferred on him. In the French tradition the official is a *fonctionnaire*, someone with specific functions to discharge within the overall complex of public powers. But in the German tradition the official is a *Beamter*, someone who holds an office (Amt) and who in virtue of that office is in a special relationship to the state. It follows that the official also stands in a special and privileged relationship with regard to the private citizen.

In a later chapter we shall look more closely at the public service in Western Germany, and in so doing will try to assess how far the traditional conceptions of the official and his role are maintained. For the immediate purpose it is necessary to emphasise that the identification of the executive with the state (and remembering that the executive has for most of modern German history not been headed by a group of politicians owing their places to popular election) has worked against acceptance of the fusion of government and politics which is inherent in a representative form of government. It has added support to the view already discussed which sees a separation between the area of political pressure and argument, and the making of authoritative decisions in government. It has equally favoured the maintenance of a professional bureaucracy whose authority is acknowledged to a far greater extent than is conceivable in those political systems in which the state has been envisaged in purely instrumental and functional terms. Despite the fact that in the Federal Republic political leadership has been far stronger than in the past, and more widely diffused at different levels of the political system, it is also true that in the analysis of German government, the structure and operations of the administration must occupy a major position. This is not merely because the area of public administration is wide or its powers extensive. It is also because the administration has to a considerable extent a political role, being involved as a politically active element in many political decisions. That this is so is a sign of the continued influence of the idea that in some way the bureaucracy "carries" the state.

# CHAPTER 2

# The Political Framework of the Federal Republic

## THE REVOLUTION OF DESTRUCTION AND ITS AFTERMATH

The Federal Republic of Germany has now been in existence for nearly a quarter of a century. The initial impressions one receives from a survey of its system of government and the development of its political life in this period are ambiguous. The way in which politics has evolved since 1949 suggests a sharp break with the past: here the sense of change is strong. There have been decisive innovations in the organisation and behaviour of the major political forces, and social attitudes and structures have been substantially modified both in the aftermath of war and under the impact of rapid economic growth and ever-increasing urbanisation. On the other hand, as Chapter 1 has suggested, when we examine the formal structures of government, the constitutional and legal concepts underlying them, and the activity of the whole complex pattern of public administration, we can detect signs of a continuity with the evolution of Germany before 1933.

This is not to argue that we are faced with straightforward case histories of innovation in political behaviour and party organisation, and of restoration in the methods and procedures of government. In reality these two areas are interdependent, each influencing what happens in the other. Whilst the impact of the experience before 1945 and in the years immediately after was to give a powerful impetus to a reshaping of German political behaviour, this had to go forward within a particular framework of institutions. And, in the absence of radical changes imposed by external

21

forces or internal revolution, these necessarily had to express earlier experience of how public authority should be constituted and exercised. Hence the interwoven themes of restoration and change by which the development of the Federal Republic has been characterised.

That it was possible in the years after the Second World War, when the West German state was reconstructed, to repair some of the links with the past was due in part to the fact that the National Socialist régime did not succeed in reshaping society and its underlying notions of government to the extent it claimed.

The National Socialist epoch has rightly been regarded by many historians as revolutionary. Here was a political movement aiming ruthlessly at the destruction of traditional political forces and at a radical transformation of the whole society. Yet the Nazi attempt to create a mass society ruled in a totalitarian fashion by a party élite was muddled in conception and incomplete in execution. Partly this was no doubt just a consequence of the shortness of time allowed to the rulers of the Third Reich for the carrying out of their revolution: six years of peace and six years of world war was not enough for the realisation of their appalling programme. But the thinking of the Nazi leadership was also (with only a few short-lived exceptions) characterised by a failure even to begin to grasp the extent of the social, economic and governmental restructuring of the society which was necessary if their revolution was to be enduring in its effects. The impact of the party on the social structure of the country was negligible in comparison with the effects on traditional élites of decimation in war; the economy remained largely in the same hands, though during the war years it was subject to extensive central control and direction; the educational system, despite ideological "Gleichschaltung", retained all the old landmarks—a tripartite division of schools, reasonably extensive provision for vocational technical training, and an academic university education for a middle-class minority destined mainly for the professions.

The poverty of Nazi thinking on the methods and techniques of revolution was revealed vividly in the takeover of the existing governmental institutions. The Third Reich never received a constitution—shadows of Weimar institutions lingered on to the end. The administrative structure remained largely intact, though modified by the introduction of provincial party chiefs (Gauleiter) who competed with the traditional authorities. The vestiges of a federal system survived, but the Länder ceased to have any autonomy and their administrative services were at the mercy of local party bosses and of inflated Reich Ministries and special agencies. German public law was not destroyed or rewritten: it was in many fields of public action simply ignored and informally suspended. The traditional bureaucracy was not reshaped. It was purged haphazardly, its political influence diminished and it had to compete with an ever-increasing number of party agencies. Ultimately the bureaucracy was powerless to influence, let alone control, the capricious excesses of the régime.[1] The same was true of the army, which the party manipulated and used for its purposes, but which survived as some kind of corporate body distinct from the party until its involvement in conspiracies against the régime and the imminence of military defeat brought about its final subjection.

Nazi rule was characterised above all by an extraordinary degree of improvisation in the techniques of government. Hitler's great insight was into mob psychology, and all else bored him. His power rested on a unique ability to arouse, concentrate and harness popular resentments against real or imaginary enemies. But his method of government was to leave all to improvisation, so that eventually the state became an anarchy of competing groups within and around the party, held together by the efforts of a few extraordinary individuals and by the habits of obedience engendered by the traditional structures of authority which continued mindlessly to operate.[2]

The allied victory in 1945 signalised the formal disappearance of the German state: for a while German sovereignty was in abeyance, and the occupying powers were free to rule Germany as they saw fit. In the East the Soviet Union rapidly established the basic components of a single-party system of government. In the West a far more confused and "open" situation prevailed. After a short period of extreme hostility towards the defeated German people, the three Western powers began, with different degrees of emphasis, to envisage the restoration of German self-government. They adopted this policy for a number of reasons. For the Americans the ideological argument played a major part, that is to say that the only way to "re-educate" the Germans in democratic self-government was to give them the chance to govern themselves again. For the British, and

[1] For an analysis of the predicament of the bureaucracy under the Nazi régime see H. Mommsen, *Beamtentum im Dritten Reich*, Stuttgart, 1966.

[2] Few books convey the style and atmosphere of Nazi government better than Albert Speer, *Inside the Third Reich*, London, 1970.

more slowly for the French, the economic case for allowing the Germans to manage their own affairs rapidly became overwhelming. To allow the Germans to rebuild their economy—and to do the job themselves—was gradually accepted as the only way of escaping a burden which none of the Western governments wanted to bear indefinitely. Then there was the impact of the confrontation of the Soviet Union with the U.S.A. which, from early 1947 onwards, made it increasingly obvious that a reconstructed Western Germany was required as a bulwark against the expansion of Soviet influence and control. This fast exerted an increasing influence on all three occupying powers in the two years before the establishment of the Federal Republic. Finally there was the problem posed by the decomposition of German society itself. Here was a country reduced to ruins. In 1946 industrial production had fallen to about 33% of its 1936 level, the population was swollen by an influx of refugees from the eastern territories of the old Reich, and many of the essential forms of social organisation and control were either dissolved or threatened with dissolution. It was soon accepted that only the Germans themselves could and should attempt to check and reverse these processes of dissolution.

## THE RECONSTRUCTION OF POLITICAL INSTITUTIONS

It is important when contemplating the manner in which a structure of government was restored in Western Germany to appreciate that the Western occupying powers had divergent interests in relation to the future of Germany and had no common doctrine defining the shape and character of the political and governmental system which they wished to see introduced. In the period up to late 1948 French interests were most clearly defined, successive French governments being anxious to prevent the re-formation of a unified German state (whether embracing East and West, or merely the three Western zones). They viewed with scepticism programmes for "re-educating" the Germans in modes of democratic government and considered that the maintenance of a divided Germany, with at least part of it under French tutelage, would best serve French national interests. On these grounds, when it became clear that the other two occupying powers were determined to press towards economic and political fusion of their separate occupation zones, the French became supporters of a decentralised reconstruction of Western Germany with renewed emphasis on federalism. The British Government was less specific in defining its interests. Although attaching importance to preventing a revival of German military power, it sensed from the outset of the post-war period that the political configuration of the world had changed decisively. The dominance of the U.S.A. and the U.S.S.R. as the two major world powers rendered the threat of German revival largely academic. It was appreciated too that the maintenance of British claims to a world role depended on a willingness to co-operate closely with the U.S.A. Above all, as mentioned already, British policy was marked by a hard-headed preoccupation with reducing the financial burdens of governing occupied Germany, even if this involved granting self-government to the Germans more rapidly than had been foreseen in 1945. On the other hand, the British, like the Americans, took more seriously than the French the need to pursue political re-education in Germany, and attached more importance to restructuring political institutions in order to encourage representative and responsible methods of government. Yet it would be an exaggeration to suggest that the British Government had very coherent ideas for the reshaping of German politics and government. The clearest example of a desire to offer the Germans an institutional model was at the local level, where in the British zone local government was largely reorganised on something like the separation between a politically responsible council and executive officials accountable to it such as is found in the United Kingdom.[3] When it came to thinking about the overall structure, little emerged beyond a preference for a reasonably strong central government: the British had little understanding of the subtleties of German administrative federalism.

Of the three occupying powers the U.S.A. was most powerfully committed to reforming German political attitudes and to encouraging a pluralist society in which there would be a vigorous interplay of interests conscious of their ability to participate in the making of political decisions. The U.S. Government was the first to permit the revival of political life at provincial and local levels, whilst pursuing at the same time a programme

---

[3]Formally this system of local government survives in North Rhine Westphalia and Lower Saxony, though in practice it has undergone important changes which bring it much nearer to the traditional German pattern of a strong executive balanced by a mainly deliberative legislative body.

of political re-education. But though the Americans were anxious to encourage the growth of a more flexible and adaptive social structure and a more democratic style of politics, they were reticent in pressing particular governmental structures on the Germans. There is little trace in the Federal Republic of the separation between legislature and executive in its American form, and where it does occur (for example, in the popular election of mayors in those areas of South Germany with the "Stadtratsverfassung" tradition), it is indigenous rather than imported. The German bureaucracy was an object of suspicion to the American authorities, but apart from imposing a measure of denazification to remove objectionable personnel, nothing decisive was undertaken to modify the kind of public service developed in Germany. When it came to designing a constitutional structure for the whole country, the U.S. Government was prepared to respect the wishes of the German delegates charged with the task, and made its influence felt only to the extent of encouraging the federalists and those who desired to see the introduction of judicial review of the constitutionality of public actions. Perhaps indeed the Federal Constitutional Court is the only institutional monument to American influence during the post-war years of occupations, and even the creation of this organ of control can be adequately explained in terms of native public law doctrine applied to the political experience of Nazism.

Thus we find that when the way was opened to the reconstruction of German political life and government, circumstances favoured the growth of an amalgam of tradition and change. The traumatic experiences of violence and disorder which had characterised the Nazi period, the disappearance from the higher levels of public life of nearly all those who had been actively associated with the defeated régime, and the control over the licensing of political parties exercised by the occupying powers favoured the simplification and moderation of party divisions which was to be the principal claim to originality of the Federal Republic. In contrast, when it came to the institutions of government and many of the formal rules of the political system traditional experience and precepts reasserted themselves. The occupying powers had no intention of writing a constitution for the Germans, even though in 1949 they maintained the right to approve and amend the draft Basic Law. Nor did they seek systematically to remodel German governmental institutions whilst they still had complete responsibility for the governing of the country. Here and there the

Germans were offered new devices, but even in such cases the occupying powers could not ensure that they would work as intended in their new social and political environment.

The provisional constitution of 1949—the Basic Law as it is entitled—was, therefore, in essentials a thoroughly German product.[4] Subject to very broad requirements relating to democratic government and the need for decentralisation of political power laid down by the occupying powers—with which in any event the writers of the constitution were in full sympathy—the drafters were left free to draw on their own historical experience. For the most part they were practical men, already deeply involved in provincial government and in political reconstruction. Most had been avowed opponents of the Nazi régime, and though their experience stretched back to the Weimar Republic and beyond, none had played a major part in national politics before 1933.

It is not surprising that the constitution which emerged was a sober and cautiously drafted document. It seeks to define in considerable detail both the principles on which the new state is to be based and the methods by which it is to be governed. Whilst asserting the sovereignty of the people (in Article 20), it also affirms that the exercise of this must be mediated through adherence to the separation of powers. Though there is reference to the conventional division between legislative, executive and judicial powers, the theory is conceived rather in terms of a comprehensive articulation of the state structure, with powers precisely specified, the conditions on which they can be used laid down, and the appropriate institutions defined. The Basic Law opens by reaffirming in decisive terms the sanctity of human rights, specifying them in some detail in the first nineteen articles and making them generally enforceable against public authorities. Though the Basic Rights have an individualist character, they are given a social dimension by the commitment of the Basic Law to the definition of the Federal Republic as a "sozialer Rechtsstaat".[5] This term

[4]For the best account of the framing of the Basic Law see J. E. Golay, *The Founding of the Federal Republic*, Chicago Univ. Press, 1958. For ample evidence of continuity in German constitutional concepts see the collection of successive constitutional documents from the mid-nineteenth century down to the Basic Law in H. Hildebrandt (ed.), *Die deutschen Verfassungen des 19 and 20 Jahrhunderts*, Schöningh, 1950.

[5]This phrase occurs in Art. 28 (1), Basic Law, where the Länder (provinces) are enjoined to maintain the principles of the "republican, democratic and social Rechtsstaat". It also appears as "Social Federal State" in Art. 20.

is difficult to translate, but it means a state founded on the rule of law and in which social and economic rights as well as the concomitant responsibilities of government are recognised. As to the form of government a parliamentary system was re-established, but with significant modifications as compared with that prevailing under the Weimar Republic. The popularly elected chamber, the Bundestag, has extensive legislative competence, though this is shared with the second chamber, the Bundesrat, representing the interests of the Länder or provinces. Whilst the Basic Law protects the Bundestag against arbitrary interference by the executive and makes dissolution extremely difficult,[6] the Federal Government has also been strengthened against the risks of party irresponsibility in the Bundestag. Only the head of the Government, the Federal Chancellor, is directly accountable to the Bundestag in the sense that he can be removed from office by a vote of no-confidence. But for this to happen it is necessary that the Bundestag should at the same time elect his successor, and with the emergence of a quasi-two-party system this has become virtually inconceivable.[7] Apart from enjoying considerable security of tenure the Federal Chancellor has also been strengthened *vis-à-vis* the members of his Government, and at the same time the President has been reduced to a mainly representative and honorific role.

A large part of the Basic Law is concerned with the determination of the federal structure, in particular with the place of the Bundesrat in the legislative process and with the division of competences between Federation and Länder. We shall consider at various stages later on the significance and character of German federalism. In connection with this outline of the Basic Law it is sufficient to emphasise that a federal structure was seen as an obstacle in the way of the centralisation of powers. It is, moreover, one of the conditions in the Basic Law which is declared to be inalienable in principle.[8] Many of the remaining provisions in the Basic Law deal with issues affecting the administration of justice and public administration

---

[6]Each Bundestag except the sixth (1969–72) has lasted for the prescribed four-year term. The erosion of Chancellor Brandt's majority in 1972 and the resulting impasse revealed how difficult it was to engineer a dissolution, though this was finally done.

[7]Art. 67, Basic Law. The one attempt so far to use this provision at national level failed in April 1972 when the CDU/CSU could not muster the required majority to replace Chancellor Brandt.

[8]Art. 79 (3), Basic Law.

generally. There are in addition sections added later to cover such matters as defence and a state of emergency.[9]

The Basic Law does not make easy reading. It is weighed down by administrative detail, it has been very much added to, and it lacks the touches of vision which appear in some earlier constitutions. Nevertheless for over twenty years now it has, in a very real sense, provided the framework within which West German politics and government have evolved. The Basic Law was, as experience has shown, a courageous and successful attempt to provide a basis for the reconstruction of German political life. Yet it also reveals at many points a reassertion and restoration of older traditions shaping the structure and operations of government. There is the return to the particularism of German history, explicit in the complicated structure of administrative federalism; the reaffirmation of faith in legal principles and judicial decisions as embodied in the statement of basic rights, in the provision for an all-embracing system of administrative law adjudication, and in the creation of a Federal Constitutional Court (in itself an innovation) as a means of resolving disputes to which public authority is a party; the reconstruction of parliamentary life and institutions on the foundations of the previous German experience of parliaments and how they should operate; the reaffirmation of the "well-earned rights" of the public service, tempered as we shall see later by political patronage and by the effects of a changed social situation; the guarantees for local self-government which represented a return to the values of earlier years when vigorous civic life in towns and cities was an important compensation for the weakness of representative institutions at the national level.

We should, however, guard against attaching a pejorative flavour to the term "restoration". In the context of post-war Western Germany it is not surprising that many political leaders sought to rescue something from the wreckage of the past, and were supported in this by public opinion. Not unnaturally they regarded the Nazi experiment as a nightmarish aberration, something to be guarded against in the future, but also to be forgotten. Most Germans could not accept the rejection of the whole of their modern history, back to the early years of the nineteenth century. Their view of the past became curiously discontinuous—a time stretching

[9]The seventh amendment, 1956, and the seventeenth amendment, 1968, refer to defence and a state of emergency. Both are very complex.

up to 1933, then a blank period to 1945, and then a new start. In reconstructing a system of government they had to connect up again with those parts of the past which could still be claimed as worthy elements in the national tradition. Hence "restoration" had a psychological justification as well as a practical value.

## THE RESHAPING OF THE PARTY SYSTEM

The collapse of the Weimar Republic imprinted one lesson very firmly on the minds of those politicians who were active after the end of the Second World War in the reconstruction of the West German state. This was that it was essential in the future to try to escape from the fragmented and unstable party system which had undermined government and opened the way to totalitarian solutions. It is this conviction which explains a number of provisions in the Basic Law of 1949 and in subsequent legislation[10] which were intended to protect governments against the effects of party instability and to discourage the emergence or survival of small parties and factions. However, the founders of the Federal Republic were probably too pessimistic in their evaluation of how the political attitudes of their compatriots would develop. The West German voters quickly showed their preference for a greatly simplified party system, dominated by two broadly based parties and contrasting sharply with the pre-1933 pattern of numerous conflicting groups committed to the defence of particular ideologies or sectional interests and largely indifferent to the needs of government.

Within four years of the inauguration of the Federal Republic in 1949 the voters had already repudiated most of the smaller political parties which had emerged when the Western occupation powers had permitted organised political activity to start up again, and which in the elections of 1949 had gained 80 of the 402 seats in the first Bundestag.[11] In the 1953

[10]Notably in both Federal and Land electoral law.

[11]In the Bundestag election 1949 the three main parties, Christian Democratic Union/Christian Social Union, Social Democratic Party and Free Democratic Party, had already secured 322 seats. The remaining eighty were distributed as follows:

| | |
|---|---|
| KPD (Communist Party) | 15 |
| BP (Bavarian Party) | 17 |
| DP (German Party) | 17 |

*(continued opposite)*

elections the minor parties could secure only forty-five seats, most of which went to the conservative German Party (DP) and to the transitory Refugee Party (GB–BHE). By 1957 a three-party situation was fully confirmed, since the small German Party with seventeen seats was already a dependency of the dominant Christian Democratic Union. Since 1961 only three parties—the Christian Democratic/Christian Social Union, the Social Democratic Party and the Free Democratic Party—have been represented in the Bundestag or have had any serious chance of being so represented. In the 1969 Bundestag elections, for example, the CDU/CSU, SPD and FDP gained 94.6% of the votes cast, the two large parties alone having 88.8% of the vote between them. Nor has this con-centration of support on two major parties and a single surviving minor partner been confined to national politics. Similar developments have taken place in the Länder and in local government, though in some cases more gradually than at national level.

The extent of the change in German political attitudes and loyalties is not to be measured merely in terms of the smaller number of parties. It must also be assessed in relation to the different nature of the post-war political parties and to a different popular view of what an election is about. All three major parties, and in particular the Christian Democrats and the Social Democrats, have consciously tried to become comprehensive parties, appealing to all sections of the community and accessible to a wide range of organised interests. Inevitably this meant that their ideological wine had to be diluted with the water of political pragmatism. For the Christian Democrats this process was relatively easy. The movement was founded as a deliberate effort to bridge social, political and religious divisions. Its principles were formulated in extremely broad terms so that they could appeal to widely differing social and economic groups. For the Social Democrats the retreat from ideological rigidity took rather more time and caused some heart-searching. But even before the party adopted a

---

| | |
|---|---|
| Z (Centre Party) | 10 |
| WAV (Association for Economic Reconstruction) | 12 |
| DReP/DKP (German Right and Conservative Parties) | 5 |
| NG (Notgemeinschaft) | 1 |
| SSW (South Schleswig Electors Association) | 1 |
| Independents | 2 |

revised programme of moderate social reform in 1959[12] it had gone a long way towards "de-marxification" and acceptance of many of the policies pursued so successfully by its Christian Democrat rivals.

The high level of agreement between the major parties on basic issues during the sixties underlined the shift which has taken place in the character and purpose of elections. Increasingly they have become contests for political leadership between two competing political groups, each confident of its ability to form and maintain a government. In such contests the personality and popularity of the alternative party leaders have come to play a major part. As early as 1953 Konrad Adenauer set the stage for this kind of election. His longevity as Chancellor and his repeated success in the elections of 1953, 1957 and 1961 underlined decisively the advantages in electoral terms of firm party leadership, a lesson which was taken to heart by the Social Democrats in their long haul towards political power which culminated in Willi Brandt's election to the Chancellorship in 1969. Though the third party, the Free Democrats, has managed to survive,[13] and has indeed been able to play a major part in government both before 1966 in coalition with the CDU and after 1969 with the SPD, the competition for power is essentially between the two big parties and is so perceived by well over 80% of the electorate. The emergence of an essentially two-party situation was confirmed by the termination in 1969 of the Grand Coalition between the CDU and SPD, and the rapid formation of an SPD/FDP coalition. Since that date the rivalry between Government and Opposition as competitors for government office has been more clearly defined than ever before. National politics have become dominated by the contest between two rival teams of political managers, each placing more emphasis on proving its competence in government than on offering sharply contrasting programmes to the electorate.

The political experience of the Federal Republic suggests overwhelmingly that major and irreversible changes in the organisation of political interests and activity have taken place. It has become legitimate to underline

---

[12]Known generally as the Godesberg Programme after Bad Godesberg where the party congress which accepted the new programme was held.

[13]The FDP has suffered considerably from the polarising effect of the two main parties. It achieved 11.9% of the vote in the 1949 Bundestag elections, 12.8% in 1961, 9.5% in 1965 and 5.8% in 1969. In 1972 the decline was apparently checked when the party got 8.4%.

the similarities between the politics of the Federal Republic and those of both Britain and the U.S.A. Nevertheless, qualifications have often been suggested which would throw some doubt on the completeness of the changes which have affected German politics.

One of these qualifications concerns the extent to which the new political stability might in future be endangered by a renewal of popular support for authoritarian radicalism, particularly if there were any serious break in the pattern of continuous economic growth. Until the end of the sixties this risk was nearly always seen in terms of a revival of the radicalism of the Right. More recently the threat—assuming that it exists—can be seen more obviously on the Left.

In the early years of the Federal Republic there were sporadic, and for the most part localised, signs of renewed support for neo-Nazi extremist groups. A combination of factors removed this danger—rapid economic revival, the social integration of refugees from the East, the success of Adenauer's governments in re-establishing the new German state, the electoral provisions penalising small parties,[14] and the banning by the Federal Constitutional Court of the extremist Socialist Reich Party in 1952. The formation of the National Democratic Party in 1965 on the ruins of a number of earlier Right-wing movements and its modest success in 1966–7 in gaining a few seats in several Land parliaments suggested that there was an under-current of resentment against the established parties which could in suitable conditions (e.g. economic depression, worsening external relations) undermine their position. The National Democratic Party secured its best result in the Baden-Württemberg Land elections of April 1968 with 9.8% of the vote, its average in other Land elections being nearer 7%. In the national election of 1969 it was already on the wane and with only 4.3% of the votes failed to gain any seats in the Bundestag. Thereafter its disintegration as an effective party was rapid.

The most plausible explanation of this short-lived revival of Right-wing radicalism lies in the mood of disillusionment caused by the modest economic recession of 1965–7 and the failure of the Christian Democrats under Chancellor Erhard to demonstrate a continued capacity to govern. Though the resolution of the political crisis of 1965–6 by the formation of a

[14]The most important sanction against small parties is the 5% clause, operative in national and most Land elections, which effectively denies seats to parties gaining less than 5% of the popular vote.

CDU/SPD coalition was widely held at the time to be an encouragement to political radicalism, in retrospect this effect seems to have been of marginal significance, at any rate as far as political developments on the Right were concerned. In the first two years of its life the Kiesinger,Brandt coalition demonstrated a capacity for firm action by successfully tackling a number of problems, chiefly financial and economic. This, combined with a renewal of the upward trend of economic activity, was enough to bring back in 1969 to both major parties many of those who had given protest votes to the National Democratic Party.

The problem of Left-wing radicalism is more complex, and moreover continues to play a big part in West German political life. In the fifties Left splinter groups could gain little support, partly because of the pre-vailing Cold War climate and partly because of the intense preoccupation in West German society with economic reconstruction. The German Communist Party was finally banned as unconstitutional in 1956, a decision which later probably had the effect of encouraging the emergence of radical splinter groups within the SPD and on the fringes of that party. During the sixties the Federal Republic began to experience social changes similar to those affecting most Western countries, characterised above all by the emergence of a younger generation conscious of its separateness from the rest of society, and by an explosive expansion of higher education. Left-wing protest groups began to proliferate and the universities have ex-perienced a crisis of purpose and structure which is by no means resolved yet.

The political expression of these developments has been confused. Numerous radical groups have been formed and re-formed, though none has recently taken shape as a political party campaigning in elections. The Communist Party was allowed to reappear in 1969–70 under a slightly different name, though it has so far failed signally to attract support. Some of the more desperate radical groups have resorted to acts of political terrorism, but by 1972 these had died down and most of the leaders were in jail awaiting trial.

Perhaps the most important aspect of political radicalism on the Left is the extent to which it finds expression within the SPD, exerting pressure on the leadership to shift its politics in a more radical direction. So far, however, the present leadership has made few concessions and has stuck firmly to the programme of moderate social reform which has guided the party since 1959. To a large extent this reflects a shrewd appreciation of the tactical situation in which the SPD, along with the other parties, finds itself. To have a chance of governing—either alone or more likely in coalition with the Free Democrats—both major parties must compete for the centre. In the 1972 election the SPD had the advantage of substantial achievements in normalising relations with the Soviet bloc and the DDR, a highly respected leader, and a programme of social and economic action which stuck firmly to balanced progress within the existing framework of society. The bulk of the electorate saw the party in this light. The Opposition's efforts to underline the dangers of creeping radicalism inside the SPD back-fired, though equally it must not be forgotten that a significant proportion of voters did in fact qualify their approval of the SPD by ensuring that the Free Democrats were strengthened. There is every reason to believe that the present SPD leaders are keenly alive to the fact that the maintenance of the party's now strong position depends very much on their ability to restrain the enthusiasts and dogmatists within the party. So far this has been done successfully at the national level, though owing to the dispersion of power inherent in the West German political system, the national leadership cannot prevent more radical elements from gaining influence in local and provincial politics. This in turn establishes the pressures which so far the national leadership has generally resisted.

A second qualification to the broad characterisation of West German party development which has been offered here lies in the continuing influence of a tradition of coalition politics. This has found expression in two directions: in the survival of a third party which has rendered some form of coalition government inescapable at the national level, and in the activity within the major parties of a considerable number of groups, factions and tendencies claiming an influence on policy-making and the distribution of political offices. Apart from demonstrating the survival of a group of traditional Liberal voters[15] the tenacious hold on life of the FDP also testifies to the mistrust which a section of the electorate still feels

[15]This was almost certainly the case until about 1967-8. Since then an attempt has been made to appeal to younger and perhaps more radical voters, with less emphasis on engaging the support of business interests and the educated middle class. The 1969 election results did not suggest that this policy had paid off, but those of 1972 suggest that there may be new reservoirs of support for the FDP.

towards the dominance of two large parties, each unrestrained by the need to moderate its policies in deference to the claims of a third group. The strategic position of the FDP did, however, also help to produce circumstances in which the preference for coalition politics found expression in a Grand Coalition of the two major parties. When the CDU realised in 1966, following the withdrawal of the FDP from the Erhard Government that co-operation with the FDP was no longer feasible, the party experienced no great difficulty in envisaging the prospect of collaboration with the SPD. Likewise the bulk of the SPD leadership quickly saw advantages in finally acceding to a share in national government, and at any rate for two years was able to co-operate very successfully with the CDU in implementing a range of financial and economic policies which had been blocked by the differences within the old CDU/FDP coalition. Acceptance of a Grand Coalition was in part due to the realisaion by the SPD that this was the best way to ensure recognition of its status as *the* alternative government. But it was also made easy by the long experience of coalition policy-making within the Bundestag and of participation in national affairs by SPD-controlled governments in the Länder.

Some observers of German politics concluded over-hastily that the Grand Coalition heralded an era of "Proporz" politics in the Austrian style. Events have disproved this thesis. Indeed the years since 1969 have been marked by a far sharper tactical differentiation between the SPD and the CDU than was present in the sixties, and their behaviour in national politics has come to resemble more closely that of the two parties in Britain, with each keen to exploit for electoral purposes the difficulties experienced by its rival. In essentials the two-party concept has triumphed over the coalition preference, though its application still remains modified by the reluctance of the electorate to confirm its irrevocability.

Turning to the aspect of pluralism and diversity within the parties, it must be said that this has imposed considerable restraints on the discretion and autonomy of the party leaderships. The Social Democrats, building on a long tradition of working-class solidarity and organisational unity, have been least affected by internal divisions, at any rate until the beginning of the seventies. The old leadership with experience of the Weimar Republic (and of persecution at the hands of the Nazis) gave way gradually at the end of the fifties to younger leaders whose political experience has been chiefly or wholly within the framework of the Federal Republic.[16] But even the SPD must take account of a dispersion of political power and influence which stems partly from a structure of government which ensures that at the provincial (Land) and local level the prizes of office are worth having, and partly from the existence within the party of groups with distinctive and usually conflicting views on policy questions. The composition of the collective party leadership depends only to a limited extent on the preferences of the official leader, and rather more on the balance of forces within the party, which in turn reflects genuine positions of influence in the parliamentary process or in the management of public affairs away from the federal capital. The SPD is, however, free from one major potential source of internal division, that is to say organisational and financial dependence on the trade unions. Though supported by the German Trade Union Federation (DGB), the party has no official links with the unions, nor can they claim any special rights within the party.

In the Christian Democratic Union the earlier complexity of German party divisions is still mirrored more faithfully. Here is a party which was avowedly built up as a coalition of disparate and often conflicting interests and points of view.[17] It brought together previously separated Catholics and Protestants; it appealed to peasants, farmers and larger landowners, to big industry and to small shopkeepers, to advocates of a market economy suitably tamed by social conscience and to protagonists of the most generous social welfare provisions, to the predominantly urban working class of the Rhineland between Bonn and Düsseldorf and to the conservative and often nationalist rural populations of Schleswig-Holstein and Lower Saxony. This catalogue of appeals to groups with differing traditions and political views could be extended still further. And above all, linked with the party in permanent alliance is a distinct Bavarian wing, the Christian Social Union, constituting a powerful and independent faction whose demands, especially in relation to the distribution of political patronage, must be respected by the managers of the CDU itself. This proliferation of

---

[16]Nevertheless, it is significant that the two men most closely associated with the SPD's rise to power, Brandt and Wehner, have been deeply influenced by their differing experiences of political opposition and emigration before 1945.

[17]For a good account of the early years of the party see A. Heidenheimer, *Adenauer and the CDU*, Nijhoff, 1960.

separate and often conflicting interests within the Christian Democratic movement, some of which are now subject to erosion in the wake of social and economic change, has meant that the party has never been the homogeneous and coherent instrument of government which the dominance of its first leader, Dr. Adenauer, and its remarkable record of success at the polls would suggest. Its organisation has remained decentralised and policy-making requires extensive intra-party discussion and compromise. This is not to deny that the party has succeeded in forming and sustaining effective governments: indeed its record compares favourably with that of major parties in other parliamentary democracies. But in assessing the operation of German government and the processes of policy-making, it must be remembered that the party in power from 1949 to 1969 has been a coalition of groups, loosely held together and firmly entrenched in different layers of the governmental system. Here the influence of earlier particularism and of the contemporary decentralised institutional structure was strongly at work.

The Free Democrats also exhibit many of the characteristics of internal diversity which are found in the Christian Democrats. Their party organisation too is decentralised and subject to regional or local pressures. In particular there has been a record of internal argument within the party, provoked partly by genuine differences of policy and political outlook, and partly by the clash of personal ambitions.

The regrouping of political forces in Western Germany over the past twenty-five years has produced a party system which is far better adapted to the functional requirements of a parliamentary form of government than any which Germany has previously known. But the larger, more coherent and united parties of the Federal Republic have absorbed some elements of the earlier multi-party situation. They include within themselves groups which still have a sense of their own distinctiveness—though the grounds for this are many and varied—and which find through the German system of government itself means of maintaining their positions within the power structures of the parties. The Federal Republic appears to have solved the twin problem which faces any complex democratic society: that of organising and maintaining political parties which are capable of mediating and harmonising a substantial proportion of the interests and demands present in the society, and that of securing stable government capable of responding to the policy needs expressed in the political life of the country. Given the earlier experience of modern Germany the magnitude of this achievement should not be underestimated. Here is a major element of innovation.

## THE SOCIAL AND ECONOMIC CONTEXT OF POLITICAL RECONSTRUCTION

The political reshaping of the Federal Republic has been strongly influenced by the social and economic trends of the post-war period. In particular the major features of the economic policies pursued after 1949 have had a big impact on the role of government in society.

Critics of West German society, both inside and outside the Federal Republic, have tended to underline the absence of profound social change after the Second World War and the survival of many traditional attitudes in social behaviour, in particular in the family.[18] But though it is a fact that no social revolution took place after 1945, it is equally true that post-war West German society has acquired many characteristics which distinguish it sharply from what it was earlier in this century. Most striking perhaps has been the rate at which urbanisation and industrial development have gone ahead. The agricultural population has declined steadily. In 1939 it amounted to 17% of the total population; by 1960 it had fallen to slightly less than 11% in the Federal Republic and the reduction has continued down to the present time. *Pari passu* the proportion of the population employed in industry and services has risen and there has been a major expansion of nearly all the larger and medium-sized cities. The small country towns have declined in significance and huge areas around the large cities have become essentially suburban regions for commuters to the major centres of business and industry. Mobility has increased enormously, with the result that in some areas of rapid expansion (for example, Baden-Württemberg) a high proportion of voters have come in from other parts of the country. Equally there was a huge influx of refugees, initially from the territories lost to Poland, Czechoslovakia and the U.S.S.R., later (and up to 1961) from Eastern Germany. They have been absorbed in the West with remarkable success, their presence

---

[18]See, for example, the critique of society and politics in R. Dahrendorf, *Society and Democracy in Germany*, London, 1968.

acting as an additional impetus to social and economic mobility.[19]

The rapid progress of urbanisation has favoured the emergence of a more open and secular society. Traditional constraints and conventions have been eroded, especially in recent years as the total commitment to economic reconstruction has weakened and more critical questions have been asked about the purposes of industrial growth and the problems which it presents. But the overall effect of the social and economic development of the past two and a half decades has been to encourage a far more pragmatic approach to political issues and to direct attention away from questions of political ideology and belief to specific policies and the solution of concrete problems. Almost certainly the fact that the Federal Republic has a highly decentralised system of government has assisted this trend: there has been plenty of scope below the level of the central government for initiative and energy to be directed to the practical tasks of reconstruction and redevelopment which faced the country in the years after 1945.

The war and its aftermath also had a sharp impact on the position of the traditional élites. The aristocracy was shattered, losing most of the influence which it had had in administration and the armed forces, as well as its land in the East. The war years and after led to some changes in the ownership of industry, though the rise of a new managerial élite owed more to the pace of reconstruction and expansion of post-war industry than to any positive steps to dispossess or weaken those who had previously controlled large parts of private industry. In political life, and to a lesser extent in the public service, new men had to be found to replace those who had been associated with the Nazi régime. In the absence of any coherent governing groups there were in the Federal Republic many opportunities in all sectors of society for new people to rise to the top: to a considerable extent the idea of "la carrière ouverte aux talents" prevailed. Self-made men came to the fore in politics, administration, industry, banking, commerce and the professions. This is not to say that family and social connections, as well as favourable educational opportunities, became entirely irrelevant. But undoubtedly they became less significant as

[19]Between 1945 and 1960 it is estimated that approximately 13 million people moved into Western Germany, most of them from the eastern parts of the former Reich and from Eastern Germany.

determinants of career achievement than they have been, for example, in Britain or France.

The emergence of something like a classless society—at any rate in the Scandinavian or American sense of "classless"—sustains the pragmatic and cautious approach to political issues which has characterised the evolution of the Federal Republic. Those who have risen by their own efforts have tended to see problems in very practical terms and to be suspicious of policies which might endanger what they have achieved. The strength of these attitudes has permitted a wide range of policy issues to be successfully tackled without the wear and tear of serious ideological arguments. For example, public support for housing has proceeded without very much conflict about public versus private ownership; industrial relations were established on a basis of regulation broadly acceptable to both sides in industry; taxation policy has (at any rate until very recently) been evolved without any obsession with its potentialities as an instrument of income redistribution.

Another aspect of the renewal of personnel in many of the key areas of society is that it has eroded much of the rigidity and authoritarianism of the past. This is most obvious in politics where, with a few major exceptions, the leadership soon passed to people whose experience was entirely of the pragmatic bargaining style of the Federal Republic. In the public services this process was slower, but gathered speed in the sixties. On the other hand, the emergence of new élite groups has also brought uncertainty. They could not have the self-confidence and inherited values of some of the groups they replaced, and it is not surprising that the Federal Republic has experienced some difficulty in stabilising conventions and accepted codes of behaviour in public life.

The social changes of the past twenty years have owed much to the economic performance of the Federal Republic. Much has been written about the "economic miracle" presided over by Professor Erhard who was Economics Minister from 1949 to 1963. We are not concerned here to describe or assess this "miracle", but only to mention a few aspects of the economic thinking on which it was based. For fairly obvious reasons a majority of West Germans after 1945 rejected state planning, control and ownership. Erhard's unique contribution was to convince most of his countrymen that reliance on market economy principles, tempered by steady improvement of the social services, would guarantee a successful reconstruction of the German economy. Entrepreneurial initiative and the pursuit of profits were encouraged; the liberalisation of trade was pursued and exposure to market competition was preached as the best way to efficiency and rising output; the state disavowed any planning role and in the interests of price stability pursued orthodox financial policies.

In many parts of the Western world post-war German economic doctrine has been regarded as old-fashioned and simplistic. Yet the proof of the pudding remains in the eating. In the conditions of post-war Western Germany the neo-Liberal market economy doctrine was accepted enthusiastically and the results of its application were impressive. Even allowing for special factors, in particular Marshall Aid and the absence of a defence budget for some years, the economic policies pursued produced a rate of revival which nobody foresaw in the immediate post-war years.

The commitment of the Federal Republic to market economy policies had important consequences for the role of government. It meant that there was no sudden growth of direct public intervention in the economic sector and that the bulk of economic legislation was of a regulatory kind, much of it in the German tradition of the public regulation of the conditions on which enterprises can be run and professions practised. More positively, governments sought to ensure that obstacles were not placed in the way of new economic developments and that taxation inducements were available to encourage them. Broadly the West German rejection of central planning and increased governmental involvement in industry and commerce had the effect of restraining the rate of increase in the responsibilities of government and administration. This in turn was to help the survival of the traditional structure and methods of administration. Since the German central administration was not asked to bear a burden of new economic functions for which it was not on the whole well equipped, it naturally escaped for a long time much of the criticism which elsewhere has been directed against centralised bureaucracies trying to perform tasks for which they are usually ill adapted. Only in the last few years, and for reasons which have little to do with the economic role of government, have demands been raised for some modernisation of the system of public administration.

It must not be assumed that the post-1949 approach to economic policy implied no state intervention or a dogmatic rejection of public subsidies and ownership. For historical reasons the Federal and Land Governments inherited extensive public industrial holdings, and there has always been a big sector of municipal enterprise. For many branches of industry (and especially agriculture) there have been measures of public financial support. The crucial point for the politics of the Federal Republic has been that, on the whole, there has been little ideological argument about public enterprise and measures of government support: they have been judged pragmatically on their merits and run in harness with policies favourable to a high level of private investment, an expanding volume of international trade and the maintenance of price stability.

To sum up, the social and economic climate of the Federal Republic has done much to support the growth of pragmatic and non-ideological politics. In this environment an active pluralism in political life has taken root. This is seen not only in the political parties and their behaviour, but also in the part played by the network of organised interests in the society which seek to influence the course of public policy at all levels. Equally the changes which have taken place have eroded much of the former deference to authority; attitudes towards government have become more instrumental and politicians are judged more by what they achieve than by the programmes they proclaim. There is some irony in the fact that the recent revival on the Left of dogmatic political thinking committed to "overcoming the system" is as much a reaction against the restraints inherent in the politics of bargaining and compromise, up to now generally taken as a sign of political maturity, as a protest against the materialism inevitably associated with the single-minded pursuit of economic prosperity. Nevertheless, despite these signs of dissent, "the system" shows remarkable stability and continues to enjoy the support of the vast majority of the Federal Republic's citizens. Against this background we can begin to examine the structure and operations of government.

# CHAPTER 3

# *Federal Executive Leadership*

THE powers of government are exercised at several levels in the Federal Republic, but it is on the Government in Bonn that most political attention is concentrated. This is not surprising: it stands at the centre of national political life and enjoys pre-eminence in the shaping of public policy.

The framers of the Basic Law stood under the shadow of the failure during the Weimar Republic to secure executive leadership which was both effective and responsible. Most of them appreciated well enough that in the final analysis government in a democracy can be no stronger than the forces supporting it. Its ability to govern must depend on the behaviour and policies of the political parties, just as whether it is "responsible" or not also depends on how the parties use the institutional framework of the political system to maintain a balance between the need for coherent direction of national affairs and responsiveness to the demands expressed in the interests and opinions they represent. Therefore, the hope of securing effective and responsible government would depend mainly on whether the party system overcame the weaknesses of the Weimar period.

Nevertheless, the builders of the Federal Republic were determined to do whatever could be done by institutional means to prevent a recurrence of the paralysis of government and resort to an irresponsible presidential authority which became inevitable before 1933. Three conditions were seen as particularly important in this respect: neutralisation of the presidency, a strengthening of the position of the head of the Federal Government, and the imposition of penalties on Parliament should it seek to use its authority irresponsibly. The principal constitutional provisions relevant to the executive embody these aims. The President has been reduced to a figurehead not very different from a constitutional monarch of the British or Scandinavian type. Later in this chapter we shall return briefly to the significance of this office. The Federal Chancellor has indeed been strengthened, both by making him the only minister who is in a strict constitutional sense responsible to the Bundestag and also by emphasising more clearly his prerogatives in relation to other members of the Federal Government. Finally, though the Bundestag has the right and duty of electing the Chancellor, it cannot remove him without electing a successor. In this way the parliamentary arm of government has been compelled to envisage the responsibility and responsiveness of the Government in terms other than those which focus on the ability of the legislature to dismiss it. Such are the principal constitutional devices which underpin the Federal executive.

## THE FEDERAL GOVERNMENT

What is formally entitled "the Federal Government" consists of the Federal Chancellor and Federal ministers. The roles of these two components differ substantially, which means that it is necessary to look at them separately. Nevertheless Chancellor and ministers are in many ways interdependent and it is important to consider the extent to which the Federal Government has collegial qualities. This is one reason for beginning with some comments on the ideas built into the constitutional definition of the Federal Government as an entity embracing both Chancellor and ministers.

The structure of the Federal Government is dealt with in Section VI of the Basic Law. The provisions here manage to combine three rather different principles, all of which have their roots in the past. There is first the idea of strong governmental leadership, expressed in the formal definition of the pre-eminent role of the Chancellor. This goes at least as far back as the Reich constitution of 1871, which provided that the Chancellor would assume responsibility for all the formal decisions of the Imperial Government in virtue of his counter-signature. This tradition is maintained in the Basic Law. Under Article 65 the Chancellor is responsible for determining the "guidelines of policy", and under Article 64 he proposes the appointment and dismissal of ministers to the President.

Alongside the "Chancellor principle" there is an element of collegiality in the structure of the Federal Government, expressed most clearly in the provision in Article 65 of the Basic Law that the Federal Government resolves disputes between ministers. In other words, the Cabinet is intended collectively to determine contested issues and in this way to assume some kind of collective responsibility. This element, a commonplace in any system of cabinet government dependent on parliamentary approval, can be traced back in Germany to the Liberal movement of the last century, one of the aims of which was to substitute government by a collectively responsible group for the traditional Council of State whose members were individually dependent on the Crown and owed no obligation to each other. Yet it is interesting, and of some practical significance, that this reference to the collective duties of members of the Government does not really underline their joint responsibility as a central group for the taking of political decisions. The emphasis is far more on helping to resolve disputes within the group rather than on the group having a positive responsibility in which all share. Against this background it is not surprising that the element of collective Cabinet responsibility and solidarity has been fairly weak in the practice of German government. Whether or not it has been strengthened is a point to return to later.

Finally there is the element of individual ministerial responsibility and autonomy. Individual ministerial responsibility in the sense that each minister could be subject to a withdrawal of parliamentary confidence and thereby forced to resign was known only for the brief period of the Weimar Republic. The consequences in terms of coalition instability were not encouraging. But individual responsibility in the sense of being charged with the autonomous management of a sector of governmental affairs goes back much further, for example to the type of executive organisation which developed in Prussia in the first half of the nineteenth century. Essentially the individual minister was regarded as a high official to whom the control of a department was entrusted. Indeed, under the Empire there were no ministers in a strict sense at all, merely state secretaries drawn from the bureaucracy, and even when the growing scale of government compelled some recognition of their departments as autonomous Reich agencies, nothing equivalent to a "Ministry" or "Cabinet" developed. Not surprisingly the "responsibility" of a departmental head was seen only in terms of his duty to run his department on behalf of the Chancellor or, more precisely, the monarch. Something of this bureaucratic notion of individual responsibility survives in the Basic Law, for Article 65 states that, subject to the rights of the Chancellor to determine the guidelines of policy, ministers shall manage their departments on their own responsibility. There is no question here of responsibility to Parliament in a constitutional sense, though in practice a minister is obliged in many ways to account to the Bundestag for his actions. It is far more the principle of autonomy in the exercise of powers properly conferred on ministers and in the administration of policy which is expressed in this provision. In some respects, therefore, the underlying concept of a minister remains ambivalent: he is an amalgam of political leadership and bureaucratic authority.[1]

The presence of these three elements in the structure of the Federal Government underlines the continuing importance of earlier experience in the shaping of the political executive. How they have worked out in practice has, of course, depended very much upon personalities and party relationships, and upon the constraints imposed by the increasing complexity of the work of government itself. There is no doubt that Dr. Adenauer preferred to emphasise the principle of strong leadership by the Chancellor, and that he found it congenial to regard most of his ministers as loyal subordinates whose job was to manage their departments independently, but with due regard to his control of major policy issues. Nor did he hesitate to intervene in the affairs of particular departments when political circumstances seemed to require such action on his part. Subsequent Chancellors have been much influenced by the conventions which he established, though in theory they have expressed a preference for a more collegial style of government. In practice this has been difficult to achieve. Professor Erhard was afflicted by dissensions within the CDU/FDP coalition which he headed, and this made it impossible either for him to assert the authority of his own office or to secure something more like a Cabinet style of leadership. The CDU/SPD Grand Coalition under Dr. Kiesinger got nearer to a genuine collective responsibility than any previous Government, chiefly because of the close party balance in the Cabinet which enforced a higher degree of solidarity and collective decision-making. This inevitably meant that the Chancellor was somewhat weak-

---

[1]This point is underlined by the generous pension provisions for those who have held ministerial office: they are treated in this respect rather as if they had been civil servants.

ened. Under the SPD/FDP coalition headed by Chancellor Brandt since 1969 the style of Cabinet government has remained ambiguous. In principle the coalition parties, and particularly the SPD, favour a more collegial style of political leadership. But the position of the Chancellor in his party has been strong and like the first Chancellor he was determined to play a dominant part in some sectors of policy, notably in foreign affairs, whilst leaving to some of his more outstanding colleagues wide discretion in the control of their own fields of action. Thus the most recent experience of the Federal Government has been marked by a reassertion of the "Chancellor principle", though with a greater readiness on the part of the Chancellor than in earlier years to leave to Cabinet arbitration and decision areas of policy to which he was not personally committed or which, because of their inherent complexity, cannot easily be brought within his control.

The way in which relations within the Federal Government have evolved has been strongly influenced by the exigencies of coalition politics as well as by the idea that a minister must manage his own department independently. The need to satisfy various demands within the political parties has meant that a lot of importance has been attached to how functions are shared out, and that their recipients have tended to regard their departments as fiefs to be administered jealously and guarded against encroachment by others. The demands of coalition politics have also imposed limits on the ability of Chancellors to assert their rights of policy direction. Even Adenauer had frequently to make concessions in internal policy for the sake of maintaining the minimum necessary degree of Cabinet unity. Indeed the rights of the Chancellor have sometimes been subjected to what might be described as "treaty limitations", as for example in the ill-fated coalition agreement of 1961 on which Adenauer's last Government had to be based. But though the needs of coalition politics have undoubtedly strengthened the hands of individual ministers and of the party groups they represent, this has not generally worked in favour of reinforcing the Government as a whole *vis-à-vis* the Chancellor: instead it has underlined the differences on which Governments have had to be based and confined the Cabinet generally to its role of arbitrator of unbridgeable differences rather than reinforcing its claims to a collective control of policy.

However, it is possible that changes are in the making which may gradually modify the relationships within the Federal Government. The vast majority of candidates for political office now have behind them a parliamentary experience and see themselves much more as political generalists than as specialists in particular fields of public action. In public discussion of the Government there has too, in recent years, been more interest in its political role as the main agency for the determination and co-ordination of policies, and political parties have responded by projecting their cabinet "teams". (That the SPD was less keen on this in the election of 1972 suggests, however, a shrewd awareness of the advantages of having a strong leader who can be trusted to exploit the prerogatives of the Chancellor's office.) These developments will probably take some time yet to acquire a clear shape. For the moment the somewhat conflicting elements which have just been outlined continue to determine the shape and character of the Federal Government. So we must turn to look more closely at its two principal components, the Chancellor as its animator and leader, and then at the ministers who support him.

## THE FEDERAL CHANCELLOR

Much has been written about the Chancellor and his role in the government of the Federal Republic.[2] His office has been seen as the keystone of the political system, the guarantee of stability and coherence in the new democratic structure of German politics. Undoubtedly much of the attention paid to the Chancellorship is attributable to the fascination exerted by Adenauer, the first holder of the office, a man of political genius and tenacity of purpose whose long and successful tenure established the Chancellorship as the key position in German political life. That in the popular imagination elections have come to hinge on the qualities of the candidates for the Chancellorship is to a large extent the result of Adenauer's style of leadership. Equally it was he who developed conventions governing the role of the Chancellor in relation to the other elements in the political system which left no doubt about the wide discretion which the head of Government could claim to exercise.

As already mentioned, the Chancellor is the only minister constitu-

---

[2]See, for example, W. Hennis, *Richtlinienkompetenz und Regierungstechnik*, Tübingen, 1964; J. Amphoux, *Le Chancelier fédéral dans le régime constitutionnel de la Republique Fédérale d'Allemagne*, Paris, 1962.

C

tionally responsible to the Bundestag. Formally the President proposes a candidate for election, but in practice he has had no influence over the nomination. To be elected a Chancellor candidate requires the support of a majority of members of the Bundestag, but there are provisions for a minority Chancellor being proposed for appointment. Only in that event has the President the discretion either to appoint him or to dissolve the Bundestag. Thus the constitutional provisions were designed to place the responsibility for electing a Chancellor squarely on the shoulders of the Bundestag. In fact the Bundestag as an institution does not play a big part in the choice of Chancellor. Political convention has established the leaders of the two main parties as the obvious candidates, and their positions depend on intra-party relationships. In so far as neither of the major parties has normally been able to count on securing an absolute majority, arguments about the terms on which a Chancellor candidate will be supported by the third party have always been necessary and have been conducted in the relative privacy of party negotiating committees. In addition, within the Christian Democrat Party the CSU wing has often aspired to a special influence over the selection of the leader. The constitutional clause guarding against the dangers of a minority government has so far remained a dead-letter, since the multi-party situation which it was intended to cover has never occurred.[3]

The same may be said of the right of the Bundestag to censure a Chancellor and enforce his removal. The procedure here was to be the famous constructive vote of no-confidence, enshrined in Article 67 of the Basic Law. The Bundestag can strike down one Chancellor only by setting up another. Until April 1972 the possibility of invoking this procedure remained academic. The attempt to use it then failed, underlining that it is unworkable in a quasi-two-party context as a means of exchanging governments. The only way out then is an appeal to the electorate for which the Basic Law makes no straightforward provision. Just as the British Prime Minister's right to dissolve Parliament is often pictured as a sword of Damocles poised to discipline dissident members of the majority party, so the obligation to elect a successor has been thought of as the unpleasant

---

[3] The possibility of a minority Chancellor appeared in mid-1972. But this arose from the near-equality of votes between the SPD/FDP coalition and the CDU/CSU Opposition. It did not reflect the situation envisaged in the Basic Law, and for that reason the constitution could not offer satisfactory ways out of the impasse.

penalty attaching to groups in the Bundestag irresponsible enough to bring down a Government. But penal dissolutions and constructive votes of no-confidence belong to the myths rather than the realities of politics in societies in which majoritarian parties seek, by demonstrating their own solidarity, to convince the electorate that they are fit to retain power. One awkward consequence of the inapplicability of the constructive vote of no-confidence is, however, that a dissolution can be secured only by rather artificial manoeuvres. The Opposition must be persuaded to renounce its right to try to elect its leader to the Chancellorship, whilst the majority must guarantee that their leader slips into a minority when he asks for a straight vote of confidence. Only in these circumstances, with the Bundestag making no use of its right to elect a successor in the period following its rejection of a Chancellor's request for a vote of confidence, can the President dissolve the Bundestag.

In relation to his colleagues in the Federal Government the Chancellor is equipped with formidable powers. The most important of these are his right to nominate ministers, his control of policy, his right to determine the internal organisation of the Government, and his ability to co-ordinate the work of the Cabinet through the Chancellor's Office. Of these possibilities only the first two are expressly referred to in the Basic Law. The nomination of ministers, as indeed the determination of their number, rests with the Chancellor and in theory leaves him wide discretion in the selection of his colleagues. In practice this discretion has often been severely reduced by the constraints rooted in party behaviour and expectations, as well as by the need to have regard to a number of other factors operating in German social and political relations. The major party constraints have arisen from the necessity of having coalition Governments. And since 1949 only on one occasion (1957) was it not strictly necessary to constitute a coalition, though even then Adenauer preferred a pseudo-coalition for tactical reasons. With the exception of the years 1966–9, there has always been one dominant party in the coalition, the CDU/CSU until 1966, the SPD since 1969. But this situation has given the minor party (or parties in the early fifties) a disproportionate influence on the allocation of ministerial posts. Moreover, the CDU/CSU has never been a completely unified party, and between its two wings there has always been substantial argument about the sharing-out of the fruits of office. Consequently all Chancellors, including Adenauer at the height of his power, have had to regard

Cabinet-making as an occasion for bargaining and the balancing of claims, and have had to pay some attention to the claims urged upon them by their own supporters. Nor have the demands voiced within the parties been the only factors restricting the Chancellor's discretion in the choice of ministers. The requirement of a fair confessional balance has had to be met, places must be given to representatives of all the major regions of Western Germany, and the influence and experience which particular politicians have acquired in the Bundestag committees and in specialised intra-party groups must not be overlooked. Thus, for example, the claims of the social committees within the CDU could not be neglected in appointing the Minister of Labour and Social Affairs, nor of the farmer's interests in the choice of a Minister of Agriculture. Equally an SPD Chancellor is alive to the desirability of having in his Cabinet some members with a trade union background.

As a result of these constraints the making of governments has often been a long-drawn-out affair, an extended bout of bargaining designed to produce solutions acceptable both in terms of satisfying personal ambitions and of meeting substantive claims to influence particular policy areas advanced by various key groups. Under Adenauer forming a government once lasted as long as eight weeks. Only the formation of the Brandt government in 1969 can be regarded as a really fast operation, facilitated both by the previous tenure of office in the Grand Coalition of several ministers and the desire of the FDP to reach a rapid agreement with the SPD in order to forestall criticism of the new course within the party.

Of the Chancellor's formal powers the most important is the right to determine the guidelines of policy, the Richtlinienkompetenz. The use which can be made of this right depends upon the party relationships within the Government as well as upon the Chancellor's own capacity and his conception of how his authority is to be used. The political stability of the Federal Republic has favoured a generous interpretation of the Chancellor's prerogatives and the development of the office as one of decisive political leadership, so much so that in the late fifties it became common to refer to the West German system of government as "Chancellor democracy".[4] In the case of Adenauer there was much to be said for this characterisation. In contrast it was a major criticism of Chancellor

[4] See F. F. Ridley, Chancellor Government as a political system and the German constitution, *Parliamentary Affairs*, XIX (4), 1966.

Erhard (1963–6) that he failed to understand the nature of his office and did not provide the firm control of the Government which public opinion expected. But whilst three out of the four Chancellors since 1949 have shown in varying degrees a desire to establish themselves as undoubted heads of government, there are practical obstacles facing a Chancellor who wishes to make a continuing reality of his policy competence across the whole field of affairs. Chief amongst these is the autonomy of ministers within their departments and the strength of departmental particularism in the bureaucracy. Any Chancellor finds it hard to overcome the opposition of ministers in charge of major departments, particularly if this opposition gains support in the Bundestag, amongst the Länder or in the area of organised interests. Moreover, in the German system of government as elsewhere, many home policy initiatives are made in response to specific problems and demands, and in the nature of the situation are likely to come from the competent executive agencies. Thus it is not surprising that in internal affairs Chancellors have used their policy-making rights more in the shape of arbitration and occasionally as justification for imposing a veto, than with the aim of actively evolving new policies. In view of the very important restraints limiting the discretion of Governments unilaterally to formulate and carry out major policy changes, it is natural that the Chancellor's powers should have been used generally in this moderate way. Any other course would have carried the risk of serious loss of prestige when it became clear that the Chancellor was not in a position to assert his will successfully. To some extent this happened to Professor Erhard when, in 1965, he committed himself to oppose expenditure increases which powerful groups in the Bundestag were determined to secure.

What has just been said does not apply in the field of foreign relations. Like the British Prime Minister the Chancellor can, if he so wishes, act more or less as his own foreign minister, and indeed it is now widely expected that he will assert his pre-eminence in this field. This owes much to the example of Adenauer, who by force of circumstances and inclination treated the handling of foreign policy as his major task. (Until 1955 he was, moreover, his own foreign minister.) Of his success in determining the course of German foreign and defence policy for more than a decade there can be no doubt. Both Dr. Kiesinger and Herr Brandt have shown a similar preference for foreign affairs, though the former had to compete with the latter as his foreign secretary and so had less opportunity to demonstrate his own control of foreign policy. When Brandt assumed the Chancellorship in 1969 he rapidly revealed the same ascendancy in the direction of foreign affairs as Adenauer had asserted, though allowing to his foreign minister, the FDP leader Walter Scheel, more latitude to make a public contribution to policy than Adenauer had ever granted to his collaborators.

Clearly it is easier in foreign affairs, and to some extent in the related area of defence policy, for the Chancellor to develop and pursue his own policies. Political issues of a more traditional kind are dominant and the implementation of foreign policy does not call for the complex executive apparatus and the same degree of bargaining with organised interests which impose so many constraints on the formulation and execution of social and economic policies. Modern communications and the trend towards personal contact between heads of government have helped forward this emphasis on the Chancellor's foreign-policy leadership. However, it may not be an unmixed blessing that Chancellors have been so easily tempted to specialise in foreign affairs. As a result there has often been a lack of leadership and coherence in the conduct of internal policy. Under Adenauer this was masked during the first eight or ten years of his Chancellorship by his extraordinary resilience and his ability to switch attention rapidly to home issues which had become acute. Then his skill as a political tactician usually enabled him to impose a solution which took his Government safely round a dangerous corner. But in his declining years there were clear signs of drift in many sectors of home policy. This was to have serious consequences in the later sixties when men of less masterful qualities have had to try to make good some of the earlier neglect of emerging problems. Yet habits die hard, and during his first three years of office Herr Brandt, despite the urgency of the problems in education, in the control of public expenditure and in taxation policy, allowed his preoccupation with foreign policy to weaken his leadership in home affairs. This meant that there was no striking progress with the programme of internal reform to which the SPD/FDP coalition was ostensibly committed, and that such progress as was made depended far more on the efforts of other members of the Government than on the Chancellor himself.

The extent to which the Chancellor can realise the potential of his office depends too on the means at his disposal for shaping the organisation of his Government and for making a continuing impact on the conduct of business. For this reason the Chancellor's right to determine the internal organisation of the Government and the role of his staff, the Bundeskanzleramt, are important factors in the evaluation of the Chancellorship.[5] Authority over organisation, the "Organisationsgewalt" in German, has traditionally been within the discretion of the executive, and at the Federal level has come to rest formally with the Chancellor himself. This means that he determines the distribution of ministerial functions and the number of ministers, as well as the internal procedures of the Cabinet. Generally German Governments have been small. Adenauer started with fourteen ministers and gradually increased to twenty-two. Some of the additions were required by new functions, others reflected the Chancellor's willingness to manipulate the number of portfolios to meet the needs of Cabinet-making. In some instances ministerial office has been conferred almost as a gesture of friendship, on Heinrich Krone who became Minister without Portfolio under Adenauer in 1961 and in 1964 Minister for the Affairs of the Defence Council, and on Ludger Westrick, Erhard's State Secretary in the Chancellor's Office, who reached retirement age as an official in 1963 and stayed on as a minister.[6] Chancellor Brandt inherited twenty departments and reduced the number of ministers to fifteen. No legislation was required for this reallocation of functions. Such a drastic reduction was facilitated in part by the fact that in 1966 seven parliamentary state secretaries had been appointed and this was increased to sixteen in 1969. Thus the total number of ministerial posts became larger, though the appointments to the junior positions rest effectively with individual ministers and not with the Chancellor, a significant limitation on his patronage. When re-forming his Government in 1972 Brandt encountered some of the usual difficulties in coalition-making. He was not able to keep his Cabinet as small as in 1969 and ended up with seventeen ministers.

In general the Chancellor's right to fix the size of his Government and the allocation of functions allows him relatively modest scope for in-

---

[5]For a predominantly legal treatment of the Chancellor's powers in respect of government organisation, see E. W. Börkenförde, *Die Organisationsgewalt im Bereich der Regierung*, Berlin, 1964. Also S. Schöne, *Von der Reichskanzlei zum Bundeskanzleramt*, Berlin, 1968.

[6]To some extent this was a precedent for Chancellor Brandt's appointment of Professor Ehmke as minister in the Bundeskanzleramt, i.e. effectively as his State Secretary. In December 1972 Ehmke was, however, replaced by a permanent official.

fluencing the attitudes of his colleagues, actual and potential. The scale of patronage is too narrow, and in any case the possession of ministerial office is by no means the only attractive goal for those engaged in politics. Moreover, the Chancellor's organisational competence stops short of intervention in the internal structure of departments, whilst many administrative arrangements below the level of ministers require legislation. In principle the Chancellor can determine the working methods of the Cabinet, for example by encouraging the use of committees. But in fact there has been relatively little formal delegation within the Cabinet, and only in recent years have there been signs of a more serious effort to develop Cabinet committees. This aspect of the functioning of the Cabinet will be taken up again when we turn to ministers and their role. Meanwhile it is worth noting that the reluctance of Chancellors before Brandt to encourage a committee style of operations owed something both to Adenauer's interpretation of the concept of the Chancellor as the ultimate arbitrator of policy, and to the reluctance of individual Cabinet members to contemplate their own exclusion from parts of Cabinet business. In addition, legal considerations were important, emphasising the formal right of all ministers as the only constitutionally sanctioned body which could properly be associated with the Chancellor in the decisions of the Government.

As regards the conventions governing the conduct of business in the Cabinet, the Chancellor can shape these according to his preferences. There is, however, a formal body of rules for the work of the Federal Government, promulgated in 1951 on the basis of the procedures adopted under the Weimar Republic.[7] Thus the Chancellor operates within a framework which is more clearly defined than that which exists in cabinet systems which have relied more on informal procedures. It is doubtful, however, whether this seriously inhibits a strong Chancellor from managing the Cabinet in his own style. Certainly Adenauer was able to use a technique of bilateral discussion and pressure to secure compliance with his wishes outside the Cabinet room. And in general he made no secret of his low opinion of the value of extended Cabinet discussions. Furthermore, the Chancellor has at his disposal the Chancellor's Office, which

[7]*Geschäftsordnung der Bundesregierung*, originally published in 1951 (*GMBl*, p. 137), and revised subsequently down to 1970 (*GMBl*, p. 50). Also in Lechner-Hülshoff, *Parlament und Regierung*, 3rd ed., pp. 338 ff.

enables him to exert influence in several ways on the conduct of the Cabinet and on the actions of individual ministers.

The Chancellor's Office has played a major part in the operation of the Federal Government. That it should have become a key organisation is not surprising. The idea of a strong Chancellor required for its translation into reality effective means of administrative support. Equally, the relative weakness of the collegial element in the Cabinet and the absence of numerous powerful committees meant that the Federal Chancellor's Office could give more priority to its role as *his* support team than to servicing the Cabinet as a collective decision-making group. This type of development was encouraged by Adenauer who rapidly built up a strong and loyal office to serve him. Indeed until 1955 foreign and defence questions were also handled directly by the Chancellor's Office.[8] From 1953 until 1963 the Office was headed by Hans Globke, the closest adviser of the Chancellor and an official with an outstanding aptitude for holding together all the threads of government activity whilst maintaining outwardly an implacable discretion on behalf of his master. Under Globke the Office received the organisational shape which, subject to one major modification, it has had ever since. Broadly speaking, it has a range of senior posts covering all the main areas of the Government. The holders of these are responsible for maintaining contact with the departments, for communicating the Chancellor's views on policy issues arising out of the work of individual departments, for watching the preparation of legislation and arranging for its submission to the Cabinet, for processing Cabinet business in these fields, and for seeing that departmental co-ordination takes place. Their influence and effectiveness depends in part on the extent to which they can operate with the full support of the Chancellor himself. Under Adenauer the Chancellor's Office acquired great authority as the principal link between the Chancellor and individual ministers, and there is little doubt that Globke had an influence greater than that of most departmental ministers. Subsequently the Office has been less powerful,

---

[8]This again was a precedent for Chancellor Brandt's method of relying extensively on State Secretary Bahr in the working out of his Eastern policy: Bahr was in the Chancellor's Office and not in the Foreign Affairs ministry from 1969 until December 1972 when he entered the Bundestag and was appointed a Minister without Portfolio. (In German *Sonderminister*, an odd term which suggests special assignments. The FDP also claimed such a post in Herr Brandt's second Government.)

though in recent years one development points in the direction of re-asserting its key position in the work of the Government. This is the decision to attempt to set up a planning unit in the Chancellor's Office.

Already in 1964 under Erhard some moves were made to develop a planning staff. But they had little success, and the experiments initiated under Kiesinger likewise had no decisive impact, though they did contribute to strengthening the idea of having such a planning staff. It is only since 1969 that a major expansion of the planning side has taken place, chiefly under the inspiration of the ministerial head of the Chancellor's Office, Professor Ehmke. Though there have been objections voiced in the Bundestag and by the Finance ministry to the ambitious character and generous scale of the post-1969 arrangements, Brandt succeeded in securing a major expansion of that part of his Office responsible for long-term planning. Organisationally the planning staff remains separate from the executive side of the Office, which continues to operate much as before. The functions of the planning staff can be summed up as information, communication and analysis. They are expected to assemble information on departmental plans and projects, to co-ordinate and present this both to the Chancellor and to the Cabinet, and to elaborate analyses of future developments and alternative courses of action. In principle the planning staff is expected to serve both the Chancellor and the Cabinet: to support the former in the exercise of his policy functions and the latter in arriving at collective decisions. So far it is difficult to estimate how far these intentions have been realised. Exponents of government reform point hopefully to the possibilities now presented for more rational and co-ordinated policy-making, and for building up a quantitative assessment of policy commitments across the whole field of Federal Government activity. On the other hand sceptics have suggested that the experiment merely involves an increase in the paperwork of the central machinery of government without seriously affecting the tortuous bargaining processes through which in practice most major decisions are taken.

Alongside its functions in support of the Chancellor, which allow one to describe the Chancellor's Office as the executive arm of the head of government (and one of considerable size too, with a total staff of 410 in 1972[9]),

[9]Of the 410, 207 were officials (Beamte) and 158 employees on contract (Angestellte). In addition, there were 756 people in the Federal Press Office, which is attached to the Chancellor too. Source: Bundeshaushaltsplan 1972, Einzelplan 04.

the Office also services the Cabinet. This is essentially a secretarial function, supervising the drawing-up of the agenda, circulating papers, taking minutes and follow-up action. But given the character of the German Cabinet as predominantly a board of departmental directors and the weakness of committees, these functions have not had the dominating place which they have in the work of the British Cabinet Office. Moreover, there is a factor of political commitment which cannot be overlooked. Globke, when State Secretary in the Chancellor's Office, took an active part in Cabinet meetings, and it is obvious in the case of Westrick and Ehmke that as ministerial heads of the Chancellor's Office they have had equal rights in the Cabinet with other members. Further, members of the Chancellor's Office down to the lower ranks of the administrative level of the civil service are expected to show political support for the ruling party. After twenty years of colonisation by the Christian Democrats there was a drastic changeover of personnel with the advent of the SPD/ FDP coalition in October 1969. The Chancellor's Office cannot, therefore, be regarded as a neutral and purely bureaucratic tool of administrative support. Nor is there much rotation between it and the ministries to diffuse experience of this central position throughout the federal administration. It is a politically committed organisation, required to assist the Chancellor actively in the exercise of his powers. This is underlined by the fact that the Federal Press Office, the principal information and publicity agency of the Government, comes within the domain of the Federal Chancellor's Office too. Without such support it would have been far harder to build up the Chancellor's leadership in the manner of Dr. Adenauer. Despite shifts in personal style, the maintenance of a strong personal executive apparatus is likely to remain a high priority for future Chancellors.

This outline of the position and powers of the Federal Chancellor has underlined the extent to which the strong leadership by the head of government has been established as a decisive convention and expectation in the Federal Republic. That there are constraints, some of them substantial, affecting the exercise of the Chancellor's powers is obvious, and several of these will emerge at later stages of this study. It is equally clear that the success of a Chancellor in asserting his claim to leadership must depend on his personal qualities and his political and administrative skill. A weak Chancellor is always a possibility. But there is no doubt that for the purposes of classification the German type of Cabinet government deserves the epithet "prime ministerial" or even "presidential". The prerogatives of the Chancellorship are great and the political system has in its evolution since 1949 been strongly influenced by their active use.

## FEDERAL MINISTERS

There is in the Federal Republic no constitutional distinction between the Government as the totality of ministers and the Cabinet as an inner executive authority. Until 1966 there was complete identity between Cabinet and Federal Government, the former term being in effect merely a popular way of describing the Government. With the appointment of parliamentary state secretaries to support ministers in the Bundestag, *de facto* a new layer of ministerial offices emerged. But technically the parliamentary secretaries are not "ministers", even though increasingly they appear on behalf of ministers in both the Cabinet and the Bundestag instead of the permanent state secretaries who head the department. After Herr Brandt took office there were fifteen ministers in the Federal Government, and this fell to fourteen in 1971 when Finance and Economics were brought together under Professor Schiller. The number rose to seventeen in December 1972, but the group remains small, so that there is no serious problem affecting the size of the Cabinet or of the wider ministerial team, although as German practice allows the attendance of a range of official advisers, Cabinet meetings can still become rather unwieldy.

Ministers share in a collective responsibility as members of the Federal Government, but their autonomy is underlined by the provision that they manage the affairs of their departments "on their own responsibility". The collective role of ministers has generally been muted. This is in part because they have been overshadowed by the Chancellor and most of them have seen their Cabinet role far more in terms of defending a departmental point of view than of making a contribution to general political debate about government policies. Equally the sense of collective solidarity remains weak and differences of opinion between ministers are openly acknowledged. This is underlined by the fact that there have been so few resignations from the Government in circumstances in which ministers have been brought to this step by a conflict between their own commitments and the demands of collective Cabinet responsibility. In over twenty years there have been only three cases of resignation accompanied by a reasonably clear assertion of a difference of opinion with the rest of the Government: Gustav Heinemann who left the first Adenauer Government in 1950 over defence and foreign policy issues, Paul Lücke who resigned from the Grand Coalition in 1968 after its refusal to go ahead with revising electoral law on the straight plurality principle as originally envisaged, and Karl Schiller who left the SPD/FDP coalition in 1972 over economic issues. Alex Möller, Minister of Finance, gave no reason for his resignation in 1971.

A number of factors explain the limitations of the Cabinet as a centre of policy-making. Of major political importance has been the coalition character of all Governments. Sometimes this has involved very formal attempts to pin down the terms on which a coalition would be maintained, though the tendency in recent years has been to avoid such rigidity. Nevertheless coalition relationships do mean that many policy issues have to be prepared outside the Government, both in special groups representing the parties to the coalition and in separate party committees. This explains, for example, why the floor leaders of the parties in the Bundestag will often attend Cabinet meetings. Inevitably the result of this situation is that the more difficult political decisions are really taken outside the Cabinet. The same applies if the Chancellor feels able to decide unilaterally or in independent negotiations with particular ministers or party potentates.

Then there is the continuing influence of a tradition which has emphasised the importance of technical competence as the major quality demanded of ministers. Undoubtedly this tradition is now in decline. The political generalist has been encouraged by the environment of post-war German politics, and ministers such as Gerhard Schröder, Franz-Josef Strauss, Helmut Schmidt, Herbert Wehner, Georg Leber and Gerhard Stoltenberg can be cited as examples of men capable of turning their talents to a variety of political tasks. Nevertheless there have been plenty of ministers who were definitely cut out for one job only, and who saw themselves as competent only in their chosen field of specialisation. This emphasis on specialised experience has been buttressed by the conventions governing tenure of office. Generally German ministers serve for long periods, usually for the full four years of a Government's normal life, and often for far longer. Dr. Erhard was fourteen years Minister of Economics, whilst Hans-Christian Seebohm survived for seventeen years as

Minister of Transport. It is not surprising that in such circumstances a minister becomes deeply committed to his own particular field. There is too the powerful influence of departmental particularism, though this is by no means a peculiarly German problem. What is of some importance in this context is the German emphasis on the formal definition of powers and competence which tends to reinforce the natural separateness of competing organisations, and the absence of much movement of officials between departments owing to the absence of any central personnel agency. In consequence the leading officials tend to be very committed to the interests of their departments and pass this outlook on to their ministers. Nor are the latter often able to stand out successfully against departmental pressures. Once again the respect for professional competence tends to make the minister willing to accept the arguments urged on him by his officials and to see his main task in acting as a mouthpiece for his department.

Finally, the limitations affecting the collective action of ministers almost certainly owe something to the style and content of much Cabinet business. The Federal Government and administration are very much concerned with legislation: the division of functions in the German federal system dictates this. Consequently a large part of Cabinet business involves the approval of draft measures to be presented to the Bundestag and Bundesrat. There is not much delegation of such business to committees: the Government as a whole has to examine and approve proposals prepared in the departments. By its nature this type of activity concentrates attention on the technical details and the niceties of legal definition. Again the expert comes into his own. There is in this context less room for general political argument since this is likely to have taken place earlier in the process of formulating policies prior to embodying them in draft legislation.

As already suggested, the Federal Government resembles to some extent a board of technical directors rather than a collective political leadership. Formally there are circumstances in which the Government must arbitrate, for example where ministers are in dispute with each other. This does sometimes happen, a notable case being the vote in Cabinet on whether to invoke powers to control the inflow of foreign funds which led to the resignation of Professor Schiller in June 1972. But often the Cabinet is an unsuitable forum for the resolution of such disputes, and they are more likely to be settled by the informal intervention of the Chancellor. Alternatively they simply persist, and since the German view of the secrecy of Cabinet deliberations is not unduly rigid, it is quite common for their existence to become a matter of political gossip. Moreover, it is by no means unusual for a minister to mobilise opinion against a colleague with whose policies he is in disagreement.[10] The ties of collective responsibility and solidarity are by no means strong enough to cover up such conflict.

As members of the Federal Government all ministers have equal rights. But three of them—the Ministers of Finance, Interior and Justice—have a slightly enhanced status owing to the fact that if they enter an objection against proposals affecting matters within their competence, they can be overruled only if half the Cabinet and the Chancellor vote them down. In practice this provision of the rules of procedure for the Federal Government is important only in the case of the Finance minister. As the minister responsible for drawing up the budget and for controlling overall expenditure, he clearly has an interest in being able to restrain the demands of his colleagues, if necessary by challenging the Cabinet to take the responsibility of ignoring his better judgment.

Reference has already been made to the relatively limited use of committees by the Cabinet. Until the mid-sixties there were only two, the Economics Committee or Economics Cabinet and the Defence Council. The latter, which was first constituted in 1959, was a rather special case, having a wider attendance than a purely ministerial committee, and was intended to provide a forum alongside the Defence ministry itself for the discussion of major defence questions. It was presided over by the Chancellor, who later delegated this task to a Minister without Portfolio, who for two years between 1964 and 1966 became formally Minister for the Affairs of the Defence Council. Thereafter this curious experiment in parallel policy-making was abandoned, though the council itself continues to exist under a slightly different name. The Economics Committee, dating back to 1951, was nominally chaired by the Chancellor, though Professor Erhard and his successors in the office of Minister of Economics have usually been *de facto* chairmen of this group. Whether the committee has been an effective means of delegating business from the Federal Government remains uncertain. There have always been tensions between the Finance ministry and the Economics ministry, and with the

[10]Interesting evidence of this is to be found in G. Braunthal, *The West German Legislative Process*, Cornell University Press, 1972.

development of medium-term financial planning since 1967 the influence of the former has tended to increase. The commitment to five-year expenditure forecasts led to the setting-up of a Finance Committee or Cabinet in 1966 in which the Finance minister had the leading role. This small committee has acquired some weight in virtue of its important function of preparing the finance plan for approval by the whole Cabinet. Steps have been taken in recent years to develop a few *ad hoc* committees for special subjects, for example for all-German affairs, for education and research, and for planning and regional policy. But there remains considerable reluctance to delegate full authority to restricted ministerial groups to act on behalf of the Cabinet.

The relative weakness of a sense of collective Cabinet responsibility and the restricted use made of Cabinet committees as decision-taking and co-ordinating bodies means that German ministers often work in relative isolation from each other and do not feel a strong need to carry their colleagues with them at each stage in the formulation of policy. There has to be co-ordination, but this is more likely to take place at the official level, and a minister then prefers to confront his colleagues with what appears to be the considered and final view of his department. Nor has the relationship between the Bundestag and ministers made it necessary for them to lean on each other and to work closely together as a group. Though ministers appear regularly before the Bundestag and its committees, there is not a lively atmosphere of political accountability. Moreover, the Bundestag has not generally expected ministers to show a high degree of collective solidarity, and its members often fail to react to knowledge of sharp disagreements within the Government. Indeed it was by no means unknown for Adenauer to disavow the actions of his ministers, and there have been many cases of ministers publicly disagreeing on policy measures. To a large extent this reflects the coalition condition of German politics and the presence within the major parties of quite distinct groups which pursue their own interests and represent their own points of view regardless of the wishes of the party leaders. There are signs that this situation is slowly changing as the Federal Republic moves towards something very like a two-party system. Certainly since 1969 the Government–Opposition dichotomy has become more sharply delineated. If this persists, it may set up pressures to emphasise more clearly the collective character of Government deliberations and decisions.

## MINISTERS AND THEIR DEPARTMENTS

In the light of what has just been said about the role of ministers in the Federal Government, it is to be expected that ministers see their principal function as the management of a department of state. Nearly all ministers have a department to run: the appointment of ministers without portfolio has been a rarity, and on the whole has proved troublesome when it has been resorted to. Notwithstanding this Herr Brandt decided in late 1972 to satisfy the demands of coalition arithmetic by including two such ministers in his second Government.

The five "classic" ministries are Interior, Finance, Justice, Defence, and Foreign Affairs, all of which have their origins in nineteenth-century Prussia. Of these Justice has nowadays relatively limited executive functions, though its opinion on constitutional and all other legal questions arising in the course of legislation has to be sought. Rather surprisingly it is one of the few ministries which since 1949 has experienced a rapid turnover of ministers. Of the other four "classic" ministries Interior has tended to lose functions with the gradual separation from it of services which have expanded to the point at which a distinct departmental structure was required for them (e.g. land-use planning). Moreover, the police service is in the main the responsibility of the Länder. Defence has grown rapidly since its re-establishment in 1955, whilst Finance remains a major department despite the competition in questions of economic policy and management from the powerful Economics ministry. The latter was from 1971 to 1972 linked with Finance to form a super-ministry, but no integration of the two wings took place and at the end of 1972 two separate departments under their own ministers were re-established, though with some shift of functions (in particular monetary and credit policy) from Economics to Finance. Between 1969 and 1972 there were eight other departments: Transport, Labour and Social Affairs, Agriculture, Housing and Planning, Health, Education and Science, Inner German Relations, and Overseas Aid. In addition the Chancellor's Office was also headed by a minister. The opportunity had been taken when forming the SPD/FDP Government in October 1969 to dissolve and redistribute the tasks of five departments: the Ministry for Federal Property, the Ministry for the Bundesrat and Affairs of the Länder, the Ministry for Refugees and the Ministry for Family Affairs, whilst the Ministry of Posts was brought into Transport, apparently as a step on the way to reconstituting it as a public

commercial enterprise. The distribution of functions between departmental ministers is now marked by a relatively high degree of stability. In
the reconstructed Government of December 1972 only minor changes
were made to permit the appointment of a slightly larger team. Housing
and Planning was extended to give more emphasis to its responsibilities for
the urban environment, whilst Education and Science was bereft of some of
its research functions to help constitute a new Research and Technology
ministry (to which Posts was assigned too).

The overall organisation and functions of the departments will not be
examined in the present context. Here we are concerned with the role of
ministers as political heads of the departments. It will be clear from the
preceding list that nearly all the departments have substantial policy-
making responsibilities. But since Western Germany is a federal state in
which much of the implementation of policy rests with the Länder, the
emphasis in the federal departments tends to be on legislative functions,
the allocation of financial resources and the formulation of general policy
guidelines. Except in the case of the Defence and Foreign Affairs departments ministers have to assign considerable priority to giving legislative
shape to the policies which they sponsor. This imposes a need to co-operate
closely with the appropriate Bundestag committees as well as with interested groups within the ruling parties and organised interests outside
Parliament. But since federal departments have relatively little executive
administration, ministers are not heavily burdened with individual casework and decisions, and most of them do not have to answer in detail in
the Bundestag for the activities of their departments.

A minister is the supreme authority in his department, and technically
the officials act on his behalf. Traditionally ministers have taken a close
interest in personnel questions and have a decisive influence on all senior
appointments. Germany has not developed the technique of the ministerial
"cabinet" in support of ministers. A minister's private office normally
enjoys only a modest influence and would not aspire to a policy-making
role on the minister's behalf. For his immediate support a minister relies
on his state secretary and a few key senior officials, as well as more recently
on a parliamentary state secretary. Appointments at the level of state
secretary and ministerial director (under-secretary in British terms) are
political. A minister could, if he so wished, ignore the political views of
his senior officials and treat them as loyal, politically neutral, civil servants.

But in fact this rarely happens and it has become normal for ministers to appoint to senior posts in their departments officials of whose political loyalty they are certain, and who are likely to be in sympathy with the style and aims of the ministers whom they serve. These practices undoubtedly present difficulties for a bureaucracy which is in theory politically neutral. From the point of view of ministers they are held to be justified by the need to ensure that the department will support wholeheartedly the aims of the political leadership. Perhaps a more serious argument is that the strength of the German bureaucratic tradition requires the injection of an element of patronage, both to strengthen the minister who dispenses it and to facilitate a partial renewal of personnel which may inject new ideas and fresh energies into an otherwise rigid administrative structure. In the other direction it might, however, be argued that the preference for political appointees at the levels of the administration most likely to be in frequent contact with ministers makes it more likely that they will be surrounded by advisers who speak too often with one voice and lack any incentive to express a critical opinion on proposals and problems with which ministers must deal.

As regards the recent institution of parliamentary state secretaries, they were envisaged partly as support for ministers, partly as a means of providing near-ministerial experience for younger aspirants to high office. Not surprisingly the experiment has run into various difficulties. There have been complaints about the lack of definition of the role of parliamentary secretaries, and much ink has been spilled trying to give legally satisfactory form to the office. The innovation had, too, to face the suspicion of most state secretaries, the official heads of administration in the departments, who feared that their authority would be undermined by the appearance of politicians who might aspire to the status of deputy ministers. So far the parliamentary secretaries have remained in a twilight zone. They cannot claim to be deputy ministers, and indeed cannot under the present rules cast a vote for their ministers in the Cabinet.[11] Nor can they deputise for a minister inside a department. In a few cases ministers have asked their parliamentary secretaries to supervise the work of part of a department. This is a reasonable step, but under the working con-

---

[11]Ministers must be represented formally by another minister in the Government, who alone can cast a vote on behalf of the person he is representing. Detailed provisions are contained in the *Geschäftsordnung der Bundesregierung, op. cit.*

ventions of a German ministry carries the risk that the political appointee becomes no more than an additional head of an administrative division. In the Bundestag parliamentary secretaries have been able to take over oral questions on behalf of ministers, which has proved a more welcome arrangement than the appearance of the state secretaries, and they have since 1969 been members of Bundestag committees. This latter was, however, a dubious measure, motivated at the outset mainly by the desire to guarantee the Government's slender majority in committees, and left the parliamentary secretaries in an ambiguous relationship both with the committees and with their ministers.

What is striking about this experiment is the difficulty which political leaders experience in devising new modes of political co-operation and direction, and in allowing these to develop flexibly and informally. The penchant for a legal definition of relationships and powers in the governmental system militates against pragmatic adaptation to circumstances, and to some extent reinforces mutual suspicions amongst office-holders. It reflects too the continuing tendency to regard a traditional bureaucratic pattern of relationships as a suitable model for political co-operation. Undoubtedly there are now influences working in the other direction, but they have not yet proved strong enough to overcome the anxieties aroused by the prospect of relying on conventionally sanctioned standards of political behaviour rather than on legally defined norms to which behaviour is expected to conform. Until this transition has been made relations within the Federal Government are likely to continue to reveal the tensions and rigidities which arise from too intense a preoccupation with defining exactly what powers are assigned to each of its members.

Despite these critical comments on the style of ministerial leadership, it has to be granted that ministers in the Federal Republic have shown a high average level of competence as departmental chiefs. They generally come to office with a fairly wide experience of politics and government, gained sometimes in the Bundestag committees, but often owing much to the diffusion of responsibilities in the federal system which makes it common for aspiring politicians to make the first steps in a successful career at the local or Land level. Furthermore, the ease with which a transition can be made from various branches of the public service to parliamentary activity means that many ministers will at some stage in their careers have had administrative experience, even if only for a short time.

All this tends to exclude the pure amateur who has acquired little specialised knowledge, and it produces a situation in which few ministers have merely a parliamentary apprenticeship on which to build success in office. The fact that tenure of office tends to be long also works in favour of continuity in policy-making, and allows ministers to acquire great familiarity both with the working of their departments and with the conditions and problems in the external environment of which they need to take account. Admittedly a price has then to be paid in terms of reluctance to envisage new approaches to policy questions. But a balance has always to be struck between the benefits of continuity and the need for innovation: the Federal Republic tends to prefer to make haste slowly.

The strength of ministers lies generally in their capacity to come to grips with the problems of administration and to take an effective part in the complex and often slow process of defining policy and bringing it to the statute book. Their weaknesses lie in the poor public exposition of proposals and in a reluctance to think aloud boldly about the problems which are going to confront the society. The performance of Professor Leussinck, Chancellor Brandt's "non-political" expert brought in to head the Ministry of Education and Science in 1969,[12] provides an apt illustration of this thesis. Following the reforms of 1968–9, which conferred on the Federal Government substantial responsibilities for future developments in higher education, Professor Leussinck was expected to move rapidly to formulate policies for tackling some of the acute problems in this field—especially in relation to the financing and planning of future expansion, the internal structure of universities, the level of student admissions, and the problems of political discontent so widely felt. But though his period in office brought a number of schemes to the work-bench and set in motion new procedures of Bund/Länder co-ordination, Leussinck made next to no political impact on the problems: his aims and priorities remained obscure. And this probably resulted far more from an inability to expound arguments in a public forum than from the actual absence of ideas and plans. Yet because issues and choices were not clarified, it remained difficult to mobilise consent for decisive policy initiatives and to make progress.

[12]Professor Leussinck retired quietly from office in March 1972.

## THE SOCIAL CHARACTER OF WEST GERMAN
## GOVERNMENTS

A brief account of the social composition of post-1949 Federal Governments will help to make clearer the character of the social changes which
took place after 1945, and their impact on politics. It may also convey
something of the style of West German political leadership. Eighty-two
ministers held office up to and including the SPD/FDP Coalition of 1969–
72. By family origin the majority of them came from the middle- and
lower-middle-class strata of society, their parents being in the professions
or in business (which often meant small-scale enterprises). But owing to
the effects of the war, many of them (and especially those who had not
embarked on a career when the war came) did not have all the benefits of
a settled middle-class educational background. They have been essentially
self-made men, starting from scratch. Of this total of eighty-two ministers,
probably only seventeen or eighteen can be said to have working- or
artisan-class origins, i.e. just over 20%. The Christian Democrats shared
in power for most of the period in question, and so just over half of the
working-class group were members of this party. Of the eighteen SPD
ministers in the scope of the survey eight were of working-class origin,
a higher proportion than in the parliamentary party as a whole, a large
part of which now has a middle-class background. Only four post-1949
ministers can be described as aristocrats by birth, and of these only one
(Brentano)[13] came from a family with a tradition of political activity.

One characteristic stands out prominently, the high proportion of those
who acquired an academic training. Fifty-nine, or nearly 75%, come into
this category. And of these no less than thirty-four, or nearly 60%, had a
law qualification. Though many of those who were educated before the
war owed their opportunities to the advantage of having had parents
with the financial resources to pay for academic training, many of those
who gained their education during and after the war owed it mainly to
their own efforts and ability to secure support outside the family. That
law is so dominant reflects the continuing role of this subject as the equivalent to a general education in the humanities in Britain: it opens many
doors and is a safe bet for a young man with no firm commitment to
another area of study. Of the other academic disciplines, technical subjects
and economics have been modestly represented at the ministerial level.

[13]Heinrich von Brentano: Foreign Minister 1955–61.

When we turn to religious affiliation, the available evidence indicates that thirty-two out of eighty-two (well under 50%) were Catholic. Of the remainder nearly all appeared to be Protestant. These figures are interesting in so far as they do bear out the claim that the Christian Democratic movement has been successful in bridging the confessional gap and indeed in rendering the whole question of religious affiliation less central to the shaping of German political life. Finally, only three women achieved a place in the group (though a fourth has appeared since 1972).

These remarks do not go very far in the analysis of the ministerial personnel of the years 1949–72. They merely underline some of the more obvious social and educational characteristics of the group by which the Federal Republic has been governed. The broad conclusion which emerges is that ministers as a category do not have the usual characteristics of a political élite. They do not reveal to any significant extent those bonds of social solidarity which are created by factors such as education in institutions with well-established traditions like the older British and American universities, or the French *grandes écoles*, socialisation in an officer corps or a sharply class-conscious trade-union movement, a sense of close family ties and shared family interests, or even the frequenting of the same clubs. There has been nothing exclusive about ministers as a group: most have been self-made men, rising rapidly in a new political system, and rather uncertain of themselves in terms of social categorisation. What most of them have revealed, however, is a capacity for responding pragmatically to the needs of a quickly changing society in which not only the problems to be solved, but the style of politics too, have been markedly different from the experience of the past. Credit should be allowed for this success.

## EXECUTIVE STABILITY AND CONTINUITY

Compared with some countries of Western Europe the Federal Republic appears to have become a model of stable and coherent governmental leadership. Though it is the changes in the party basis of politics which have had a major effect here, the institutional framework cannot be discounted as a factor encouraging governmental stability. The strengthening of the Chancellor's position has been crucial. Protected against easy dismissal by the Bundestag, and with the prerogatives of the office clearly stated in relation to his ministerial colleagues, the Chancellor has had a firm constitutional basis for asserting his leadership. At the same time ministerial office has generally offered sufficient scope for ambitious politicians to be able to make a constructive contribution to the work of government. Undoubtedly Adenauer was tempted to devalue ministerial office, particularly during the years up to 1955 when much was still fluid in German political life and the major tasks associated with re-establishing full German sovereignty encouraged the Chancellor to hold all the strings in his own hands. But gradually, as a new generation of more self-confident politicians emerged, it became apparent that even a Chancellor as dominant as Adenauer had to rely extensively on the co-operation and initiative of members of his Government. Though the sense of collective solidarity and responsibility has remained weak, the second decade of the Federal Republic saw a move in the direction of a more collegial style of government, supplementing and supporting the leadership which the Chancellor is expected to provide. That in recent Federal and Land elections so much has been made of the potential ministerial teams offered by the parties underlines this shift of emphasis as compared with the earlier years of the Federal Republic.

Finally, there has been since 1949 no question of a dual executive, the one half parliamentary, the other presidential and perhaps plebiscitary. Reacting against the dualism of Weimar the framers of the Basic Law reduced the rights of the Presidency to a minimum, depriving the office of popular authority by providing that the President should be elected every five years by an assembly consisting of the members of the Bundestag and an equal number of delegates from the Länder parliaments. There is practically no significant political action which the President may take on his own initiative, so that his functions are reduced to two. First, when a Government has to be formed, he has the duty of finding out who is likely to be able to secure the necessary support in the Bundestag. Had the party situation developed differently and remained characterised by division and instability, this would have been a significant function. But in fact the emergence of two dominant parties has left the President nothing to do but to confirm the decisions of the party executives. When Adenauer retired in 1963, it was clear, despite his personal opposition, that Erhard would have to succeed him. When Erhard ran into difficulties in 1966 there were some signs that the then President (Lübke) preferred his replacement by a new leader heading a Grand Coalition. The issue was settled by the parties and by the action of the CDU/CSU in nominating

Dr. Kiesinger as successor to Erhard to lead a coalition with the SPD. In 1969, once the FDP had agreed to join with the SPD, there was no shadow of doubt about the choice of Chancellor.

Secondly, and more important, the President has a representative function. At home he is expected to set an example of fairness and impartiality, to stand above party politics, and to serve as a model of civic virtue and responsibility. Abroad he must be a symbol of the political moderation of the Federal Republic. In these respects the three holders of the office have lived up to expectations. President Heuss, a lifelong Liberal and leading figure of the FDP, contributed greatly to establishing the style of the office in these terms. Though he occasionally ventured into political controversy, he drew back before conflict with his masterful Chancellor threatened to call the Presidency into question. His CDU successor, Lübke, was a man of limited talents who nevertheless tried dutifully to emulate the example already set by Heuss. The *faux pas* which he made from time to time were of a kind calculated to cause amusement rather than genuine political controversy. Persuaded to leave office shortly before the end of his second term, he was succeeded in March 1969 by the elderly SPD politician, Gustav Heinemann, a man of courage and high principle who could be relied upon to sustain the dignity of the office.

Just as in the analysis of contemporary British government the monarchy receives but cursory attention, so in the treatment of German government there is but little to say about the Presidency. The office has symbolic value, and in some circumstances—acute political crisis or the threat of openly unconstitutional action—it could act as a long-stop, compelling active politicians to pause before doing serious damage to the political system. Occasionally the suggestion is made that there should be a return to popular election of the President, not to strengthen his powers, but to encourage the participation of the people in political life. But there is little evidence of widespread support for such a modish change, and it is as reasonable to assume that the present method of indirect election, which is itself favourable to the selection of elderly men prepared to withdraw from the arena of political controversy, will be maintained. Not least, having removed the dangers of a dual executive, party leaders remain suspicious of any changes which, by lending popular legitimacy to the office of head of state, might introduce an element of instability into the structure of German government with which they are now so familiar.

CHAPTER 4

# The Federal Administration

The Federal Government operates for many purposes through the federal administrative system. It is important to pay some attention to the structure and character of this for at least two major reasons. First, the powers exercised by the federal governmental organisation are decisive for the achievement of most of the major public policy objectives: they determine the framework within which a great deal of executive activity then takes place. And second, as far as organisation and procedures go, much that is true of the federal administration is true with modifications of detail for other levels of the governmental system too.

We shall begin by considering the structure of the federal ministries, and then go on to examine some of the conditions within which they must work, what will be called the external relations of the federal executive apparatus. Then some of the relationships and processes within the federal administration have to be considered, particularly those which bear on the significance of recent steps towards strengthening the planning function and improving the management of public expenditure.

## THE FEDERAL MINISTRIES

*Allocation of functions*

At the outset the Federal Government lacked some of the ministerial functions normally found in sovereign states, notably defence and foreign affairs. This was a direct consequence of the fact that under the terms of the agreement with the Western Powers establishing the Federal Republic, its sovereignty was restricted in certain ways. Nevertheless a foreign affairs department was re-formed in 1951, though political control of it remained until 1955 with the Federal Chancellor who was his own foreign minister. Defence did not emerge as an officially recognised ministerial responsibility until the Federal Republic was brought into NATO in 1955 and recovered full sovereignty.[1] The first Government of Dr. Adenauer, formed in 1949, reflected in its size of fourteen these and other limitations on the powers of the new state. Gradually the Government became larger as new ministries were formed, partly to take over new functions, partly to satisfy the demands of coalition arithmetic. By the sixties a membership of twenty to twenty-one was normal for the Federal Government, though it has now fallen below this level.

The distribution of functions between ministries calls for a few comments. There are some departments with major responsibilities which constitute the core of the federal administration. Foreign Affairs, Defence, Interior, Justice, Finance, Economics, Labour and Social Affairs, Transport and Agriculture come into this group. Some of these have substantial administrative services of their own in virtue of extensive or exclusive federal responsibilities. This is the case with Defence and Foreign Affairs, and to some extent with Finance. But others, notably Justice, have very limited administrative functions and remain extremely small organisations. Then there are some departments which are well established by now, but whose powers are restricted in various ways, notably by the federal structure. Housing and Planning, Health and Family Affairs, Education and Science can be put under this heading. Here the Federal Government has responsibilities, but they are hedged about by the restrictions stemming from the powers conferred on the Länder and by the fact that the federal administration has few or no executive responsibilities. Finally there have been and still are departments which owed their survival to the importance of special interest and claims, or to the need for patronage. The former Ministries for Refugees, for Federal Property, for the Affairs of the Bundesrat, and for Family Affairs (now in Health) belonged to this group, whilst as surviving examples of this phenomenon one may count the Ministry

[1]The Paris treaties of October 1954 and subsequent agreements integrated the Federal Republic into the Western defence structure and resulted in abolition of the Occupation statute. In this way practically all the restrictions on full West German sovereignty were removed.

for Inner German Relations and the Ministry for Economic Co-operation. The latter both survive in part because it is thought that there are sound political reasons for underlining these areas of policy by having separate departments with their own ministerial chiefs.

There are substantial differences in the political weight and influence of departments. Foreign Affairs, Defence, Interior, Finance, Labour and Social Affairs, Agriculture, Transport are near the top of the scale; Health, Housing and Planning, Inner German Relations, Economic Co-operation, Research and Technology (a late 1972 creation) probably come towards the bottom, whilst somewhere in the middle are Justice, Education and Science, and now Economics. Until late 1972 the latter would have come much nearer the top, but it has had to take second place to a strengthened Finance ministry. As for Justice, though the department has prestige as a "classic ministry", its responsibilities are to some extent of a formal nature and it has not been very attractive to ambitious politicians wishing to make a name for themselves by pushing through major programmes of social or economic change. Some departments have gradually expanded owing to the assumption of new functions at the federal level. This is particularly true of Education and Science which grew slowly out of a department of Atomic Energy Questions (1955) into one for Scientific Research (1962), and finally after 1969 into Education and Science. The greater emphasis on education became unavoidable in the later sixties as a result of the growing demand for more federal intervention and support in the higher education sector. A similar trend is probably at work in the area of Housing and Planning where the greater interest in questions affecting the control of the physical environment is working in favour of some strengthening of the federal influence.

*Scale and structure*

Taken as a whole the central administration of the Federal Government is on a remarkably modest scale. In 1954 it employed only 10,109 people, with 86,968 in subordinate federal agencies (these figures exclude the Post Office, though not the Ministry for Posts). The corresponding figures for 1960 were 14,034 and 224,548, and for 1971, 18,729 and 277,353. There has clearly been a big increase in the overall size of the federal administration, but it should be remembered that in 1971 just over 171,000 personnel were employed in the subordinate agencies of the Defence ministry, over 40,000 in the tax and customs administration of the Finance ministry, and over 20,000 in the border police which come under the Ministry of the Interior's supervision. When these large blocks of personnel are deducted from the totals the restricted scale of the federal administration emerges more clearly, especially in relation to the central ministries themselves. These have not yet attained 20,000 personnel and have so far not quite doubled in total size in the course of the seventeen years 1954–71, during which the Federal Republic passed from the early stages of reconstruction to the achievement of a highly developed welfare state. Many of them remain very small: for example, the Ministry of Justice had barely 500 staff in its central organisation in 1971, the Ministry of Labour and Social Affairs only just over 800.

Let us turn now to some features of the structure of a federal department, illustrating these by references to the Ministry of the Interior as it was in 1966–7 after the formation of the Grand Coalition. At the top of the ministry was the Minister, flanked by a newly created post of Parliamentary State Secretary, the responsibilities of which were at that time quite undefined.[2] Heading the permanent administration were two state secretaries. The presence of two top officials in a big department is now not unusual: if such a provision is deemed necessary, it is then normal for the work to be clearly divided between the two, often with one of them controlling the key divisions of the department, and therefore in a stronger position. Political considerations may determine who holds these top official posts: at this time the Minister belonged to the CDU (Paul Lücke) and one of the state secretaries certainly stood close to the same party. The other was, however, more of a non-party career official, a type who now appears increasingly less at the highest levels of the bureaucracy. Below the state secretaries the department was organised into nine divisions; five of these were large enough to be split into two or three subdivisions (twelve in all). Though at this level politically motivated appointments are also possible, Interior is a department in which the tradition of neutral state service remains fairly strong and there is a preference for the experience and skill of career officials. In consequence some of the key posts have been

[2]More recently the Parliamentary State Secretary has taken over the supervision of three divisions of the ministry, an arrangement which makes him resemble in function the State Secretaries.

held for long periods by the same person regardless of changes of minister. The divisions of the ministry indicated its principal areas of activity: Constitutional Questions and Civil Service law comprised Divisions 1 and 2, both formidable preoccupations in the Federal Republic, but especially Civil Service law with its three subdivisions. Public security was another large division under which all the law and order functions assigned to the federation were grouped. The police forces in the normal sense do not, however, come under the federal ministry, being controlled by the Länder. Another division dealt with civil defence, and four more looked after the social, non-law and order tasks of the department, viz. Sport, Cultural Affairs of the Federation, Physical Planning and Communal Affairs, and Miscellaneous Social Payments. The latter covered a curious collection of assistance provisions, including war indemnities and war graves maintenance. Under Communal Affairs there was little of major importance, again owing to the fact that either the Länder are responsible or there are questions of finance involved which fall to the Finance ministry. To complete the picture there was a central organisation and personnel division.[3]

Below the division or subdivision are subject sections or Referate as they are called in German. These numbered ninety-eight at this time and averaged roughly seven or eight in a division or subdivision. These sections constitute the basic operational units in all German ministries, the points of obligatory reference for all business coming into them and the level at which proposals are formulated for upward transmission to the top levels of direction. These posts are held by permanent officials of relatively senior rank, nearly all of them in a department like Interior being qualified in law. The total number of officials of the higher service, i.e. those with an academic qualification, was 183, a figure which again underlines the relatively small and intimate scale of the organisation. Indeed the scale is still such that a significant proportion of the officials in charge of sections can expect to have direct contact from time to time with the ministers or leading officials, and operate as a matter of course as the main contacts with Bundestag committees, organised interests, etc.

Within the area of responsibility of the Interior ministry and subject to

[3]The broad allocation of functions has not changed much subsequently. There are now ten divisions, with an additional one for refugees and the war-injured (transferred to Interior in 1969).

its supervision and direction are a variety of executive agencies, dependencies as they might be termed. These numbered fifteen in 1966, excluding agencies connected with the border police. Some were research establishments without political importance such as the Archaeological Institute in Berlin, the Federal Institute for Eastern European Studies in Cologne and an Institute for Surveying in Frankfurt. Two others had functions in respect of foreigners seeking asylum in Western Germany and of refugees. Another was the Federal Archives in Coblenz. Four agencies of broader political significance are the Federal Statistical Office in Wiesbaden, the Federal Office for Protection of the Constitution in Cologne, the Federal Office for Crime Detection (Wiesbaden) and the Federal Administrative Office (Cologne). The latter is a kind of general administrative unit, formed in 1959 with the aim of relieving various ministries of executive tasks. But though it has acquired a rather extraordinary collection of tasks, notably in relation to immigration laws and naturalisation, it has not been as successful as was hoped in counteracting the tendency of other departments to prefer to maintain their own dependencies. The Office for Crime Detection has played an increasingly large part in overcoming some of the problems inherent in a decentralised police system trying to cope with criminals who recognise no administrative (or even national) boundaries. The Office for the Protection of the Constitution is essentially concerned with collecting information about the activities of groups subversive of the constitutional order: it has no police functions and resembles to some extent an internal counter-espionage organisation. Its regular reports have been a useful source of information about the scale and variety of political extremism to the Right and to the Left. The Federal Statistical Office is, of course, the main instrument for the preparation and publication of national statistics.

The relationships between these dependent agencies and the Ministry of the Interior are in many cases relatively distant. All of them have been set up on the basis of some formal instrument, a decree, decision, agreement, or sometimes a law. This means that their powers and duties are fairly strictly defined, and in some instances the Bundestag will have had the opportunity to ensure that an effective separation between the parent department and the dependency has been achieved. The ministry exercises varying degrees of supervision: in some instances over policy and personnel (the "Fachaufsicht" or general administrative supervision), in others only a control over the proper use of powers (the "Rechtsaufsicht" or control of legality). In practice these subordinate agencies control their own personnel within the budgets agreed with the ministry and would come for support on policy questions only when the issue was new powers, a revision of existing powers or some major departure from current practices. Generally they are expected to operate autonomously and to take their own decisions, many of which, like any other administrative act, are subject to the possibility of control by the courts, administrative and constitutional. Naturally the discretion of these bodies is subject to other limits too: finance, for example, and the need to seek approval from the ministry or even from the Bundestag for some kinds of action (e.g. in the case of many of the statistical exercises of the Federal Statistical Office a law is required). But on the whole by removing from the departmental organisation very many executive tasks, they do provide for a genuine measure of delegation and deconcentration. It should be emphasised that in the case of the dependencies of the Interior ministry none has any kind of regional or local organisation: they are essentially single-tier agencies.

The organisational pattern which has been indicated for the Interior ministry is reproduced with variations of detail in all other federal departments. Naturally some, notably Defence, and more recently Finance, are on a larger scale and reveal somewhat more complexity in organisation. In the case of Defence there is, of course, an extensive country-wide executive structure supporting the central unit. But the model of a relatively small ministry at the centre, concerned chiefly with policy, statutory regulation and resource allocation, and supported according to need by a range of dependent executive agencies, is common throughout. This achieves a rough separation between policy-making and administration which is by no means confined to the federal level: it appears throughout German government.

Both the structure and working style of the federal departments express a continuing preference for a fairly rigid hierarchical system. Indeed the basic elements in the structure and guidelines for the conduct of business are laid down in a document approved by the Federal Government.[4] In theory action is initiated at the level of the Referenten, the officials in charge of subject units, and it passes upwards according to its importance to subdivision and division heads, and thence to the state secretaries and ministers. Contacts between divisions tend to be of a fairly formal nature,

[4]*Gemeinsame Geschäftsordnung der Bundesministerium*, originally approved in 1958.

and the development of mixed teams, operating across organisational boundaries, has been rather hesitant. The emphasis on the responsibility of the line officials has been strong, which means that *pari passu* staff units with across-the-board functions (e.g. planning or organisation) have been relatively weak. An exception to this is the position of the finance divisions which has generally been fairly strong, chiefly due to their responsibility for putting together the annual expenditure programme, supplemented now by medium-term financial projections.

There are relatively few means of encouraging co-ordination from the top. Division chiefs have direct access to the state secretary and the minister. Neither of the latter has a substantial personal staff, though ministers do have a private office and a press section at their disposal. However, a minister does not have a "cabinet" acting on his behalf, which means that for securing a departmental response he is very dependent on the co-operation and sympathy of the senior permanent officials. It is not surprising that in this situation there should be strong support for the practice of making political appointments to senior official posts in order to ensure responsiveness to ministerial requirements.

In most federal ministries the majority of general administrative posts are held by lawyers. Given the large amount of regulatory or rule-making work which falls to the federal departments, there is a practical case for this arrangement. But undoubtedly it has its drawbacks in terms of uniformity of experience and a tendency to formalism in the approach to administrative activity. In some departments the character of the work has encouraged the employment of officials trained in other disciplines, and where the functions are of a predominantly technical nature (e.g. in parts of the Transport ministry) it has always been normal to entrust them to the appropriate type of specialists. Yet to a rather surprising extent the federal administration retains its legalist qualities, despite the many doubts which have been expressed about their shortcomings in relation to the kind of responsibilities which government now assumes.

## THE FEDERAL DEPARTMENTS AND THEIR EXTERNAL RELATIONS

So far we have been mainly concerned with organisation and structure. We must now turn to consider the pattern of relationships and pressures

D

surrounding the federal departments in the daily management of their affairs. Naturally it will not be possible in a short account to offer a detailed examination of these; the emphasis will be on trying to summarise the position in respect of some of the main aspects of interaction between the federal ministries and other actors in the governmental system. In particular we will look at relationships with Parliament, with organised interests, and with consultative bodies of various kinds. The links with the Länder are dealt with mainly in Chapter 5.

Traditionally Government and Parliament have kept each other at arm's length in Germany. But this distance has been much reduced in the Federal Republic, where the Bundestag has achieved a political strength previously unattainable for German parliamentary institutions. Particularly important is the fact that the ministerial personnel now come predominantly from the Bundestag: much of their active political experience is acquired in a parliamentary setting. Though the idea of the "specialist" minister survives, it usually means a parliamentary specialist and only rarely a non-political expert without a seat in the Bundestag. The Minister for Education and Science from 1969 to 1972, Professor Leussinck, is a recent example of the latter. The impact of the Bundestag on the work of the ministries is, however, much more marked in the area of legislation than in the sphere of general political accountability. The Bundestag does not as a matter of normal practice create a climate of continuing public debate and confrontation which ministers must take into account when deciding what to do. There are, it is true, opportunities for debate in plenary session both on bills and on Government statements, the Opposition can and does make use of its right to interpellate (which also results in debate), and there is a question hour. But the cumulative impact of the activities on the floor of the Bundestag remains modest. This is partly because it is doubtful whether the majority of German politicians set a high value on public debate and confrontation for their own sake; the Bundestag meets only about sixty times on average per year and this frequency is itself some indicator of the importance attached to its plenary sessions. Neither is there much zest for public argument, nor much desire to subject the executive to a continuing and detailed scrutiny of its actions.[5]

[5]This is in any case subject to some limitations as far as the Federal Government is concerned, since the actual administration of so many services rests with the Länder or other decentralised agencies. See also Chapter 7.

As a result it cannot be said that the departments work in an environment in which it is necessary to pay continuous attention to the problem of how to explain and justify Government actions before a critical Parliament with an active Opposition forcing the pace.

This view may, however, need some qualification in the light of experience in the years since 1969. The division between Government and Opposition has become sharper. Though the FDP survives in alliance with the SPD, there is a shift to something much more like a two-party situation. The habits of coalition-style politics show some signs of weakening; the Opposition has adopted a more critical stance in many Bundestag debates and sought to exploit such debates for the sake of influencing the electorate. Similarly the Government has on occasion been tempted to assert its right to get decisions through in virtue of its majority and without regard for the traditional preference for a broad cross-party measure of agreement. How firmly these trends are established depends substantially both on the future relations between the Free Democrats and the SPD, and on the continued cohesion of the CDU/CSU in opposition. If the FDP remains committed to its present senior partner and if the CDU/CSU holds together as an Opposition anxious to establish its claim as the alternative Government, then the sharpened confrontation between Government and Opposition is likely to persist. But should either of these conditions not be fulfilled, the trends of the past few years may prove to be no more than a temporary departure from well-worn paths.

The really effective and close relationships between the departments and the Bundestag arise in the passage of legislation. And since the legislative process in the Bundestag is above all a committee process, this means that it is the ties with committees which count. The Bundestag operates a system of specialised subject committees, with roughly one for each federal department. The main task of these committees is to examine draft bills and to report them back for approval by the floor. In practice this means that the bulk of legislative amendment takes place in committees. In addition committees do consider other matters, notably expenditure proposals (especially in the Appropriations committee) and many reports submitted to Parliament by the Government.

How do the federal departments deal with these committees? Sometimes the contact is at the political level, with a minister, or more frequently now a parliamentary secretary, attending committee sessions (which are as a rule private). More usual is the presence of officials on behalf of ministers, and in fact under Article 43 of the Basic Law the Federal Government or its agents have access to committees as of right. The result of this situation is that it is officials who maintain most of the contacts with committees, and in fact they attend often in substantial numbers, each specialist for a particular part of a bill feeling that he ought to be there.

As to the role of officials in committees, they do not appear as witnesses facing the members. They are there far more as participants and advisers, having every right to join in the discussions, though clearly the extent to which they do so depends on the technicality of the issues involved and on the personality of the chairman. There have been and are strong chairmen who occasionally give officials a rough handling, but on the whole the officials are more likely to receive considerate treatment. The official is, however, potentially the victim of divided loyalties. His first obligation is to defend the measure proposed by his minister. But at the same time a committee is entitled to call on him for support in drafting amendments which may run counter to the departmental draft, and he is obliged to give such help. In fact officials in their relationships with committees have to develop considerable political tact and often must make their own judgment of the kind of political bargain which can be struck. Moreover, in the highly complex bargaining ambience of many committees officials may be tempted to play politics rather too freely: it is not unknown for the representatives of one department to undermine the position of another on a legislative draft.

Over the years officials develop very close relations with committees of the Bundestag. They get to know the personalities involved intimately and can assess very shrewdly the network of political interests in play. (Equally this knowledge operates in reverse to the advantage of committee members.) Generally the officials, as permanent representatives of the departments, enjoy a reputation for skill and expertise which secures respect for their views, at any rate so long as important political interests are not at stake. They maintain a certain style of independence *vis-à-vis* committees, and rarely assume that studied deference so common in the Anglo-Saxon tradition. One especially significant aspect of relations with committees is that it is not unusual for senior officials to be invited to party meetings, especially those of the "working circles" of the parties in the Bundestag. These are the groups which bring together all the committee members from each of the main areas of government action for the purpose of settling party policies. They play a vital part in determining the subsequent course of action in the official Bundestag committees, and are the forums in which the necessary compromises are often hammered out. It was during the long period of CDU dominance when the higher administration was quite extensively colonised with CDU adherents or sympathisers that the practice grew up of inviting officials to such party meetings if it was felt that their advice would be useful. Since the change-over, first to a Grand Coalition of the two major parties in 1966 and then in 1969 to an SPD/FDP coalition, this intimacy between officials and members of the Bundestag at the party level has obviously diminished, though there are signs that similar links are gradually being established between the bureaucracy and the SPD. This practice throws into sharp relief the manner in which the senior officials of the Federal Government become committed politically, or at the very least are brought right into the intra-party arguments. That they gain insights and information which can be used for departmental purposes to outmanoeuvre troublesome critics is not the least of the consequences of this blurring of roles.

In these remarks on relationships with the Bundestag we have stressed the advantages enjoyed by the departmental spokesmen *qua* experts. It must not, however, be forgotten that on the other side of the coin is the accumulated experience of committee members and the relatively extensive sources of information and support inside and outside the Bundestag on which they can call. There is little doubt that generally the Government has its way—80% or more of all measures passed originate with the departments. But the committees can and do insist on adequate explanation of drafts and will frequently make numerous amendments of detail. Occasionally substantial changes are made, though when this happens this is usually the result of party objections rather than the expression of committee solidarity against the Government. It is not without significance that in the final presentation of measures to the Bundestag written reporting plays a major part: it is not difficult to understand from the style and content of reports on bills why the Bundestag floor often finds so little need for extensive debate. The pre-digestion of measures in a context of committee-department relationships which have a strongly bureaucratic flavour ensures that few loose ends or contentious items remain. This is one more example of the assimilation of politics and administration.

It is dangerous to generalise about the scale and importance of the Bundestag contribution to legislative output. Much depends upon the prestige and influence of particular committees and of their chairmen and leading members. In some cases, for example Interior, Law (Recht), Finance, Agriculture and Labour, the committees have a strong position and it is to be assumed that the departments chiefly concerned with them pay careful attention to the points of view and interests known to be powerfully represented in them. For rather special reasons the same has been true of the Appropriations committee which has to scrutinise and recommend approval of the annual budget. But in other fields the departmental position is often stronger, and provided the minister concerned is determined to get a measure through and has the backing of his colleagues and party, then the departments can count on getting their way. Yet there is always some uncertainty in the legislative process: interests are tenaciously represented in the Bundestag parties and there is a general expectation that proposals will be negotiated rather than imposed. As a result the business of getting measures through is for the departments time consuming and tricky: their officials need to have a keen sense of the political undercurrents in the parties and the ability to strike a bargain at the right moment. In this area of relationships the federal administration cannot afford to ignore a complex and subtle party political environment.

We come now to the difficult area of relations with organised interests. Perhaps the best starting-point is the requirement in the orders of business for the federal ministries that the interests affected by any proposed measures shall be heard. Of course, this is not an open-ended commitment. Departments must themselves act as filters and select those interests which have a substantial claim to be heard. Overwhelmingly this means pressure groups which have a national organisation and operate at the federal level. Given the highly developed organisation and bureaucratisation of interests in the Federal Republic, this restriction does not, however, go very far towards keeping down the number of bodies claiming a right to be heard: lobbyism is big business in Bonn and the federal departments are the main (though by no means the only) recipients of attention.

There is no satisfactory typology of interests which can be employed, but it is worth referring specifically to two types of interest which are of major importance. The first is the broad group of economic pressure groups, ranging from the employer organisations on the one hand to the trade unions and consumer groups on the other. They have close ties with crucial areas of the federal administration, for example the farmers' organisation (Deutscher Bauernverband) with the Ministry of Agriculture, the Federation of German Industry (the BDI) with the Economics Ministry or the Trade Union Federation (DGB) with the labour affairs divisions of the Ministry of Labour and Social Affairs. Gradually the staff of these departments, who for the most part enjoy relatively long tenure of particular posts, tend to become advocates for the points of view of the organisations with which they habitually deal. Nor is this a specifically German problem: in any country a Ministry of Agriculture spokesman who regularly opposes the farming interests will find himself in an untenable position.

A second category of great importance comprises interests which have a quasi-public status. These are very numerous and diverse, and their range has tended to increase as the role of government has widened. Chambers of Trade and Agricultural Chambers of Trade are good examples of bodies with recognised public status and duties. The local authority associations, notably the Deutscher Städtetag, are similarly public bodies in all essentials. The public service unions come into the same category, and a wide variety of professional associations also have a statutory basis. In the educational and research sector there are now many bodies financed out of public funds, but able and willing to press their claims on public authorities just like private interests.

The close links between organised interests (of both the private and semi-public variety) and the machinery of government encourage a close assimilation of styles between the two sides: the kind of people who operate in the interest group area resemble those in the administration, they may often be ex-officials, and they are anxious to conform to the conventions of the official world. Thus it becomes more and more difficult to distinguish where the boundaries are, what the extent of conflict may be, and at what point on the scale running from the achievement of declared public policy aims to satisfaction of private interests affected bargains are struck. Instead the organised interests and the world of government appear often to be engaged in a single co-operative (and some would say manipulative) venture. This is facilitated by the relatively high level of organisation of pressure groups and associations in the Federal Republic. Their incomes tend to be fairly substantial, staff are well qualified and paid, and office services are good. Thus they are properly equipped to keep a close watch on all developments of importance and to maintain effective contacts with the ministerial departments. There is a professionalism about the world of pressure groups and lobbies in Western Germany which is more reminiscent of Washington than of many other European capitals.

In relation to the Federal Government organised interests of course owe their influence in part to the political importance of their claims: the roles of the agriculture lobby or of the public service unions are clear cases of this. Though pressure is brought to bear first on the departments, and preferably at the earliest possible stage in the evolution of a new policy, the organised groups do not hesitate to press their claims at the political level if that seems necessary in order to gain satisfaction. Federal ministers are a target for demands, and at the same time have many close and unavoidable links with the interests which provide opportunities for the exchange of views. Neither do the organised groups interact with the federal departments merely as the sources of demands which have to be taken account of in the conduct of affairs. In addition they are involved in a co-operative role owing to their wide representation in many consultative organs, and are able to reinforce their pressures and opinions by activity in other parts of the political system, notably in and through the political parties in the Bundestag. That the Bundestag has opportunities for exerting influence on legislation means that the action of organised interests there is directed to substantial objectives: if opposed strongly at the departmental level, they appreciate that there are real possibilities through the parliamentary committees of securing some of the concessions demanded by their members.

Thus the departments are involved often enough in a complicated process of political bargaining in which they have to strike a balance between the desiderata of Government policy, the impact of the groups upon party political forces, and the desirability of maintaining a high level of administrative co-operation and readiness to provide information on the part of the organised interests. That the German central departments are themselves nearly all non-executive means that they are *more* rather than less dependent on outside interests for providing much of the raw material of experience of statutory schemes which is so important for the successful formulation of policies.

The Federal Republic shows many signs of a highly organised, rather bureaucratised pluralism. The central Government is naturally, as the main policy-maker, the recipient of the largest share of the pressures of the articulate organised interests, though the extensive decentralisation of the German political system also means that there are important interests to be defended at other levels. The interplay between Government, bureaucracy and parties on the one hand, and interests on the other, is often taken to justify sinister conclusions about the distortion of the public interest and the oligarchical position of large private groups, especially in the sector of business and banking. Undoubtedly there are dangers, and these have been underlined in recent years by the numbers of cases in which members of the Bundestag have been involved in allegations of undue susceptibility to financial inducements held out to them by private business concerns. In relation to the administration there is very little evidence of such dubious methods, though even here it is probable that the links are sometimes too close and friendly to allow the public service to retain as high a level of objectivity as would be desirable. Yet it must also be remembered that there is a vigorous competition of interests in the German political system, and a recognition by most shades of political opinion that such pluralism is necessary and beneficial. This situation of itself offers some protection against the grosser distortions of public policy by private pressures: the political and administrative sides appreciate that a balance between claims has to be maintained, and that this is expected both by public opinion and by most of the organised groups which participate in the elaborate processes of bargaining by which most issues are resolved.

As in many other Western states the operation of government in the Federal Republic has in the past two decades or more been modified by the steady growth of consultative and advisory bodies. The traditions of German administration were unsympathetic to this trend, particularly due to the emphasis on the sole right of officials to take decisions involving an exercise of sovereignty. But all this has changed under the influence of post-war political developments and above all as a result of the recognition that, as the state now performs a vast range of functions directed to extending social and economic welfare, it is no longer practicable for public agencies to proceed by autonomous decisions. They have got to consult, take advice, gather information, co-ordinate interests, and maintain the continuing co-operation of non-governmental bodies involved in the various sectors of public provision.

The growth of consultative bodies attached to the federal departments, and indeed to all other levels of government, has been rapid. They vary widely in status and functions as well as in size and membership. There has been extensive use of rather grand advisory councils—nearly every department has at least one—but generally they have only a limited practical influence. There are exceptions to this, as, for example, the Finanzrat (Financial Council) and the Konjunkturrat (Trade Cycle Council), which have a statutory basis and are attached to the Ministries of Finance and Economics respectively. These bodies represent the federation, the Länder and the local authority associations, and have the task of making recommendations about levels of public expenditure and the co-ordination of public spending programmes in the former case and economic prospects and measures in the latter. Their opinion has often to be sought on action taken or planned if it involves subsequent measures by the Länder or local authorities. Then there is a wide range of commissions and committees in narrower areas of public action, many of which are in practice serving to associate the relevant organised interests with continuing implementation of policy. Another type of advisory body is the specialised group which may have an *ad hoc*, once and for all task, or may operate as a standing source of expert assessment. An example of the former was the Electoral Law Commission composed of seven professors which was set up after 1966 by the Grand Coalition, of the latter the Experts for the Appreciation of the General Development of the Economy who report annually to the Minister for Economics (Sachverständige zur Begutachtung der gesamtwirtschaftlichen Entwicklung). The influence of these expert groups is variable: if political factors are dominant the Government is usually inclined to trust its own judgment of what it is expedient to do. If the issue is rather more open, then the opinions of qualified experts still carry great weight. It is perhaps significant that the layman plays an insignificant part in nearly all kinds of advisory body: the specialist is preferred and where the taking of evidence becomes relevant, that too tends to come from "qualified" sources. Affecting this whole phenomenon of consultation and advice is the realisation of the need nowadays to engage a broader range of skills and knowledge in policy-formation than was thought necessary earlier on. In this way the administration finds itself exposed to new constraints: it has to show that official policies are not out of touch with outside research and analysis in the fields relevant to them. Whatever advantages this may have, there is also a price to be paid in terms of increased delay and complexity in reaching decisions.

We have pointed to some of the major areas of interaction with institutions and interests external to the federal administration. All of these impose a substantial burden of co-ordinating effort on the federal ministries. These relationships clearly have major implications for policy-making at the federal level, imposing on it the character of a bargaining process in which compromises have to be struck between what departments want and what organisations external to them will let them get. The Federal Government can rarely determine policies unilaterally, at any rate in all sectors of internal development, and it remains acutely conscious of the need to make haste slowly. There is in addition the dimension of relations with the Länder which complicates the picture still further. This aspect is, however, central to a consideration of the federal structure of Western Germany and better dealt with in that context.

## RELATIONS BETWEEN THE FEDERAL DEPARTMENTS

The federal departments have, of course, relationships with each other, and these too present several important problems. Both in theory and in practice the departments in Western Germany have a high measure of autonomy and each tends to pursue its own interests and policies without too much attention to the manner in which these affect the objectives of the others. But equally the changing character of government functions has meant that the ministries are much more dependent on each other and more closely interlocked. It follows, therefore, that there is some tension between the claims of departmental autonomy and those of co-ordinated policy-making.

Traditionally German ministries have emphasised their independence of each other, being attached to what is often called the "Ressort" or "Department" principle. This owes something to a political habit of coalition, but perhaps more to the preference for the formalisation of procedures and relationships and the precise definition of powers. Thus a situation has arisen in which departments and other administrative agencies are acutely aware of their powers and seek jealously to preserve them. Often there has been hostility and suspicion between ministries, and it is not unusual for the subordinate agencies of the departments to try to hold their supervising authority at arm's length. These conditions are changing as the outlook of the civil service changes and as they are exposed to the influences of a society in which highly formal conventions of behaviour are gradually giving way to a more informal style. Nevertheless, the legal approach to the regulation of relationships continues to be powerful in public administration and this sets limits to the extent to which informal co-operation and mutual confidence can be developed within the federal administration.

There are certain characteristics of the civil service which help to explain the rather sharp demarcation lines between departments. As will be pointed out in a later chapter, the German civil service lacks any élite group or corps which is capable of transcending the loyalties and interests of those in particular agencies. There is no genuine "administrative class" or "grand corps" whose members are distributed throughout the machinery of government. The majority of officials make their careers within a single department, often staying in the same area of activity for a long time. There is no central agency which can move personnel about and guarantee an interchange of experience. Inevitably in these circumstances officials develop a very strong commitment to their own ministry or agency, and *pari passu* a degree of suspicion towards those from other agencies. As we shall explain later, there are factors which help to moderate the divisiveness produced by this situation, but they are not strong enough to make working co-operation between departments easy. And above the administrative level, the tendency for ministers also to be specialised and to stay in the same office for a long period adds emphasis to the claims to departmental autonomy.

The main counterweights to the centrifugal influences just outlined are to be found in the Federal Chancellor's Office and the Finance ministry. The significance of the former as the administrative support for the Chancellor has been dealt with in a preceding chapter. In the present context it is necessary to emphasise that, though the Office undoubtedly buttresses the political role of the Chancellor, its opportunities to function as a co-ordinating instrument for the federal administration as a whole are restricted. There is only modest use made of Cabinet committees to co-ordinate the work of different departments, and thus limited opportunities for the Chancellor's Office to operate as a central secretariat. It would be unusual too for the Office to play a leading part in official-level interdepartmental committees, though it is quite regularly brought into such groups. There is now also a planning section in the Office, which has direct ties with planning officers in all the departments, ensuring both a flow of information and regular meetings. Yet it is doubtful whether this activity has yet had a significant bearing on most current issues: the demands of current politics take precedence over plans for the future and in consequence the planning organisms usually find themselves on the sidelines.

Two conclusions can be drawn from the relative weaknesses of the Chancellor's Office as a co-ordinating instrument. Past experience suggests that the Office has been most influential when it has enjoyed the full support of a masterful Chancellor. The style of action then has been not so much co-ordination by bringing departments together, but selective and often forceful intervention to ensure that initiatives which cut across the aims of the head of Government were brought into line or modified. This was the style made familiar in the mid-fifties and up to 1963, and it has not really been reproduced since then, in part because no Chancellor has had the unchallenged position *vis-à-vis* his colleagues which Adenauer could claim. But if this interventionist style is less easy to achieve now, this alone underlines the need for developing a more co-operative style which would allow the Chancellor's Office to perform a more closely integrated co-ordinating role in relation to business coming up from the departments. Second, the tendency of the departments to view the activities of the Chancellor's Office with some suspicion has undoubtedly been strengthened by the way in which it is staffed. There is no regular interchange of personnel between it and the departments which, if it were practised, might do much to promote closer working relationships. Equally it would encourage throughout the federal administration more awareness of the need for central co-ordination well in advance of the stage at which disagreements assume the character of sharp political controversy.

It is a feature of many governmental systems that the Finance department enjoys special powers in relation to all other agencies. Broadly these powers stem from its responsibilities for the budget and for the general oversight of expenditure programmes. The federal Finance ministry is no exception in possessing a privileged position *vis-à-vis* other departments. The federal Minister of Finance is responsible for presenting the annual budget for the approval of his colleagues before its transmission to the Bundestag, he has similar duties in respect of the five-year finance or expenditure plan required since 1967, and he has the right of initiative in most taxation matters.[6]

[6]There are divisions of competence here: customs policy, for example, rests with the Economics ministry.

Inside the Federal Government the Finance minister can in certain circumstances be overruled only by a majority of his colleagues plus the Chancellor, though Finance ministers have generally tried to avoid invoking their privileged position in disputes with their colleagues. Further, under Article 113 of the Basic Law there are powers which the Federal Government can use to counteract a parliamentary determination to raise expenditure estimates without corresponding revenue adjustments. The Finance minister would have to take the lead here, though his ability to stand up to pressure on his budget depends ultimately on whether he has the backing of the Chancellor.[7]

Supporting the more formal powers of the Finance minister is the administrative apparatus of what is now by Federal German standards a very large ministry. In 1970 (that is to say, a year before the temporary link-up with the Economics ministry) the department had nine divisions, twenty-three subdivisions and nearly 150 subject branches. The budget division alone has more staff than several other departments in total.[8] As a result of its revenue responsibilities the Finance ministry also disposes of substantial executive services. Clearly the institutional resources and powers of the Finance ministry allow it to play a major part in co-ordinating and scrutinising the financial demands of the whole federal administration. The department sits on very many interdepartmental committees and working groups, it has extensive bilateral dealings with the spending agencies, and takes the lead in the top-level organs responsible for expenditure recommendations and decisions, the Financial Planning Council, the Finance Cabinet (a committee of the Federal Government), and the Federal Government itself. Undoubtedly the introduction since 1967 of medium-term financial projections and the gradual strengthening of the Federal Government's powers to co-ordinate within agreed guidelines the rate of growth of all public expenditure has strengthened the Finance ministry still further.

Yet despite the pervasive role of this department its effectiveness as a

[7]Experience of Art. 113, Basic Law, for example in mid-1965 before the election of that year, has underlined the difficulty of resisting pressures for higher expenditures and the weakness of the Finance minister's position if the Chancellor refuses to stand firm.

[8]Detailed staff statistics and comparisons with other agencies can be found in A. Zunker, *Finanzplanung und Bundeshaushalt*, Metzner, 1972, pp. 57–66.

co-ordinating instrument remains limited. This is in part a problem of institutional dispersion and competition. It has to work with agencies at federal and sub-federal levels which actively seek to maintain their autonomy. It is also an expression of a rather old-fashioned separation between financial programmes and their policy content and significance. The right of the Finance ministry to know of financial proposals and to seek reductions in them is not questioned. But there is far less appreciation of the need for a Finance minister to be continuously involved in the formative stage of policies with financial implications. As a result the department is not so closely concerned with the development of policy throughout the federal administration as is, for example, the Treasury in British government. This is why its role as a co-ordinator often has a formal, additive quality which leaves difficult issues to be argued about at the top level, where the Finance minister often runs the risk of being checkmated by his colleagues in the major spending sectors.

Another aspect of the limitations affecting the Finance ministry arises out of its approach to the problem of securing efficiency and effectiveness in the departmental management of spending programmes. This results to some extent from the relative isolation of the audit process which is entrusted to the independent Federal Court of Accounts (the Bundesrechnungshof), and also from the fact of decentralisation, which means that many federal departments do not spend directly. But in addition tradition has encouraged the Finance ministry to take a rather formal view of financial management, with the emphasis on inputs in financial terms rather than on outputs as expressed in the achievement of purposes, the discharge of functions and the scrutiny of processes. The character of the monumental annual budget, the Haushaltplan, vividly underlines this fact, with its vast accumulation of detail of the cost of all the inputs. Needless to say, any changes in this would require the approval of the Appropriations committee of the Bundestag, a body whose functions of scrutiny are modelled on ideas of financial control suited to earlier phases of public expenditure management.

In the preceding paragraphs we have underlined some of the limitations affecting the role of those agencies which by reason of their functions must take the lead in co-ordinating the activities of the federal departments. But it is also necessary to stress that there are many influences working in the direction of closer relations between the departments and of a more coherent and co-ordinated control of their activities. Dominant amongst these are the longer time-scales of public action, the need for better control of levels of expenditure and the impetus towards the forward planning of commitments. The departments are all building up planning divisions, which in turn are linked to the planning section of the Chancellor's Office. Even if these changes have so far had only modest effects on how policy is actually made, they do provide the elements of a new information system which in future could serve the needs of a more coherent planning of policies across the whole of the central administration. Factors such as these have already modified the boundaries between agencies and will do so further in the future. In addition, operational needs impose an immense amount of routine co-operation on all the separate parts of the federal administration. Even if the dominant tendency is still for each part to try to preserve its own interests, there is a growing fund of experience of common problems and shared dilemmas. This constitutes a basis for the continuing erosion of the formalism and particularism which has been a marked characteristic of interdepartmental relations.

## A PLURALIST EXECUTIVE

The outstanding characteristic of the Federal executive in the broad sense of that term as embracing both the political leadership and the administrative structure supporting it is that it is by no means monolithic. It has within it strong elements of competition and conflict which can be contained only by continued efforts of leadership at several levels. This internal differentiation and division is produced by many factors. The necessity of coalition politics has always been of importance, encouraging a tendency to see particular parts of the Federal executive as fiefs held by distinctive political interests. The way in which powers are defined and distributed has supported a fairly rigid view of the conditions on which they are to be exercised. Equally this has been backed up by a system of institutional separation and specialisation throughout the federal administration which makes the integration of policy difficult and expresses a preference for a deconcentration or dispersion of executive responsibilities. The environment of German government supports these conditions. Political institutions external to the Government—notably the Bundestag and the whole structure of federalism—have powers and possibilities of influence which have to be respected in the development of policies and in putting them into effect. And finally there is a wide range of political, economic and social interests in the society which are organised effectively for the purpose of pressing their claims on government, and whose claims to do so are recognised by prevailing political values. That the structure of government at the federal level has in these conditions achieved a relatively high degree of success over the past twenty years underlines the extent to which the values of a pluralist society have been accepted, and their implications embodied in the practices of government by mutual accommodation. Should these values be seriously challenged, the effectiveness of this complex structure of government at the centre would almost certainly be called into question.

# CHAPTER 5

# *Federalism and Decentralisation in West German Government*

NEITHER the government nor the politics of Western Germany can be properly understood without taking account of the fact that it is a federal state. And not only does Western Germany have a federal constitution. It is also a state in which many other forms of decentralisation, to the benefit of local authorities for example, and of administrative deconcentration are firmly established. This makes the system of government highly complex both in formal terms and in its methods of operation. Inevitably there is a temptation to see the Federal Government as possessing the command position in relation to subordinate units which undoubtedly the central Government does often have in centralised states such as Britain and France. But it does not have this kind of position: its functions are more restricted, especially in the area of administration; it is highly dependent on co-operation and consultation with the numerous autonomous and often competing authorities in the federal system; and it lacks independent control over both personnel and financial resources available lower down in the structure of government. Moreover, there is one politically decisive fact which should not be overlooked. There is in Western Germany a lively awareness of the importance of the control of territory as a basis of political power. Thus there are many party notabilities at the Land and local level who have built up their positions in virtue of their control over the instruments of government and personnel at these different levels. This situation has effects on both the national party system and the operation of government throughout the country. It sustains some resistance to centralising demands and helps to maintain a dispersion of interests which has to be recognised in national policy-making.

## THE MAIN FEATURES OF GERMAN FEDERALISM

The roots of federalism run deep, back to the patchwork of states which originally constituted the Holy Roman Empire. Many of these survived into the nineteenth century, and when national unity was brought about by the dominant state of Prussia in 1871, it had to be on the basis of a compromise with Germany's particularist past. In essentials this compromise survives.

In the far smaller Western Germany of 1945 the occupying powers early created the basis for a revival of federalism. Partly for reasons of practical convenience, partly out of reluctance to envisage the possibility of a German central government, the zones of occupation were divided into provinces or Länder. Some of these had an historical basis such as Hamburg and Bavaria, others such as North Rhine Westphalia and Lower Saxony were new constructions, mainly out of the former Prussian territories. The Federal Republic as constituted in 1949 contained eleven Länder, excluding West Berlin. The latter is technically outside the federation, though sending non-voting members to both the Bundestag and the Bundesrat, the legislative organ of federalism. Territorial adjustments in 1951 resulted in the three south-western states becoming one (Baden-Württemberg), whilst the return of the Saarland in 1957 brought the number of Länder in Western Germany back to ten. In order of population size these are North Rhine Westphalia, Bavaria, Baden-Württemberg, Lower Saxony, Hesse, Rhineland-Pfalz, Schleswig-Holstein, Hamburg, Saarland, and Bremen.

The Länder vary widely in population, area, and resources. The largest, North Rhine Westphalia, now has over 17 million inhabitants, the smallest, the city state of Bremen, only 800,000. Of the remaining states only Bavaria has just over 10 million inhabitants, whilst Baden-Württemberg, Lower Saxony and Hesse are all above the 5 million mark. The share of the gross national product per head of population varies markedly between the Länder: from 12,010 DM per head in 1964 in Hamburg to 5520 DM in Rhineland-Pfalz, or in terms of variations above and below a national average of 100, from 170.3 to 78.3. Here the differences reflect not so much size and population as the level of industrialisation as opposed to dependence on agriculture. Bavaria, Lower Saxony, Schleswig-Holstein and the Saarland belong to the category of "poor" Länder (in all except Saarland agriculture is a major factor in their economies), whilst the others are "rich". Indeed in resources per head the richest is the small city state of Hamburg. Variations in economic resources entail variations in tax yields: in 1964 between 1030 DM per head in the Saarland to 4964 DM per head in Hamburg. This in turn is one of the factors leading to different levels of expenditure on particular services.

Constitutionally the Länder show few important variations, all being committed by the Basic Law to adhere to the democratic form of government. All have written constitutions, in some cases of formidable length and detail, and all have a system of judicial review through their own constitutional courts. All the Länder are, however, subject to the general principle that federal law takes precedence over Land law.[1] Unicameral legislatures are the rule (except in Bavaria).[2] In all Länder except the city states there is a Government headed by a Minister President, whereas in Hamburg and Bremen the Senate, presided over by the first Bürgermeister, constitutes the executive. In the case of the two city states (as well as West Berlin) the Land authorities assume the major functions of local government too. There are, however, many minor variations in constitutional and political practice (e.g. Land election law is not everywhere the same) and there are fairly substantial differences in Land administrative structures and in the organisation of local government.

Despite the fact that the Länder are no longer historic entities, in the twenty years or more of their existence even the more artificial ones have to some extent established themselves in the loyalties of their inhabitants. But the differences in culture and religion which in earlier periods distinguished many of the German states one from another have become attenuated, and in none of the Länder can one find a powerful sense of separate cultural identity. In short the Länder reflect at most a number of regional variations in what is now a basically homogeneous society.

Most federal systems reveal the influence of the American model by providing for a vertical division of functions between the Federal Govern-

[1]Art. 31, Basic Law.

[2]The Bavarian constitution of 1946 provided for an advisory Senate composed of representatives of local government and of major social and economic organisations.

ment and the member states. In theory powers are distributed so that each level is co-ordinate with the other and independent of it.[3] German federalism does not conform generally to this pattern. Though the principle of co-ordinate and independent powers plays some part in the relations between the federation (Bund) and the states (Länder), as defined in the Basic Law, it is far less important than another principle of division, namely a horizontal one in which the Federal Government and Parliament have the bulk of the legislative powers, either exclusively or concurrently with the member states, whilst the latter are responsible for the greater part of administration, i.e. the implementation of both federal and Land laws and the provision of services directly to the population. Provided the responsibility of the Länder for the autonomous administration of federal laws is genuine—and this is a problem to be examined below—then there are no grounds for concluding that this horizontal division is less "federal" than the American-style vertical division. Both can produce a situation in which there is an effective decentralisation and dispersion of public powers within the system of government, though obviously the German model is more likely to reveal uniformity in the type of services provided, in standards and in the aims of public policy.

The principle of Land administration of federal law is laid down in Article 30 of the Basic Law: "The exercise of state powers and the discharge of state functions rests with the Länder insofar as this Basic Law does not prescribe or permit other arrangements." Article 80 reaffirms that the Länder administer federal provisions as their own affair, "als eigene Angelegenheit", and under Article 84 they are made responsible for establishing their own administrative services and procedures, unless the Bundesrat has agreed to other arrangements. The Federal Government can promulgate subordinate decrees in respect of federal services administered by the Länder, but only with the consent of the Bundesrat. The same article also provides for federal execution should a Land fail to fulfil its obligations to administer federal law, but these powers have never been invoked. The nearest approach to Federal Government action against a Land was in 1955, when Bonn sought redress before the Constitutional Court against Lower Saxony which had passed a schools law (which it was fully entitled to do) allegedly incompatible with the Concordat of 1933 between the Vatican and the Third Reich. In this case the court decided in 1957 that though the

[3]K. C. Wheare, *Federal Government*, 4th ed., p. 33, OUP.

Concordat remained valid, the Federal Government could not enforce its provisions, since the Länder had full autonomy in educational matters. Indeed it is in the area of education, along with local government powers and structure, and police, that the vertical type of federalism has a foothold: here the Länder have more or less full legislative competence.

The principle of Land administrative supremacy is, however, modified in a variety of ways. Where the Federal Government has exclusive competence it may administer directly either through the federal ministries, or through higher federal administrative agencies (Bundesoberbehörden), or indirectly by making use of public law corporate agencies. Foreign affairs, external shipping and waterways, and railways are respectively examples of these different possibilities. Further, under Article 85 of the Basic Law the federation has power to legislate in such a way that the Länder are required to administer services as its agent. In these circumstances the Federal Government assumes full financial responsibility and can issue instructions on how the services are to be run. But the scope of these provisions is limited to items mentioned in the Basic Law, such as civil defence, motorway construction, air-traffic administration and the exploitation of atomic energy. There is no general power allowing the Federal Government to use the Länder as its agents, though an amendment to the Basic Law in 1969 (Article 104(a)(3)) did come near to this situation by providing that where a federal law specifically states that 50% or more of the funds envisaged are to come from the centre, then the law is to be administered by the Länder as agents of the federation. As we shall see later, the financial arrangements of German federalism make it unlikely that this provision can be extensively used. Finally, there is now provision (since 1969) for what are known as "joint tasks", notably in higher education, coastal protection and certain types of regional development, in respect of which joint planning and financing by federation and Länder is prescribed. Though the day-to-day administration remains with the Länder, the degree of federal involvement in policy-making has been significantly increased. This development will have to be referred to again when we come to consider the changing balance in German federalism.

So far we have been concerned with the manner in which German federalism rests on autonomous Land administration, subject to various qualifications. The distribution of executive responsibilities must now be related to the provisions in the Basic Law which determine the distribution of legislative competence. These are set out in Section VII on "The legislative competence of the Federation".

Formally at any rate Section VII is written in terms of the "independent and co-ordinate powers" model. It starts off by giving a general legislative competence to the Länder, from which it follows that new functions of government or any not regulated by Articles 72 to 75 fall within the sphere of the Länder. The legislative powers of the Länder are, however, circumscribed by the provisions conferring exclusive competence upon the federation in certain areas, and concurrent powers in others. The area of exclusive federal competence comprises such matters as foreign affairs, nationality laws, the monetary system, customs, and posts. Defence was added in 1956. Part of the revenue administration is federal, though here the complex provisions of Articles 105 to 108 allow considerable Länder participation.

Turning to the concurrent powers, the concept implies that the Länder may legislate only in so far as the Federal Government has *not* made use of the same powers. Further, the federation's stated concurrent powers may be exercised whenever they bear upon matters which cannot be effectively regulated on a Land basis, where individual Land regulation would damage the interests of other Länder or the national interest, and where it is generally desirable to maintain legal and economic unity, and uniform standards of living. In short, though the relevant Article 72 appears to be intended to limit the legislative sphere of the federation, in practice it has created a strong presupposition in favour of federal use of the concurrent powers in it.

There are now twenty-six items in the catalogue of concurrent powers. It is not necessary to list all these, but enough to note such examples as civil and criminal law and the organisation of the courts, public welfare, the care of refugees, immigration, labour law, a range of functions relating to regulation of the economy, financial assistance to hospitals (a recent addition) and major aspects of traffic regulation and transport services. Broadly speaking the concurrent powers of the federation extend to the regulation of most aspects of internal law and order (other than the control of the police), of social benefits, and of economic relationships. They have provided the basis for most of the extensive legislative activity of the federation since 1949. Only in a very few sectors (e.g. mining regulations) has the federation failed to use its powers or legislated in such a manner as to leave the substantive details to Land law (e.g. the 1961 law on Youth Welfare).

There is a third type of federal legislative competence, the power to enact "framework provisions" (Rahmengesetze). Originally this power extended to only five items: the conditions of public service, the legal position of the press and the film industry, hunting and nature conservancy, land use and water supplies, identity cards and the registration of persons. In 1969 the twenty-second amendment added to the list "the general principles of the university system". The "framework provision" or "general rules" article is interesting, because it provides a means whereby the federation can enunciate general principles, leaving to the Länder a duty to fill in the detail by their own legislation. Indeed a framework law pre-supposes that it will be in such general terms that there is room for the Länder to use their discretion in subsequent enactments: a framework law containing too much detail might be exposed to invalidation on appeal to the Federal Constitutional Court.

But in fact experience with this article has not been very encouraging. The clause relating to the press has never been invoked, and though frame-work laws have been passed in the other four sectors originally listed, their effects have not been entirely satisfactory. The position in relation to land use and water is both extremely complicated and to some extent inadequate to meet current national needs. Federal enactments on public service con-ditions have had some standardising effects, but have not prevented important variations, have not so far secured common action on some problems which call for it (e.g. the reform of legal training for the higher civil service), and have not excluded sharp disputes about the scope of federal powers (e.g. the appeal by the federation to the Constitutional Court against the action of Land Hesse in unilaterally adjusting judges' salaries, which the Court decided in 1971 largely in Hesse's favour. This led to a constitutional amendment[4] designed to bring the regulation of public service pay and pensions into the catalogue of concurrent powers in order to overcome the anomalies created by reliance on framework provisions.) Whether the new framework clause on the regulation of the university system inserted in the Basic Law in 1969 will operate more successfully still remains to be seen. The Federal Government began to draft legislation in early 1970, but apart from the elements of controversy

[4]Art. 74a, March 1971.

currently so intense in this field, there was also the difficulty that several Länder had already passed legislation on universities or proposed to do so. Thus either account would have to be taken of this in any federal framework provisions (e.g. by allowing a variety of schemes in internal university organisation) or they would have to run the risk of provoking sharp opposition from Länder likely to be confronted with the need to modify their existing provisions. The framework competence is subject to the general need for national uniformity of regulation[5] and, since by definition it refers to matters on which the Länder will subsequently legislate, to the approval of the Bundesrat. To this extent it is difficult to pass framework laws to which a substantial number of Länder are opposed.

It is clear that the division of legislative competence under the Basic Law confers the bulk of the responsibility for law-making, and *a fortiori* for policy-making in the broadest sense, on the federal authorities. The Länder have effectively a residual competence and their more or less exclusive powers are by subtraction concentrated in three spheres: education (up to university level), police, and the general framework of local government. The second and third of these spheres are still pretty well immune to federal intervention, the first is in terms of legislative competence still largely with the Länder, though under Article 91b (twenty-first amendment 1969) the federation and the Länder may now reach agreements on educational planning, and in the case of supra-regional developments in education may share the costs. There is also the new framework power in Article 75 just referred to.

This subsection has been concerned with the underlying principles and basic rules of the German type of federalism. But if we wish to pursue further how this system operates in practice and whether it provides for a genuine distribution of powers between different levels of government, then we must consider at least four main aspects of federalism in action: the role of the Länder via the Bundesrat in legislation, the place of the Länder in the overall structure of government administration in Western Germany, the financial relations between the federation and the Länder, and the methods of consultation and co-ordination between the two levels of government. This will provide the necessary basis for turning finally to the problem of how German federalism is changing, and to the significance within it of other forms of decentralisation.

[5] Art. 72, Basic Law.

## THE LÄNDER AND FEDERAL LEGISLATION

The organ which guarantees Länder involvement in national legislation is the Bundesrat or Federal Council which acts as the second chamber in the federal legislature. It consists of forty-one members, appointed by and from the Länder. Länder with over 6 million inhabitants have five seats each (North Rhine Westphalia, Bavaria, Baden-Württemberg, Lower Saxony), those with over 2 million four seats (Hesse, Rhineland-Pfalz, Schleswig-Holstein), and those with less than 2 million three seats (Hamburg, Bremen, the Saarland). West Berlin sends four representatives, but they do not have voting rights (i.e. they are additional to the forty-one members mentioned above).

The members of the Bundesrat are all members of their respective Land governments, headed by the Ministers President (or Bürgermeister in the case of the city states). The votes of every Land must be cast *en bloc* in plenary sessions: no member votes individually. There is no such thing as an election to the Bundesrat: the chamber is permanently in existence, renewed gradually as the political composition of Land governments changes through the effects of Land elections, and through retirements and death. It is in essence a chamber of provincial potentates, a familiar feature in German history.

The Bundesrat has a number of dignified powers and some real powers which have nothing to do with its legislative role. Its President takes precedence immediately after the Federal President and the President of the Bundestag, and acts as head of state in the absence of the former. Half of the members of the Federal Constitutional Court are chosen by the Bundesrat; it has the right to nominate representatives to a considerable number of official bodies with both executive and consultative functions. But its real authority is derived from the requirements scattered throughout the Basic Law and subsequent legislation that its consent must be given to a wide range of legislative proposals and to any administrative decrees which affect the interests and functions of the Länder. Indeed in the field of what in some countries is called delegated legislation the Bundesrat is more important than the Bundestag.

The major rights of the Bundesrat in relation to legislation are as follows:

   (i) All laws amending the Basic Law must secure a two-thirds majority in both Bundestag and Bundesrat.

(ii) Ordinary legislation may be amended or rejected by the Bundesrat, but except in the cases covered by (iii) the objections of the Bundesrat can be overridden by an equivalent vote (i.e. a majority of members or two-thirds majority as appropriate) in the Bundestag.

(iii) A substantial amount of legislation must secure the approval of the Bundesrat if it is to be passed at all—the so-called "zustimmungsbedürftige Gesetze".

(iv) Decrees or statutory instruments made in pursuance of legislative acts generally require the consent of the Bundesrat (but not that of the Bundestag).

The most significant point in this catalogue is the veto power of the Bundesrat in relation to proposals for which its consent must be obtained. The underlying idea here is that any legislation involving consequent legislative or administrative action by the Länder comes into this category, i.e. it affects the interests and duties of the Länder. It was not originally believed that this category would be very extensive. Experience has falsified this expectation, and as a result of a broad interpretation of the various articles of the Basic Law requiring the consent of the Bundesrat (especially Article 84) it has been possible for the Bundesrat successfully to claim that on average about 50% of all bills must have its consent. Moreover, few major bills would fall outside this category. Table 5.1 shows how the proportion of ordinary bills to those dependent on Bundesrat consent has fluctuated over the years 1950–60.

TABLE 5.1. THE LEGISLATIVE POWERS OF THE BUNDESRAT: BILLS REQUIRING ITS CONSENT, 1950–60*

| | No. of ordinary bills passed | No. of bills passed requiring B.R. consent |
|---|---|---|
| 1950 | 69 | 19 |
| 1952 | 65 | 66 |
| 1954 | 58 | 42 |
| 1956 | 77 | 64 |
| 1958 | 21 | 32 |
| 1960 | 57 | 55 |

* Source: K. Hesse, *Der Unitarische Bundesstaat*, 1962.

The reasons for this increase in the range of legislation subject to the need for Bundesrat approval are complex. To some extent it is simply a result of the fact that contemporary legislation usually implies extensive administrative arrangements, which in the German federal system are the responsibility of the Länder. Thus their representatives have been able to assert successfully a claim to have a voice in determining the shape of such legislation. Equally important has been the recognition by the Federal Government and administration that they are dependent to a substantial extent on the administrative experience of the Länder and their willingness to co-operate in the implementation of policies. So there has been an inclination to accept the Bundesrat's claims, both in order to benefit from the advice its members can offer and to make sure that a co-operative spirit is maintained in the Länder. In return the Bundesrat has used its powers with moderation, rarely seeking to oppose the Federal Government on major questions, though prepared to insist on many changes of detail and on occasion to delay agreement until appropriate concessions are made.

The Bundesrat possesses the right of legislative initiative, but in fact has made negligible use of it. Neither its structure which expresses separate Land interests, nor the division of legislative competence under the constitution, leaves much scope for the Bundesrat itself to operate as a source of proposals. Instead it has seen its role as being rather to scrutinise and, if necessary, modify the initiatives of the Federal Government and Bundestag, and in so doing, to safeguard Land interests. These latter include both specific material interests and the general political interest of maintaining the influence of the Länder as factors in the system of government.

The usual procedure is for all federal bills to be referred first to the Bundesrat for an opinion, after which they go on to the Bundestag, finally returning to the second chamber when the Bundestag has passed them. At the opening stage the Bundesrat has six weeks in which to consider the proposals (though this can be reduced to three weeks in cases of urgency). At the closing stage the Bundesrat may be required to decide within three weeks whether to raise objections or not, and if it does there is the possibility of invoking the Mediation Committee, a joint body of both chambers which had, at any rate until 1971, worked very successfully in ironing out differences between the two chambers.

The time limitations affecting the Bundesrat are not so severe in their effects (except just before an election when legislative log-jams are suddenly released) as might be expected. This is partly due to the manner in which the Bundesrat works. It has few and short plenary sessions. Most of the work is done by subject committees in which Land officials usually represent their ministers. Thus it is a highly qualified bureaucracy, supported by resources in the Länder capitals, which is brought to bear on proposed measures, and it is capable of operating with some speed. Yet more important is the fact that on many bills there is extensive official consultation between the federal departments and the corresponding Länder departments before a draft goes to the Bundesrat. This consultation may well continue at later stages, particularly when it is known that a measure is running into opposition in the Bundestag committees and perhaps in the Länder capitals too. Thus the Bundesrat has many opportunities through its members and their official agents to express a view and exert influence on issues which are thought to damage Land interests or excite political objections.

The political weight of the Bundesrat has depended chiefly on three factors. First on the fact that very often the Länder governments (whose delegations to the Bundesrat must vote *en bloc*) have been coalitions of a composition different from that in Bonn. Thus the Federal Government has had to reckon with political opposition, even when nominally it had a majority in the Bundesrat, which could not be overcome without concessions. Second, the Bundesrat has been wise enough to appreciate that its influence is the greater, the more it refrains from challenging the Federal Government or the Bundestag on issues of major political controversy. In other words, its chances of influencing legislation on matters to be administered by the Länder are greater if it steers clear of clashing with the Government on a big issue and thereby getting involved in party conflict. Third, the Bundesrat relies greatly on its expertise and administrative experience: its views command respect when they are known to express objections based on practical administrative needs. If the Bundesrat is urging a better formulation of proposals on the Federal Government or Bundestag, it can usually expect to get much of what it wants.

Recent political developments may be affecting the legislative role of the Bundesrat. The more clearly defined quasi-two-party position reached in 1969 has increased the probability of sharp divisions of opinion in the second chamber. And since currently there is a small Opposition majority in the Bundesrat, the temptation is to oppose some Federal Government proposals on straight party grounds. In one sense this means more attention to major questions of policy-making and thus an upward revaluation of the Bundesrat's legislative role. But at the same time if it frustrates Government proposals on big issues, then it may become exposed to the risk of having its legislative competence cut down: for many Bundesrat delegates the increase in party controversy within the chamber during 1971 must have been painful.[6]

The part played by the Bundesrat in policy-making through legislation is, in summary, critical and scrutinising rather than original or polemical. But nevertheless its influence by way of amendment of bills has been very wide, and it has emerged as by far the most effective second chamber in modern German history. Its consent is required for such a wide range of measures that it has gained a key position in many of the major sectors of contemporary legislative regulation. Yet of almost equal importance with the legislative role is the fact that through the very existence of the Bundesrat, the Länder governments receive a flow of information which helps them to appreciate and anticipate developments in national policy. In other words the Bundesrat is, or more accurately is part of, an information network which is essential if the Länder are to be in a position to react sensibly and critically to the proposals emanating from the centre.

## THE LÄNDER WITHIN THE FRAMEWORK OF GERMAN ADMINISTRATION

The importance of the Länder as administrative authorities can be seen in Table 5.2 showing levels of expenditure and numbers of personnel in

TABLE 5.2

| (a) Direct expenditure in milliards DM in 1967 | | | |
|---|---|---|---|
| Federation | 68.2 | | |
| Länder | 47.3 | Ratios, 4:3:3 | |
| Local Government | 44.8 | | |
| (b) Personnel employed | | | |
| Year | Federation | Länder | Local Government |
| 1964 | 250,000 | 977,000 | 587,000 |
| 1966 | 272,000 | 1,031,000 | 622,000 | Ratio, 1:4:2.5 |
| 1968 | 276,000 | 1,072,000 | 625,000 |

[6]These dangers became particularly apparent in 1972 when certain delegations to the Bundesrat were tempted to oppose the Government's Ostpolitik and to vote against the treaties with the U.S.S.R. and Poland. Though this danger was finally headed off after the Bundesrat had in February 1973 first voted against the treaties, but then in June supported their ratification, it showed what strains could affect the Bundesrat in conditions of sharp party controversy and rivalry.

recent years. In order to widen the comparison we have anticipated a later section by including the relevant details for local authorities. Of course such figures can easily mislead. The federal staff figures include civilian employment in defence, but not the armed forces. Nor do they bring in Posts or Railways. The Länder staff figures include teachers and the police. Nevertheless the table serves the simple purpose of illustrating how extensive is the Länder responsibility both in terms of the use of financial resources and the control of personnel.

The aspects of Land administration which are crucial to an understanding of German government concern its degree of autonomy, the extent to which it imposes a dimension of consultation and collaboration on the Federal Government, and the manner in which administrative powers (combined with a voice in the national legislature) can act as a support for the dispersion of power inside the political parties.

We will consider first the question of Land autonomy. Clearly, except in the areas of exclusive Land responsibility, the Länder cannot pretend to advance a claim to complete autonomy. Normally they are putting into effect federal provisions, and are bound by the terms of the federal statutes. This does not, however, imply lack of discretion. It is a truism that the statutory basis of modern social and economic services is bound to leave substantial control of how policy is implemented and how services are developed to those executively responsible. This is particularly so in Germany because of the style of German public law. Much of it is drafted in broad and general terms, providing a basis which must then be filled in by subordinate decrees, rather than a detailed structure of regulation. These decrees may in some cases be federal, subject to Bundesrat approval, but are often provisions determined by the Länder governments. German public law in any case allows an inherent administrative discretion to the state, for this purpose the Länder, which often renders unnecessary that degree of specific legislative regulation by the national Parliament typical of Anglo-Saxon public law systems. Consistency and coherence in law, as well as the protection of individual rights, depend ultimately on the action of the courts. All administrative acts are subject to challenge, which means that superior law, whether federal or Land in origin, must be drafted in a manner consistent with the constitution, whilst subordinate law must respect both the enabling statutes and the principles of equity and reasonableness expressed in German administrative law adjudication.

The relatively wide autonomy of the Länder does not, however, stem only from the structure of public law. It depends too on other factors in the way government operates. The Federal Government cannot give instructions to the Länder in the execution of federal law, nor can it prescribe in detail how they should administer provisions. It has no powers of supervision or specific approval such as are found in centralised systems of government, and the greater part of the financial costs of services are met out of the general allocation of revenues to the Länder rather than by specific grants from the centre. And it is of major importance that the Länder (and local authorities) control their own personnel and administrative organisation, though as we shall see later, this does not seriously derogate from the fact that the Federal Republic has a relatively homogeneous public service. Neither should it be forgotten that the Länder can supplement federal law under the concurrent powers heading.

In the area of administration directly on behalf of the Federal Government, the Länder have to act more like agents. The federation has control over both legal questions and policy, though it cannot intervene at the subordinate levels of Land administration and must normally communicate through the Land ministries. Motorway construction is one of the most important and costly services provided by the Länder as agents of the Federal Government. Since 1949 the programme has been ambitious, the cost falling on the Federal Government. Obviously the main elements in it have been determined by the Federal Ministry of Transport in consultation with the Länder, phasing and priorities have been similarly fixed, and standards too have been subject to federal control. But even in this sector the Länder have had substantial influence, mainly in virtue of their command of a large part of the technical resources needed for execution of the programme, and of their responsibility for much of the feeder-road system.

At the other end of the spectrum is the area of exclusive Land competence, where autonomy is at its widest. In relation to the powers and structure of local government there is virtually no federal interest. In education there is still practically no direct federal involvement below the university level, and even in respect of higher education, federal concern is with planning and finance rather than with executive responsibilities. The police remain substantially within Land control, though there have been moves towards strengthening co-operation with the federal crime detection services, and through its powers in respect of public service conditions the Federal Government can work against too serious differences as between the Länder. In addition there are many powers affecting the environment, personal services for the citizen, public health, and the encouragement of industrial development, which rest with the Länder and can be used autonomously. It may be helpful to an understanding of how responsibilities are divided if we break down the figures for federal, Land and local authority expenditure. This is done in Table 5.3.

TABLE 5.3. EXPENDITURE OF FEDERATION, LÄNDER AND LOCAL AUTHORITIES
IN SELECTED FUNCTIONAL AREAS (YEAR 1967)
(Figures are in milliards DM)

| Service | Bund | Länder | Local authorities |
|---|---|---|---|
| Defence | 23,314 | nil | nil |
| Law and order, courts, etc. | 400 | 4554 | 617 |
| Education (schools) | 107 | 7877 | 4274[a] |
| Higher education and research | 2033[b] | 4078 | 80 |
| Social security | 21,809 | 3540 | 4122 |
| Main subdivisions as follows: | | | |
| Employment services | 96 | 117 | nil |
| Social insurance | 11,099 | 49 | nil |
| War pensions, etc. | 6100 | 337 | nil |
| Health, sport | 144 | 2070 | 4174 |
| Food and agriculture | 3723 | 1545 | 308 |
| Support for industry | 3148 | 694 | 169 |
| Transport | 5498 | 3719 | 3073 |
| Planning and housing | 1271 | 3780 | 1843 |
| Public economic enterprise | 3827 | 1122 | 2189 |
| General finance (including pensions of public services) | 11,204 | 9696 | 3903 |
| Total net expenditure | 78,916 | 49,325 | 33,308 |
| Total direct expenditure (i.e. allowing for transfers between sectors) | 68,216 | 47,287 | 44,846 |

[a] Mainly school building.
[b] Mainly support for research.
Source: *Finanzbericht, 1970*, Federal Ministry of Finance.

In the past twenty years the preponderance of the Länder in the direct administration of services has been maintained. After an initial expansion of federal services and organisation in the years 1949–55, something like a state of equilibrium was reached in which it was recognised that most major policy decisions and the preparation of legislation should rest with the federation, whilst the Länder would retain full executive responsibility and rights of consultation. Inevitably this gave the Länder a major influence on how services were provided and developed. It also gave them considerable influence over federal legislative drafts. In the later sixties the position began to change, and the Federal Government was no longer so willing to let the Länder go their own ways autonomously. The growth of public services had produced a strong movement towards the intermeshing of federal and Länder responsibilities, and the horizontal split between policy and administration could no longer disguise the need for closer co-operation between the two levels and for better co-ordination. Thus there have recently been shifts in federation-Länder relationships which require some modification of the picture which was valid only a few years ago. We shall return to these points when looking at the recent evolution and future prospects of federalism.

In a system in which powers and responsibilities are extensively decentralised, there is inevitably a need for a complex network of consultation and co-ordination, at any rate in a society as homogeneous as Western Germany, as densely structured in socio-economic terms, and as keen to see equal standards applied everywhere. There has in fact been a remarkable growth in consultative arrangements over the past two decades, both between the Länder and between the latter and the federation. Similarly a lot of effort has been invested in devising co-ordinating and planning machinery. Many of these arrangements are formalised, so that it is possible to outline them in institutional terms.

Until 1969 the Federal Government included a Minister for the Bundesrat and the Affairs of the Länder, whose main duty was to look after relations with the second chamber and to encourage co-operation between the federation and the Länder. But this device failed to make any significant contribution to these ends, chiefly because the minister had no executive powers and had, therefore, little to contribute to the co-ordination which went on at other levels between federal and Länder organisations which did have an executive role. Moreover, the political weight of successive ministers was generally small, and they tended to be overlooked by their more powerful Cabinet colleagues. In 1969, when the SPD/FDP coalition was formed, it was decided to abandon this particular method of co-ordination and the department was abolished. In effect this was recognition of the fact that many other more effective instruments exist for linking the Federal Government with the Länder.

At the political level there is fairly regular contact between federal and Land ministers within the framework of the interministerial conferences organised by the Länder. Consultation between the Länder governments was rapidly built up after 1949, and by 1962 eleven permanent ministerial conferences were in existence, covering in fact most of the major areas of Land responsibility. Obviously some ministers meet more frequently than others: Finance ministers come together about half a dozen times per year, whilst Justice ministers meet far less often. The original aim of such meetings was to facilitate Länder co-operation and co-ordination. Though this still remains important, an additional dimension has been added through the presence of the appropriate federal ministers on many occasions. In sectors such as finance, transport, health and economic policy, it is clear that there is often a need for formal political consultation between the two levels of government, and this is one way by which it can be arranged in a manner which allows the Federal Government an opportunity to express its views before representatives of all the Länder. Nevertheless, the Federal Government does not participate here as of right, and indeed in one sector, education, it has been relatively little involved in the Standing Conference of Education Ministers. This has been the major instrument for co-ordinating Land policies and for taking decisions on uniform procedures and objectives. But it has suffered from the need to achieve unanimity, and from the fact that it was never a very satisfactory body for long-term planning in fields such as university development. Thus there has been a recent tendency to develop new forms of co-ordinating body in the education sector which brings in the Federal Government right from the start as a partner of the Länder. We shall come back to these developments below. One other point in relation to interministerial consultation is that there is some contact between the Land Ministers President and the Federal Chancellor. Paragraph 31 of the *Business Procedure of the Federal Government* indeed provides for this, though under the long chancellorship of Dr. Adenauer hardly any use was made of this possibility. His relations with the Länder were quite often strained, and his dominant interests lay in fields outside the Länder competence. His successors have in different ways tried to reactivate top-level consultation with the Länder, particularly Herr Brandt, the present Federal Chancellor. On the other hand, though this kind of consultation may sometimes be useful in securing agreement to major moves in internal policy, it can also become formal and decorative, with all the knotty problems referred back to subordinate political and administrative groups.

Though the consultative machinery at the level of ministers is important, it is probably less influential and certainly less extensive than the substantial apparatus of administrative co-ordination and discussion which exists between federal departments on the one hand and Länder ministries on the other. Much of this is informal, involving working relations between Bonn and the provincial capitals. A great deal is formalised, however, in the operation of committees. From a study of federation–Länder co-operation published in 1968[7] it appears, for example, that six ministries in Land North Rhine Westphalia were involved in about 400 federation–Länder committees. Undoubtedly many Land officials spend a lot of time travelling to and from Bonn, and equally federal officials are often *enroute* for Stuttgart, Munich or Hamburg. The growth in the number of national advisory committees set up by the Federal Government has also multiplied Länder involvement, since in many cases the Länder are requested to nominate representatives. A good example is the Science Council or Wissenschaftsrat, set up in 1958 as a result of a federation–Länder convention, to act as a standing advisory group on the development of universities. Its membership includes representatives of the Federal Government and the Länder, as well as people from universities and independent figures. Its recommendations have had no binding effect, but did have a major influence on Länder plans for university expansion in the sixties. Though still in business, the Council has recently tended to be overshadowed by the more recently established arrangements for co-ordinated planning in higher education.

Another tool of co-ordination, apart from the Bundesrat and its committees to which no further attention will be paid here, is the network of Land delegations in Bonn. The heads of such delegations are either senior officials or ministers, and usually have the title of plenipotentiary, perhaps suggesting a breath of that independent particularism which has marked German history. These delegations, varying in size according to the resources of the Länder, represent Länder interests in Bonn, maintain contact with federal departments, with Bundestag and Bundesrat committees, and with any other institutions in which Länder interests are under discussion.

[7]Renate Kunze, *Kooperativer Föderalismus in der Bundesrepublik*, Stuttgart, 1968.

In addition the plenipotentiaries communicate Länder views to federal ministers, and act in the reverse sense by passing on federal opinions to the Land capitals.

One other aspect of federation–Länder co-operation needs to be stressed. This is that much of it does require formal agreements, treaties and conventions. These may be between the federation and one Land or more, but may also be made between the Länder themselves. In the years 1949 to 1960 it has been estimated that about 340 formal agreements were entered into. Many covered trivialities like shared jurisdictions or the payment of travelling expenses to court witnesses. But others affected major questions like the Königstein agreement of 1949 between the federation and the Länder which was to determine the financing of scientific research for many years, or the agreement already referred to on the establishment of the Science Council. The need for such formal arrangements is often an embarrassment, making it harder to reach agreement quickly. At the same time it also acts as some protection for the interests and rights of the Länder, assisting them to maintain claims *vis-à-vis* each other and the federation.

As this outline has shown, there can be no doubt about the range and complexity of the arrangements which have had to be devised to bring together the Länder themselves, and to relate them to the Federal Government. This all introduces a dimension of co-operation between the centre and the states which is unique to German federalism, and for which there is no real equivalent in other federal systems, for example in the U.S.A. Clearly a price is paid in terms of the complexity and slow-moving nature of the German administrative system, though whether this of itself contributes to a lower executive output than might be achieved under more centralised arrangements cannot be demonstrated. Indeed it is possible to argue that the dependence of the Federal Government on carrying the Länder with it, particularly in the sphere of administrative action, means that there is a better chance in the Federal Republic of relating administrative means realistically to political ends, and of ensuring that a wide range of interests in the society are consulted and enabled to express views before final decisions are taken. Certainly, if we were to take as an example economic development in less prosperous areas, the Federal Government in Bonn would have to look to the Länder for advice, and would receive advice far more firmly rooted in knowledge of local circumstances than is likely to be provided by the agents of a centralised government. In this way the Federal

Republic has perhaps avoided to some extent the risk that central policy may be made in a vacuum or on a basis far too flimsy to stand up in practice.

Yet the types of administrative and political co-operation evolved after 1949 did not, in the late sixties, seem adequate to the new phase of co-operative federalism which was then being preached. In particular there appeared to be a problem in the educational sector, where the federation had no powers, but faced an increasing demand for more resources to be made available, and in the broad field of public expenditure management where it was becoming evident that the *total* autonomy of the Länder and local authorities could no longer be maintained. A number of constitutional amendments and ordinary legislation, chiefly passed in 1969, opened the way for the active co-operation of the federation and the Länder in planning policies in several important fields. The development of universities, regional economic policy, and the improvement of agricultural structure and coastal protection became "joint tasks", and for these special planning committees were set up. These comprise an equal number of federal and Land representatives and can take decisions by a three-quarters majority. For education apart from universities a special commission was constituted early in 1970, composed of all the Land education ministers and six of the federal ministers most closely concerned. *De facto* this body, responsible for producing a long-term educational plan, has to work through official committees, of which it had six in 1971. Its recommendations proceed to the Governments concerned, and the agreement of nine Land Governments is required for a decision to be taken. Even then it would bind only those supporting it. Not surprisingly, these elaborate provisions, designed to frustrate the growth of a centralising power in Bonn, have made the educational planning machine work slowly: results are barely visible yet, and major issues of scale, organisation and quality remain to be resolved.

In relation to public expenditure management there is now the Financial Planning Council and the Trade Cycle Council. Both these bodies, which also make use of subcommittees, are intended to facilitate co-operative action under the guidance of the Federal Government in order to plan the growth of expenditure, to relate expenditure to forecasts of available resources, and to co-ordinate counter-cyclical action. We will return to the problems involved in managing public expenditure programmes[8] in the final chapter.

[8]On medium-term financial planning see Professor K. M. Hettlage, The problems of medium-term financial planning, *Public Administration*, Autumn 1970.

One further observation leading on to wider political issues can be made on the co-ordination and consultation problem. The arrangements outlined here have served to underpin and institutionalise the claims of the Länder in a manner which tends to maintain their influence in the overall operations of government. The Federal Government has a restricted capacity for direct administration, and even in the framing of policy it must try to carry the Länder with it if subsequently the policies decided on are to be effectively carried out. The extensive nature of Land functions and the control of executive action which they confer—meaning in the first place control of administrative services and personnel—means that the Länder dispose of substantial political influence. Nor is this narrowly confined to the institutions of government. The German party structure reflects the decentralisation of power implicit in federalism. This has always been obviously so in the case of the Christian Democratic Union, a party built on Land constituent groups and closely linked with its highly autonomous wing in Bavaria, the Christian Social Union. But the Social Democrats have been subject to the influence of federalism too. For many years it was only in the Länder that they could build up positions of power and executive responsibility. Men like Max Brauer in Hamburg, Wilhelm Kaisen in Bremen, August Zinn in Hesse, Ernst Reuther and then Willi Brandt in Berlin, showed that it was possible to make major contributions to national political life from the secure foundation of leadership at the provincial level. Gradually the SPD party organisation has adapted itself to the requirements of the federal structure, so that now the individual Land parties play a vital part in the management of election campaigns and in fact control in negotiations with the central organisation the composition of the Land lists of candidates. These factors alone contribute to a dispersion of influence and interest within the parties which makes it impossible for the national leaderships to act without regard to the need to secure the co-operation of the lower levels on which they depend. Admittedly, all these effects are far more evident in internal policy, especially in social and economic affairs, than in such spheres as foreign affairs or defence. But this hardly detracts from their importance in a society in which bread and butter issues of economic and social progress are what matter most to the electorate.

## THE FINANCIAL BASIS OF FEDERALISM

So far we have avoided any detailed references to the distribution of financial resources under the German type of federalism. This aspect is best treated separately, if only to avoid adding to the complexities which are already apparent in the outline of the distribution of powers and the operation of the administrative system of German federalism. Obviously in any federal system the kind of effects it has on the operation of government depend in large measure on how the taxing power and the distribution of tax yields are regulated. If the member states are chronically short of revenue and dependent on central grants, then substantial formal powers are unlikely to protect them against the growth of centralised authority.

Just as the distribution of powers in the Federal Republic does not follow the "co-ordinate and independent powers" model, so the approach to the allocation of revenues departs from the traditional search for independent sources of revenue familiar in many federal states. The Basic Law, it is true, allocates certain taxes exclusively to the federation, and reserves others of minor importance to the Länder. But the most important principle is that of sharing out global tax revenues between the federation and the Länder, and more recently the local authorities too. Subject to this principle the bulk of the legislative taxing authority rests with the Bundestag and the Bundesrat, the latter having a veto in so far as any matters affecting appropriations to the Länder go. The crucial issues concern the method of apportionment, the capacity of the Länder to secure an adequate share, and the extent to which they can then use their revenues within their own discretion.

Originally the Basic Law provided that the proceeds of customs and excise, of fiscal monopolies, of consumption taxes (apart from the beer tax), of turnover taxes and of taxes on the transport of goods were to accrue to the federation. The proceeds of income and corporation tax went initially to the Länder, but could be divided between the federation and Länder, whilst a number of taxes on property and real estate, taxes on motor vehicles, and taxes with only local effect were to accrue to the Länder and local authorities. These provisions were not at that time related to any estimate of the likely expenditure of federation and Länder as determined by their respective functions. By 1951, when it was evident that the Federal Government had greater needs than had been envisaged originally, the sharing of income and corporation tax became necessary, though no satisfactory agreement on the apportionment of these taxes was reached until 1955.

Already by 1952 the federation had secured legislation to entitle it to claim 37%, rising to 38%, of the proceeds of the income and corporation taxes. It was also necessary in the early fifties, when the financial burdens arising from the social and economic consequences of the Second World War were particularly heavy, to make arrangements for equalising resources as between rich and poor Länder. In 1955 something like a permanent settlement of revenue-sharing was achieved.[9] This recognised the principle that the federation and Länder were each responsible for their own expenditures and that financial resources should be shared so that functions and needs would be more closely related to tax resources. It was provided that until 1958 the federation would get 35% of the income and corporation tax, the Länder 65%. The future share-out was, however, also to be subject to biennial revision by federal law (with the approval of the Bundesrat), and this led in practice to frequent and often acrimonious arguments between the Federal Government and the Länder. The proportions were varied from time to time, mainly because the federation demanded a larger share, but in 1966, for example, the Bundesrat refused to accept a federal claim to 39% of the proceeds of these taxes and the Federal Government had finally to settle for 37%, subject to changes in the provisions for equalisation amongst the Länder. In 1969, just before the major reforms of that year, a division between federation and Länder of 35%/65% was fixed.

One of the fundamental difficulties of this arrangement was that it required a large part of total tax revenue to be shared out with no reference to the way in which the yields of various taxes varied over time. In consequence frequent adjustments to adapt to new financial needs had to be made. But on balance the federal share declined and that of local authorities (who received funds passed on from the Länder) remained static. In contrast the Länder share increased relatively because the taxes which constituted it proved more dynamic. (The yield of income and corporation tax rose by 260% between 1955 and 1967, whilst turnover tax yield rose by only 110%.)

Another set of difficulties arose out of the equalisation provisions, which

[9]*Finanzverfassungsgesetz*, Dec. 1955, *BGBl*, I, p. 817.

had in one form or another been in force since 1950. These included an element of vertical equalisation between federation and Länder in the distribution of shared tax yields as well as horizontal equalisation between the Länder. But the scope for equalisation was not wide enough to compensate fully the poorer Länder, the provisions left room for considerable manipulation of tax yields, and the weak Länder generally resented their dependence on their more fortunate neighbours.

The situation during the sixties was dominated by the problems presented by rising levels of expenditure on the part of federation, Länder and local authorities. Federal social security expenditure continued to rise, spending on the economic infrastructure rose, defence claimed substantially more as the German armed forces were established and equipped, and in many areas, e.g. scientific research and development, the Federal Government was compelled to increase its contributions. Similarly Länder budgets rose, especially in the education sector, and local authorities embarked on more and more ambitious programmes of environmental improvement and economic development. It became increasingly evident that in this dynamic and rapidly changing situation, it was imperative to overhaul the somewhat rigid pattern of tax apportionment in order to achieve a more stable relationship between financial resources and functions at the three main levels of the system of government. Accordingly a committee of inquiry was set up at federal level in 1964, which in 1966 presented the report, usually known as the Troeger report on fiscal reform. Slowly, and in the face of numerous arguments and objections, the process of drafting a scheme for revising financial relationships was set in motion, and finally in 1969 the necessary constitutional amendments and consequential laws were passed.

The major element in the financial reforms passed by the Grand Coalition in 1969 was a change in the principles governing the sharing-out of revenues between the different levels of government. The proportion of revenues subject to apportionment was raised to about two-thirds of all tax yields, this being achieved by bringing the added-value tax into the pool (previously the turnover tax). Despite strong opposition from the Bundesrat, a compromise was finally reached which provided that, after deducting 14% of the income tax for the use of local authorities, the remainder of the income-tax yield and the corporation tax should be shared equally between federation and Länder. These provisions were included in a revised Article

106 of the Basic Law. The sharing-out of the added-value tax was left to legislation, subject to Bundesrat approval. Here the outcome was a 70% share to the federation and 30% to the Länder, though with a guarantee of readjustment after 1971 in the light of developments in the costs of services and any new burdens imposed on the Länder by federal law. Changes were made too in the arrangements for both vertical equalisation, i.e. payments by the federation to poorer Länder, and in horizontal equalisation, i.e. adjustments between rich and poor Länder. These provisions are of unusual complexity and need not be given in detail here. It is, however, worth noting that the principle of local yield is still maintained, i.e. revenues flow to the Land in which they accrue. The principle is modified in various ways to mitigate the inequities which it can produce, but nevertheless it is upheld for two reasons. One is that it helps to justify Land control of large parts of revenue administration, and the other that it offers an inducement to the Länder to encourage revenue-producing development. As far as horizontal equalisation goes, payments between the Länder were reduced from DM 1725 million to DM 1100 million. Five Länder are recipients, five are donors. Whilst the distinction between richer and poorer Länder still affects political attitudes in the Bundesrat, it must be stressed that poverty is a relative term in the German federal system. There is a big difference between tax yields and social product per head as between Hamburg and the Saarland, but this is within the context of a society in which overall standards of living and public expenditure are high. There is certainly not the kind of difference found between the poorer American states and the richer, nor between the poorer and richer regions of many centralised countries.

It was certainly optimistic to hope that the reforms of 1969 would create a long-term financial equilibrium. The expenditures of the Länder have continued to rise at a brisk rate, with education contributing a great deal to the upward trend. Local authority spending has also continued to go up, to such an extent that by 1971 many major cities were dangerously over-stretched as a result of the costs of accumulated borrowing. But at the same time the Federal Government, committed by its programme to internal reforms, also faced the prospect of needing more resources. In this situation there was soon a demand by the Länder for a reapportionment of the proceeds of the added-value tax, preferably so that the Länder share of 30% would rise to 40%. During 1971 the Federal Government resisted this claim, though finally it accepted that some solution more favourable to the Länder than that of 1969 was inevitable. Eventually a 35% share was conceded to the Länder. At the same time the rising level of overall public expenditure was pushing the SPD/FDP coalition towards a policy of increasing tax rates, a policy opposed by the FDP and by some members of the SPD too, who believed it would have harmful effects on economic growth, and supported by those anxious to improve services and in favour of more progressive scales of taxation as a means of promoting greater social equality. But regardless of the ideological element in the argument about tax levels, some increases in the overall yield became unavoidable in 1972 if the three major levels of government were to be enabled to meet the rising demands for services facing them.

Two other aspects of the financial arrangements of the German federal system need to be mentioned. One is that there has so far been relatively restricted use of what might be called federal grants-in-aid. It is a fact that the Federal Government could and did make formal agreements with Länder for special purposes and contributed funds in this way. In 1968 such specific subventions totalled DM 5000 million. But this was not a large sum in relation to total expenditures by either the federation or the Länder, nor was it so significant as to put particular Länder into a state of complete dependence on Bonn. The other point is that the reforms of 1969 also envisaged a new form of federal–Länder financing under which both sides would contribute funds and join in the planning. This was devised for the new category of "joint tasks", chief of which is the development of universities. After 1969 the federation was pledged to bear 50% of the costs of new capital development in this sector, gaining in return a foothold in the planning of such works.

We must turn now to the two questions about the financial settlement raised at the beginning of this section, namely whether the Länder can secure an adequate share of revenues, and the extent of their discretion in disposing of it. The Länder share of total national revenues amounts to roughly 35%. Whether this is "adequate" depends very much on the demands for services which it has to meet. The reforms of 1969 were intended to produce an apportionment which was reasonable, having regard to the services which have to be financed by all three levels of government. Unfortunately the contemporary social service state never reaches a point of equilibrium. In the short time since 1969 the overall levels of public expenditure in the Federal Republic have risen by at least 10% per annum, and it is apparent that the long-term trend of expenditure, much of it for services provided by the Länder, is inexorably rising, and faster than was previously envisaged. Thus the Länder have very quickly found that their revised share of tax revenues is no longer adequate to their needs. It must be assumed, therefore, that the problem of apportionment will remain acute, and that the federation will continue to be subject to pressure to increase the allocations to both the Länder and local government. Nevertheless, despite these difficulties, the volume of resources claimed by the Länder is very large. Their claims are underpinned in the Basic Law, and no changes can be made without the consent of the Bundesrat. Over the years the Länder have shown that they can strike hard bargains, and there is no reason to believe that they have yet lost this capacity. The shift towards a clearer two-party division naturally tends to make it harder for a majority in the second chamber to act against the Federal Government, but on financial questions the Länder Governments have often shown a readiness to join forces across party alignments in defence of their various interests.

As to the discretion of the Länder in spending, this is, of course, limited by federal and Land law, and by continuing commitments. The bulk of services have a statutory basis, and the Länder are expected to provide those for which they are responsible. But within such obvious limits the Länder control their own spending. They enjoy budgetary autonomy, which means that each year the various Landtage have to approve a budget, in the detailed determination of which both the Länder governments and parliaments are autonomous. In many fields the Länder can vary the amount of support they give to programmes required by federal law, and they remain free to supplement services prescribed by federal statute. Moreover, there are many sectors, notably economic development and the provision of infrastructure, in which the Länder enjoy the full rights of initiative. One has only to consider the five-year development programme put forward in 1970 by the SPD/FDP government of North Rhine Westphalia to appreciate how wide-ranging is the scope for genuine policy-making by a Land Government.[10] Certainly the opportunities granted to regional

[10]*Nordrhein-Westfalen Programm 1975*, published in 1970 by the Minister President's office.

economic agencies in several more centralised European countries fade into insignificance when compared with those enjoyed by the German Länder.

## OTHER ASPECTS OF DECENTRALISATION WITHIN THE FEDERAL STRUCTURE

It is most appropriate at this stage to make some brief references to local government and to the way in which it fits into the broader pattern of government in the Federal Republic.

Germany has a long tradition of vigorous local government, reaching back to the reforms initiated by Freiherr vom Stein in 1808. Indeed in the shape of the city states this tradition stretches even further back into the past. In the nineteenth century it was in local government that the middle class, and later the rising working class, were able to exert some political influence and gain experience of managing public services. Local government was severely weakened during the Nazi period when many of the most competent and enlightened figures in the towns and cities were forced out of office. After 1945 the sheer extent of destruction constituted a great challenge to local authorities: they faced tasks of daunting magnitude which could be undertaken successfully only by authorities vigorous and independent enough to think boldly and to take risks. Fortunately for German local government, the scale of the problems induced great efforts rather than any feelings of despair or a readiness to wait for instructions from above. Moreover, the political climate, expressing hostility to centralisation, was very favourable to a reinstatement of the older traditions of active local self-administration. Thus there was full support for a restoration of local authorities on a basis which gave them a similar status to that which they had enjoyed before 1933.

A further general comment about local authorities is worth making. This is that internally they have a tradition of strong executive leadership. The constitutions of local authorities have varied widely (and still do), ranging from those providing for a popularly elected chief executive (Bürgermeister or Oberbürgermeister) through those with an indirectly elected chief executive to those with a collegial type of executive (usually known as the Magistrat). And in north Germany there is something nearer to the British type of local government through a council and its committees.[11] But regardless of these differences, there has been a basic understanding that local councils should have a deliberative role and that there should be a strong executive charged with the formulation and execution of policy. This approach has meant that local authorities—at any rate those of any size—have been well organised to carry out their functions. They have been capable of providing local leadership and a sense of direction. A career in local government has enjoyed prestige and offered prospects of substantial achievement. One has only to think of the many names which have become associated with periods in the history of famous cities to appreciate that local government has offered and continues to offer opportunities for securing a national reputation. What is more, the political parties form the essential basis of concerted action in local government, and those who are successful at this level embody powerful political interests. No Social Democrat Government can, for example, be indifferent to the fact that much of its strength lies in the record of the party in the major cities of the country. There exists here a network of influence and interests which the party leadership both in Bonn and in the provincial capitals must respect.

Turning now to the institutional position of local government, the principle of "communal self-administration" is recognised in the Basic Law.[12] The responsibility for the detailed application of this principle rests with the Länder and the constitutional framework of local authorities is determined by Land law. The Federal Government has few direct connections with local government and cannot influence its structure or the manner in which its powers are exercised. As in other continental countries, the basic unit in Germany is the "commune" or "Gemeinde", and until recently over 22,000 of these existed. Since about 1966 a process of local government reform has been under way in all Länder, and very soon the number of Gemeinden will have been drastically reduced through amalgamations, though the total will still amount to several thousands. District authorities also exist in most Länder which function both as units of local government and for some purposes as state (i.e. Land) authorities. Superimposed on the local government structure is something like a prefectoral system, what is known in German as the "Mittelinstanz" or "middle level".

---

[11]Over the years the British model has reverted to something much nearer the German "strong mayor" system, with the significant result that it is the Clerk or Stadtdirektor who has become the key figure.

[12]Art. 28 (2), Basic Law.

These are the deconcentrated administrative units of the Länder, which obviously do not exist in the city states, nor in Schleswig-Holstein, and are responsible both for Land services and for the administrative supervision of local authorities.

The principle of communal self-administration is held to imply a high degree of autonomy for local authorities. In addition they enjoy a general competence which entitles them to provide any services which they deem to be in the interests of their inhabitants. If the foreign visitor is struck by the lavishness of a municipal theatre or opera house, or by the generous scale of a municipal zoo or wildlife park, then he should reflect that this is due in part to the sovereignty of the local authorities in deciding whether to support such ventures. The range of local functions is wide and it is still possible for local authorities to engage in a large amount of public utility enterprise—public transport, gas, electricity, water, district heating schemes, and so on. In the field of education local authorities are generally confined to school building, the control of education being a Land responsibility, though they are free to encourage and support a variety of further education institutions too. In housing local authorities have a restricted role as far as new provision goes, chiefly because it has been national policy to encourage the construction of new flats and houses by channelling subventions to a wide range of housing associations and to individuals rather than through public authorities. Judged by the high post-war levels of construction this policy has been extremely successful.

Financially local authorities, like the Länder, have few independent resources. Instead they rely on allocations from the national taxation and from the yield of specific taxes. They are now guaranteed 14% of the proceeds of the income tax, and receive a share of the motor fuel tax, and substantial allocations from the Länder. Certain taxes like the site tax (Grundsteuer) are reserved to local authorities. In the raising of loans to finance capital investment local authorities are subject to relatively few controls by the Länder other than those of legality. They have collectively been able over the past twenty years to push their indebtedness up to an extremely high level.

The Länder exercise supervisory powers over local government. These bear for the most part on legality rather than on policy and the exercise of discretion. Where local authorities are acting on behalf of a Land government, for example, in school building, there is a control of programmes and their content. This would apply too in respect of many roadworks and in some sectors of public health. But in many cases the supervision is much more formal in character and does not permit the Land administration to interfere in the details of local action. Moreover, the growth of the major cities and conurbations, combined with the ease and rapidity of communications, has led to a situation in which local leaders have direct access to Land ministers. This has strengthened their influence and diminished the role of the field administration of the Länder.

In recent years it has become increasingly necessary for the federation to draw the local authorities into the framework of overall public expenditure planning. Their current spending amounts to at least 20% of total public spending, and their share of new public investment is at a still higher level. The Stability Law of 1967 did not formally bring the local government sector into the structure of medium-term budgetary planning, but both the Financial Planning Council and the Federal Government have been anxious to ensure that local authorities, like the federation and the Länder, should be bound by the recommendations agreed on centrally for controlling the overall levels of public expenditure. Thus by 1971 the local authorities had by administrative means been required to prepare medium-term financial plans (i.e. over a five-year period) forecasting expenditure, including investment, and had been asked to observe the guidelines agreed centrally for controlling the rate of increase of expenditure. These developments do not imply any detailed intervention by the Federal Government in the local sector, nor can they be regarded as even approximating to a structure of specific programme controls operated by the Länder on behalf of the central authority. The room for local manoeuvre remains wide, and is likely to remain so as long as the overall growth in public resources, itself a reflection of the rate of growth of the national product, does not slow down sufficiently to impose really serious constraints on the ability of the federation, Länder and local government to maintain present and prospective levels of public spending.

At the national level the local authorities are represented by a number of influential associations. These have been organised around the different types of local authorities—towns and cities, smaller Gemeinden, and districts. The best known and most influential is the Deutsche Städtetag which represents the larger cities and towns. It maintains a substantial organisation and has contributed a great deal both to advising its members on technical and administrative questions, and to formulating a common policy on all questions of major interest to local government, whether coming up at Land or federal level. These "top associations", or "Spitzenverbände" as they are called, sit on many of the advisory bodies set up by the Federal Government, and thus they have an opportunity to press local authority claims when decisions on major policy issues are being formulated. Moreover, they have close contacts with both the Bundestag and the Bundesrat, and in particular with those committees of the former which deal with proposals affecting services provided by local government.

Below the level of the Länder governments local authorities are the most important examples of political and administrative decentralisation in the Federal Republic. Their powers are extensive, they are intimately involved in the structure of party political life, and they benefit from a strong tradition of autonomy. For these reasons they constitute a vital part of the governmental structure of the Federal Republic. The preference for decentralisation expressed in the federal structure and in local government extends further, though here we come to a pattern of administrative deconcentration rather than to straightforward decentralisation to politically autonomous bodies. As already mentioned, within most Länder there is a system of field administration which enables them to reproduce something like the separation between policy-making and execution which is present at the federal level, where the federal ministries rely either on the Länder for executive action or on deconcentrated federal agencies. In many Länder there are too a variety of special purpose agencies responsible for particular functions, such as the two territorial associations for land use planning in North Rhine Westphalia (Landschaftsverbände Rheinland und Westfalen-Lippe), and the Ruhrsiedlungsverband, a local-authority-based agency which goes back to 1923 and has some housing functions in the densely populated Ruhr area. Such bodies have a representative element in their organisation. Many economic tasks are also delegated to autonomous bodies, such as the oversight agency for the state-supported coal mines in the Ruhr. Indeed in the public utility sector, the local authority enterprises are organised on a basis which grants them considerable autonomy from the normal run of local administration. In cultural and educational matters too there is extensive use by the federation (where appropriate) and the Länder of semi-independent agencies.

This capacity to avoid an accumulation of executive functions and of detailed supervisory work at the policy-shaping levels of government is intimately linked with concepts of German public law and their translation into administrative practice. There are a number of legal devices which any level of government can use for the purpose of delegating tasks to subordinate agencies. These have the advantages of leaving the agencies considerable operational autonomy, establishing in accordance with general principles the kind of supervisory rights which the superior authority may exercise, and defining again in general terms the public law responsibilities of such bodies. For example, a public law economic enterprise is a particular kind of public administrative entity, whose characteristics are basically the same, no matter what level of the system of government may establish it and exercise supervision over it. To put the matter in another way, German public law avoids the need for specifying *de novo* and separately in relation to every case the characteristics and powers of every public agency which is set up. In addition it ensures that all types of subordinate agency are brought within the general principles of administrative court adjudication should they abuse their powers. These conditions explain many of the most striking differences between the German structure of decentralised public administration and the conditions prevailing both in countries with the Anglo-Saxon common law tradition (which in practice has entailed casuistic specification of powers in the public law sector) and in highly centralised continental states such as France, where the very predominance of the central state has often frustrated the search for modes of decentralisation. In the final analysis the complexity and variety of German decentralisation rests upon a structure of public law which by its nature strives to reconcile uniformity of conditions with diversity in operations.

## TRENDS IN GERMAN FEDERALISM

There are good political arguments for the decentralisation achieved by federalism; there are substantial constitutional obstacles in the way of drastically modifying its character; and there is little doubt that around the provincial network of government interests loyalties have been consolidated which are suspicious of change, particularly if this were to be in a centralising direction. Taken as a whole the record of achievement of the subordinate layers of government is impressive, and decentralisation in the Federal Republic has undoubtedly contributed much to the physical recovery of German society by encouraging the release of energies and initiative. Nevertheless it remains a fact that the Federal Republic is a relatively small and densely populated state, socially and culturally more closely knit than pre-war Germany, and achieving now a standard of technological development which brings all parts of the society closer and closer together. As against all this the system of government is fragmented and complex, and the institutional barriers which are inherent in a federal system make it difficult to deal quickly or even efficiently with many of the problems on which the public expects action. The strains arising from federalism have become more apparent in recent years, and as a result there has been a shift away from the high-water mark of decentralised government reached in about 1960 to a renewed emphasis on the need for central co-ordination and planning, combined with greater stress on the duty of the Länder to co-operate with each other and with Bonn in the pursuit of national aims. In the language of constitutional theory, this is often described as "co-operative federalism".

The causes of this questioning of the relationships established under the federal provisions of the Basic Law are not hard to identify. The financial arrangements have repeatedly caused argument and dissension, and have become more problematical, the more rapidly levels of public expenditure have risen. But their reform a few years ago opened the way to arguments about other aspects of federalism, including the whole question of whether resource distribution would be improved if the territorial basis of federalism were simplified.

There were too other factors which have had an influence. Though the Federal Republic has had no genuinely depressed or backward regions, there are parts of the country which have developed economically less rapidly than the average: Schleswig-Holstein, parts of Lower Saxony, the eastern fringes of Bavaria along the border with East Germany, for example. This stimulated the call for some positive federal action. But equally it has been the very magnitude of economic growth, bringing with it major environmental problems and underlining the need for a national view of industrial location, transport systems and population distribution, which in many parts of the country fed the call for a less rigid view of provincial competences and a more active role by the Federal Government. The evolution of national politics should not be ignored either. Public attention has been concentrated on the Federal Government and in particular on the Chancellor. The national parliamentary leaderships have been strengthened, and elections have been dominated by two competing political parties. These factors have worked in favour of a tendency to think in terms of central policy-making and initiatives. Even in Adenauer's time it was clear that Land elections were often dominated by national issues, though this has not meant that national politicians can intervene unilaterally in Land campaigns (and when they have done so, it has often done them no good). By now the political palette at Land level has lost most of the diversity which it had ten or fifteen years ago: the two major parties predominate and Land elections are inevitably regarded as a judgment on the national Government.[13] Again this serves to encourage the view that it is only at national level that decisive political action can take place.

Along with the influences which have worked in favour of strengthening the central power has been some erosion of the political content of federalism within the Länder institutions. The main problem here is the position of the Landtage or provincial parliaments. Their legislative powers have always been restricted, and over the years they have dealt with most of the areas within their scope. Increasingly they have become concerned with minor enactments and budgetary details. At the same time their authority in relation to the Land Governments has been weakened by the actual strengthening of the latter which recent changes in federal relationships have brought about. A good example is the move towards medium-term financial planning which clearly strengthens the Land Governments, and *pari passu* reduces the room for argument allowed to the Landtage. It is not known precisely what effects the slow decline of the Landtage has had on political recruitment at Land level. But undoubtedly there is a risk that as political life in them loses its attractions, the calibre of members will decline and this will eventually weaken the very capacity of the Länder for self-government. Already there is some reason to believe that political ambitions are focused chiefly on the Bundestag, and that an important route to high

[13]The Landtage are generally elected every four years and elections are staggered throughout the legislative term of the Bundestag. Though they do function as barometers measuring opinion, it is not certain that Land voters always respond to national considerations. For example, the SPD success in Bremen in 1971 suggested that a popular local figure can be decisive and may gain more support than his party could expect in a national election, and in the 1972 Baden-Württemberg election the CDU improved its position, despite Chancellor Brandt's popularity.

office in a Land government lies through service in the Bundestag rather than activity in a Landtag.[14]

We have already discussed some of the effects of this climate of criticism of German federalism, notably the changes which were made in the apportionment of revenues, hopefully intended to render less frequent and less acrimonious the arguments about how large the respective share of the Federal Government and Länder should be. Of considerable longer-term importance is the introduction in 1969 of the concept of "joint tasks" into Article 91a of the Basic Law. The Troeger Commission, which reported on financial relations within the federal system in 1966, evolved this idea and originally it was hoped to apply it fairly extensively. But the opposition of the Länder was successful in restricting the application of this new device to only three fields of activity. Subsequent legislation has provided machinery for the federation and the Länder to plan jointly schemes falling within the ambit of this device. Though the type of planning commission adopted, in which the Federal Government and the Länder are equally represented (i.e. eleven votes to each side), is cumbersome, it does represent an advance on the unanimity principle which applies in the Länder ministerial conferences and at which the Federal Government had only the status of a guest. But in this latest emanation of co-operative federalism the Federal Government has acquired in the relevant sectors opportunities for policy initiative and planning which were previously denied to it. In the case of higher education the gradual build-up of the federal Minister of Education and Science is bound to add strength to the voice of the Federal Government and to make it increasingly difficult for a Land to go its own way. On the other hand, the new machinery is complicated. Already by late 1971 the planning com-

[14]There are many examples of prominent Bundestag members leaving the national scene to take up high office in the Länder, e.g. Kiesinger to be Minister President of Baden-Württemberg 1958–66, Stoltenberg to be Minister President in Schleswig-Holstein since 1970, Vogel to be Education minister in Rhineland-Pfalz since 1966. This sort of movement supports the view that success at national level can often lead to high office in a Land. But it needs to be stressed that there are also examples of Länder political leaders who prefer to remain at that level, maintaining a secure position on the basis of their provincial support, e.g. Kühn, currently Minister President in North Rhine Westphalia, Goppel in the same position in Bavaria, and Koschnick, the President of the Senate in Bremen. Whether such people, however, owe much to success in Landtag parliamentary politics is open to question: their executive skills and capacity as party managers are probably the decisive factors.

mission for joint Federal–Länder action in university development had set up nine *ad hoc* working groups in which federal departments not represented on the main committee were participating. In addition there were two federal interdepartmental committees to co-ordinate aspects of federal policy, and above these a ministerial Cabinet committee. Plainly, even an improved federal system, intended to strengthen central co-ordination and policy guidance, remains a baffling administrative jigsaw.

The changes made in 1969 and after included extensions of the federal legislative power. The Federal Government was empowered to make framework laws to cover the principles of the organisation of universities and other higher education bodies. This was thought to be important because of the desirability of general and uniform regulation of the internal structure and government of universities.[15] Concurrent powers for Bonn were soon afterwards proposed and granted in respect of the pay and conditions of the public service, the safeguarding of wildlife and the protection of the environment. The extent of the federal competence for the environment is obscure. It is an extremely wide sector and constitutes a major preoccupation of the Länder: any substantial incursion of federal power would not only be unpopular with the Länder governments, but would bring enormous administrative difficulties too.

One step not taken was to give the federation a general framework power allowing it to lay down principles in any area of activity deemed to be of national importance. Many constitutional lawyers and also the Troeger Commission have held that only in this way can the need for frequent constitutional revision be avoided. But the objections to granting the Federal Government such a flexible means of increasing its authority remain strong, and it is unlikely that the Länder would in the foreseeable future be ready to accept such a change. Moreover, it would run counter to the strong tendency in the Federal Republic to prefer specific definitions of powers in all circumstances: discretionary formulae are not popular.

This discussion of the part played by the federal structure in modern

[15]Up to the end of 1972 this power had not been used, though draft bills were under discussion in the Bundestag for over two years. In fact it was some of the Länder which were showing most initiative in trying to legislate on university organisation, some of them prompted by a desire to avoid the generalisation of the worst follies of "reform" as pursued in the late sixties. This no doubt had a certain political convenience for the Federal Government.

German government can now be concluded by referring to three points. The first is that the operation of German federalism does ensure a very substantial decentralisation of executive responsibility to the Länder and to other subordinate sectors of public administration. That German federalism can be described in terms of administrative decentralisation does not, however, mean that it has no effects on the political life of the country, on national policy-making or on the position of the Federal Government. It does in fact support the dispersion of influence within the party structures, and in many of the ways discussed the Länder are able to modify and limit the initiatives of the centre. Second, there is no doubt that one of the most striking consequences of the federal system is a high degree of complexity in the governmental structure of the country. A lot of effort has to be put into co-ordination and consultation, there are many competing competences and interests, and the decision-making process is slowed down. It need not be assumed, however, that all this means less effective government or poorer services; at a very general level of comparison German government can be said to be as effective as government in other similar societies and has proved capable of guaranteeing a high standard of services in many sectors of life.

Third, it is likely that one of the main arguments of the mid-seventies will be about the geographical basis of federalism rather than about the distribution of powers between the centre and the Länder. The present pattern of Länder reflects to a large extent the rather arbitrary carving-up of the western part of Germany by the three Western powers after 1945 to suit their short-term administrative needs. Of the larger Länder only Bavaria has some claim to historical identity; in addition Hamburg and Bremen have historical roots, though because of their small size they are difficult to justify as units of government at the second-tier level. The other Länder vary considerably in size and resources and are all more or less composite geographical structures, in some cases taking little account of socio-economic requirements. Already in 1970 inquiries into the federal system were announced by both the Federal Government and the Bundestag. These include the geography of federalism in their terms of reference. Any changes in the boundaries are bound to aim at fewer and larger Länder (i.e. bringing the smaller ones into units comparable with North Rhine Westphalia, Baden-Württemberg or Bavaria). Amongst the most common proposals is one for six Länder and another for five. For example, six could be achieved fairly easily by amalgamating Hesse, Rhineland-Pfalz, and the Saarland, thus creating three states in the southern half of the country. In the north Schleswig-Holstein and Hamburg could be joined, with Bremen going to Lower Saxony. Along with North Rhine Westphalia this would produce three states in the northern part of the country.

Redrawing the map like this has its attractions. It would make for more equal tax yields and thus avoid some of the difficulties inherent in the present financial arrangements. It would to some extent simplify a whole range of institutions from the Bundesrat down to many federal-Länder working parties, perhaps making it easier for them to reach decisions. At any rate it would no longer be possible for a small Land to exercise its right to hold up action until its particular interests have been protected. Some argue that such changes would give federalism a new lease of life by creating more viable governmental units, better able to argue on equal terms with Bonn and more capable of developing a vigorous internal political life. There may be something to be said for such expectations, but it can equally be argued that a rationalisation of the federal structure will increase the prospect of political divisions at the national level being reproduced faithfully at the Land level, and thus decrease the chances of the Länder evolving *across* national party lines points of view different from those held by the Federal Government. At least it seems certain that a simplified federal pattern would add strength to what is already a powerful trend, namely the acceptance of standardisation and uniformity of services as a major desideratum. This is currently by far the most popular argument for extending the rights of the Federal Government to lay down the major purposes of public action and to determine the standards of service to be guaranteed.

But so far no politically acceptable proposals for further change have been formulated, still less any action taken.[16] Meanwhile the issue of federalism, its shape and effects in operation, remains high on the German political agenda. This must be so in an age when it is increasingly difficult to set any limits to the range of governmental action.

---

[16] A lengthy article of the Basic Law (Art. 29) deals with territorial reorganisation. It is worth noting that action to this end is subject to referendum, one of the few cases under German constitutional law where this is prescribed.

CHAPTER 6

# The Bureaucracy in the Federal Republic

## THE HISTORICAL HERITAGE

As in several other European countries the bureaucracy in Germany was for a long period a strong and prestigious element in the state. It began to develop in something like its modern form in the eighteenth century as an instrument of absolutist rulers. But it was shaped not merely as an instrument of order and control, for which in any case the military services were always at the disposal of the monarchical rulers. The civil bureaucracy was conceived too, and particularly in Prussia under Frederick II, as an active agent for developing the social and economic life of the society according to the precepts of enlightened despotism. There took place in the mid-eighteenth century a growth of the cameralist sciences, a portmanteau term covering all those elements of law, economics, politics, public finance, agricultural science, and forestry which were thought to be relevant to the activities of the state. A number of university institutions were reformed to provide an education intended specifically for public servants, thus establishing a link between universities and professional training for public service.

These early developments in ideas about the branches of knowledge which had a direct bearing on administration influenced the growth of the absolutist bureaucracies in Germany, and in particular training and recruitment for them. Public service was seen as a collection of offices which should be filled by those possessing the appropriate professional and technical skills and imbued with a sense of commitment to the service of the state. Though recruitment to the higher levels of the bureaucracy in the late eighteenth century and after remained to a considerable extent socially exclusive, the Prussian civil service in particular did not constitute a system

138

of outdoor relief for the nobility: public service called for hard work and self-sacrifice.

The collapse of Prussia in the face of Napoleon I did not lead to a weakening of the bureaucratic state apparatus of absolutism. Indeed defeat in 1806 prompted a vigorous reappraisal of the quality and structure of the administrative system, which in the years after 1808 was substantially improved, in part under the influence of the Napoleonic model. The first thirty years of the nineteenth century saw a rapid development in public education, and reform of the universities along lines always associated with Wilhelm von Humboldt. Though Humboldt conceived of a university as essentially a place of learning and research, he also saw it as a part (though privileged no doubt) of the state structure. Thus it was quite logical that universities should educate people for the needs of the state, whether as teachers or as officials. Gradually a system of state examinations in subjects relevant to particular branches of public service was developed, and success in such examinations qualified men for careers in public service. The classic case was law, which was (and still is) studied at a university, followed by a state examination, practical experience and a second state examination. The possession of these qualifications then entitles the holder either to pursue a private career (e.g. as a solicitor) or to enter public service (e.g. as an official or a judge). These developments played a big part in opening the higher levels of public service to the educated middle classes, who saw here opportunities for making use of their talents. Thus gradually in the course of the last century the social basis of the civil service was widened, a development which was not without political effects.

The reason for stressing the manner in which the system of higher education was long ago adapted to the needs of public service is, of course, that in this way a tradition was established which has endured to the present day. In the contemporary discussion of university expansion anxiety is often expressed about the careers for which particular courses qualify those who take them, and in reverse it is often suggested that the state has a responsibility to ensure that suitable posts are available for those qualified in different fields. And this is not just a plea for general full employment policies, but for the creation of *public* employment opportunities. These traditions have had too a continuing influence on the structure of the civil service. In the course of the nineteenth century the civil bureaucracy in Prussia developed a structure related to levels of education on recruitment. For the highest level (höhere Dienst) a university training was obligatory, and inter-nal civil service movement into this level was virtually non-existent. The public service acquired an academic character which buttressed the prestige it already had on social and political grounds. (Nor is it irrelevant that the erstwhile prestige of the academic profession in Germany owes something to the fact that is members were and are officials, educating officials.) The emphasis on specific academic attainments may have narrowed recruit-ment in modern times and slowed down the adaptation of the bureaucracy to new needs. But it also encouraged the higher levels of the civil service to see themselves as articulate and qualified experts on the aspects of state activity for which they had been trained. Officials have for long been ener-getic writers of articles, legal commentaries, technical manuals and so on, recognised by the wider public and by the academic world as competent authorities. Obviously these characteristics have a political significance: they accord ill with discreet anonymity and they create a presumption at least that officials may quite rightly be the initiators of policy in default of active political leadership. Indeed the revival of Prussia in the early decades of the last century owed much to the vision and the liberalising intentions of influential civil servants. Again, these are traditions which persist and should not be left out of account when we are considering the character and role of the bureaucracy in the Federal Republic.

There are three further points to be made by way of historical back-ground. The first is to underline the dominant influence of the Prussian model on the development of public service in the rest of Germany. It was in Prussia that ideas about the structure and working of administration and the education of officials were put into practice which were eventually accepted in all the Länder.[1] The public regulation of the bureaucracy outside Prussia came to be modelled on the Prussian example. All this meant that there was far more uniformity in the German public service than the survival of a federal state would have suggested. Likewise today this unify-ing influence persists. Despite the fact that the Länder and local authorities control their bureaucracies independently, and indeed the former are responsible for most of the training and education of officials, there is in the Federal Republic a homogeneous public service in which the characteristics

[1]This is not to deny the intellectual contribution made elsewhere, e.g. in Württem-berg or Baden. But the decisive influence was Prussian. Indeed it is still a compliment to describe an official as one of the old Prussian school.

of administrative methods and personnel vary little from one part of the country to another, or from one level of government to another.

The second point is the dominance of the legal concept of the state—the Rechtsstaat—and the consequences of this for the public service. Though the idea of the state as essentially a hierarchy of logically related legal norms had serious shortcomings, it did provide support for the conclusion that public acts too were subject to stringent requirements of legality, and this was of particular significance for German administration. It goes far to explain why it was held that the higher civil servant needs generally to be qualified in law, this providing a guarantee that he has the knowledge and techniques to operate within a body of formal rules and regulations. This opinion was, however, never extended to those parts of the public service where clearly other types of experience were needed—civil engineers for building works, surveyors for land measurement and improvement, mining engineers for the oversight of mining, to quote some examples. Here a broader view of the need for relevant professional skills prevailed. But it did become conventional to regard a legal training as the only relevant preparation for general administration, and on this arose what is nowadays referred to as the *Juristenmonopol*, the monopoly of lawyers. Once more we detect a continuing influence, though it is perhaps now on the wane: the higher levels of German administration are staffed by those who have studied law and it has been difficult to secure acceptance of the idea that other types of background may be just as good a foundation for a public administration career.[2]

The last historical observation concerns the relationship between the bureaucracy and politics. In one sense the absolutist bureaucracy was politicised, or within the realms of politics. This was simply because it was expected to carry out without question the will of the ruler, and its members could only with difficulty express dissent from the politics of their sovereigns. But in another sense the bureaucracy as it developed in the nineteenth century regarded itself as outside of and above politics. It was a permanent professional service, dedicated to the public good and the rule of law. It was the most visible embodiment of the state which itself existed to further the public interest. Of course no such ideal was realised in practice, but it did have a marked influence on the bureaucratic ethos, encouraging

[2]For some comments on these matters see the author's chapter on Western Germany in *Specialists and Generalists*, edited by F. F. Ridley, Allen & Unwin, 1968.

officials to regard political parties as expressions of divisive and partial interests in society, incapable of that insight into the common good which the bureaucracy possessed. This outlook was also widely diffused in German society, certainly down to 1933, and echoes of it linger on today in arguments about state and society. Until the end of the Empire the bureaucracy's claim to a stance above politics was not really put to the test: the political leadership from 1871 to 1918 held the parties at bay, and the bureaucracy was not exposed to serious conflicts of loyalty. Under the Weimar Republic the position changed. Parts of the civil and most of the military bureaucracy were hostile to the Republic or to particular parties in it. Though most of the public services continued to work efficiently and fairly as before, at the top levels there were examples of official disloyalty to elected political leaders and of officials aspiring to a decisive influence on policy. The political turmoil of the years before 1933 accentuated the difficulties of the higher civil service. Many feared the advent of Hitler, but felt bound by their loyalty to the state to remain silent. Others believed that the neutral, impartial bureaucracy would be able to exert a moderating influence on the Nazi Government, keeping them within the bounds of lawful practice. And some actively intrigued to assist the Nazi assumption of power, seeing in the new movement an opportunity to sweep away the paralysing influence of party strife and to reassert the unity and strength of the state.

In the outcome all found that they had been equally misguided: the bureaucracy could exercise no significant influence on Nazi policies. The notion of absolute loyalty to the state posed terrifying dilemmas when it became clear that the state in question recognised no moral limitations on its behaviour. And the idea of being above politics collapsed in the face of a ruthless determination to subject all forms of public service to the will of the political leadership. Thus the bureaucracy emerged from the Second World War weakened, discredited, and demoralised. True, there was resistance to the Nazi tyranny by a few brave members of the civil and military services, many of whom paid for this with their lives. But it was unlikely that the bureaucracy could ever again advance with confidence the claim to be able to express the enduring public interest in the state on which its privileged position had historically been founded.

Nevertheless, when the Basic Law came to be drafted, those responsible opted for the traditional principle of a permanent and professional civil service, declaring in Article 33 (5) that the law appertaining to the public service was to be drawn up in accordance with this aim. Thus in general terms an element in earlier traditions was formally embodied in the Basic Law. There is a lot of room for argument about what this amounts to, but a few essential aspects need stressing. There is the obvious fact that the German public service continues to be founded on the concept of a "Beamter", someone who holds office permanently, owing certain obligations to the state in return for which the state recognises obligations towards him (such as remuneration, pensions, security of tenure, and so on). There is a reassertion of the old idea that only those in a position of public law loyalty and service can discharge acts of sovereignty towards third parties (which then gives the latter certain possibilities of redress). There is renewed emphasis on the duty of the public service to serve impartially the whole community (the idea of a neutral bureaucracy), but a much clearer commitment to the subordination of the administration to the political leadership at different levels in the system of government, which, as we shall see, has encouraged a high degree of political patronage in the bureaucracy. Finally there is an explicit reaffirmation of the principle that all public acts must be within the law and can be appealed against if they infringe constitutional rights, and of the principle of resistance to orders or actions which subvert the democratic order or are unlawful.[3] For the bureaucracy this reaffirmation of the idea of the state as the rule of law has meant a renewed awareness of legal norms, more stress rather than less on the value of a law training, and acceptance of a degree of judicialisation of administration which far exceeds anything experienced in the past.

Thus we can see that the political and practical needs encountered in the reconstruction of a West German state after 1948–9 worked in favour of an attempt to repair some of the links with the past which had been broken. And indeed until the early sixties few challenged whether this had been a wise course to follow in respect of the public service, or whether there were not major new requirements which could no longer be satisfied by the old methods. Even now it cannot be said that the movement towards a reappraisal of the status and organisation of the public services stems from widespread dissatisfaction with what was achieved after 1949. It is rather an expression of changing social values and of an awareness of the qualitative

[3]These conditions can be found, for example, in the 1965 Federal Civil Service Law (*Beamtenrechtrahmengesetz*, BGBl, I, p. 1753, 1965), which revised and codified earlier provisions.

change in the role of government in society which has taken place. It is to the present structure and organisation of the public services in the Federal Republic that we must now turn.

## THE ORGANISATION OF THE PUBLIC SERVICES

It makes little sense in the West German context to write only about the federal civil service. This is not just because, as already shown in Chapter 5, so much of administrative activity goes on below the Federal Government level. It is also because in many important respects the bureaucracy in the Länder or in local government is indistinguishable in character from that serving the Federal Government. Two points need to be emphasised at the outset. One is that the public services are regulated by law, partly by federal law or federal "framework" provisions, partly by Land law. But diverse though the sources of public service law are, there are in it many elements which are common to all branches of the public service, and which thus guarantee a considerable degree of uniformity in conditions throughout the public sector. Yet this relatively homogeneous public service is also organised in a manner which allows each area or level of government to control its own personnel. Each separate agency embodies *vis-à-vis* its officials the authority of the state as a whole, and the head of the agency as "Dienstvorgesetzter" has rights of direction in relation to his subordinates. This applies throughout the administrative system: the Minister in a federal department, the President of the Bundestag *vis-à-vis* the Bundestag administration, a Land Minister of Education in relation to teachers in a particular Land, the President of the Federal Railways in relation to railway employees, all sit at the top of separate personnel pyramids and are alone entitled to give binding directions to the officials in their respective organisations. Given the importance which formal instructions still have in German administration, this dispersion of control of personnel contributes substantially to the decentralised pattern of management and operations throughout the public service.

Turning to the overall size of the public service Table 6.1 presents part of the picture.

As Table 6.1 shows, the federal administration is relatively small compared with the services maintained by the Länder and local government,

TABLE 6.1

| Type of public authority | Year | Total public employees |
|---|---|---|
| 1. Federal Government | 1966 | 272,126 |
| | 1968 | 276,560 |
| | 1970 | 284,988 |
| 2. Länder | 1966 | 1,031,594 |
| | 1968 | 1,073,779 |
| | 1970 | 1,154,193 |
| 3. Local authorities | 1966 | 621,970 |
| | 1968 | 624,672 |
| | 1970 | 668,943 |
| Total 1–3 | 1966 | 1,925,690 |
| | 1968 | 1,975,011 |
| | 1970 | 2,108,124 |

Notes: (i) These figures include the three categories of Officials, Employees and Industrial staff (see below).
(ii) Judges are included as Officials.
(iii) Figures for the uniformed members of the Armed Forces, for Posts and for the Federal Railways are not included in the Federal Government totals.
(iv) There are additionally about 150,000 public service employees in public economic enterprises without independent legal status.

Source: Federal Government Annual Finance Reports and Federal Statistical Yearbooks.

though it is to be remembered that the Länder totals do include teachers and the police.

Within the global figures three types of public servant are to be distinguished. There are officials, *Beamte*, who constitute about 45% of the total (rather less at the federal level); then there are employees, *Angestellte*, who make up nearly 40% of the total (rather more in the federal service); finally there are industrial staff, *Arbeiter*, who account for rather more than 15% of the total. These basic categories in public service reflect differences in conditions and terms of employment as well as in functions. The officials belong to the group which has traditionally typified the idea of permanent state service. The official stands in a public law relationship of loyalty and service towards his employer, the public authority, and in return is guaranteed security of tenure, reasonable remuneration, a pension and a variety of

F

other privileges and rights. In principle only officials can discharge functions which are regarded as requiring an exercise of sovereignty, though there are now exceptions to this rule. Employees, on the other hand, are technically in a private law contractual relationship with the public authority, do not have the same automatic rights, have contributory pensions and in theory do not exercise sovereign functions. But in reality the distinction between officials and employees has become extremely blurred. Their conditions of service have been brought very close to those of officials, and in many areas of administration members of the two groups are used almost interchangeably. Indeed the need for a wider variety of experience in general administration has encouraged the recruitment of "employees", since the terms on which they can be taken on are more flexible. It is not impossible that the two categories will be fused in the fairly near future should the current discussion of civil service law reform lead to positive results. The third category, workers, contains a wide variety of occupations, some of an industrial character, but many in the service sector too. The picture here is very confused: many people employed by the Federal Railways are "officials", though performing industrial work analogous to that carried out by "workers". The conditions of service of workers are assimilated more or less to those prevalent in private industry.

One important consequence of this classification of public employment is the way in which it is mirrored in the trade unions representing public servants. Most influential and prestigious is the Association of German Civil Servants, the Deutsche Beamtenbund, a body which represents the interests of about 720,000 officials. Given the continuing strength of the bureaucratic tradition and the fact that many of those in politics at all levels are or have been officials, the DBB is in a position to exert a strong influence on all measures of civil service regulation, particularly in view of the fact that so much regulation requires legislative action by the Bundestag or by the Landtage. Moreover, the DBB is, and not surprisingly, the defender of the traditional privileges of the bureaucracy and thus generally opposed to changes which would weaken the status of *Beamte*. Employees are organised in part under the auspices of the Deutsche Angestelltengewerkschaft, the DAG, a union which like the DBB has remained outside the main organisation of the German trade union movement, the DGB. Though it does not have the prestige of the DBB it has influence as spokesman for a large sectional interest within the public service as well as for similar groups in semi-public and private employment. There is too the Public Service and Transport union (ÖTV), a very large and articulate organisation within the DGB, whose membership is now about a million, covering a wide range of workers in public services and utilities. One advantage for such large bodies is that they can negotiate across the board, seeking terms which will have to be applied by any type of public authority for which their members work. For the different levels of government too the process of negotiation is simplified, though the very size and comprehensiveness of the unions means that they are tough partners to deal with.

A feature of public service organisation and conditions which is important is that the whole process of recruitment and training is highly dispersed. Each of the three main tiers of government recruits its own personnel, and within them the separate units and agencies are largely responsible for meeting their personnel needs independently. Each local authority and each Land recruits its own personnel, and in the Federal Government there is no such thing as a public service commission responsible for securing staff for the whole federal administration.[4] The departments are autonomous in the appointment of staff, though technically it is the President who confirms entry into the permanent federal civil service. In the case of some of the more senior appointments involving promotions, the federal Cabinet (or *mutatis mutandis* a Land Government) will give its approval. Most of the subordinate agencies coming under the supervision of federal departments enjoy a similar degree of independence in the selection of personnel.

At first sight it is surprising that a system so fragmented can operate effectively at all. That it does work is due in part to the strength of the tradition of public service in Germany which still attracts a large number of people into public employment. Thus particular agencies have not on the whole found it hard to recruit staff for the vacancies they advertise. In part too the system is held together by the unifying influence of public service law. Though the system of recruitment, for example, is highly decentralised, the rules governing it and the requirements which applicants must meet are for the most part rigorously defined and are the same, either

---

[4]The Ministry of the Interior has certain general responsibilities and powers in civil service matters stemming from its responsibility for civil service law. But it is not a central personnel department, still less a central organisation and management agency.

throughout the whole system of government or throughout a particular sector (e.g. the Federal Government service or a Land administration). Thus a person seeking to enter the higher career grade in general administration will have to have the same educational qualifications whether he is applying to a Land ministry in Kiel, the Federal Ministry of Labour and Social Affairs, the Federal Railways, or the department of the Oberstadtdirektor in Essen.

Since recruitment to public service is based on the assumption that applicants should have qualifications appropriate to the category of service they seek to enter, it has been assumed traditionally that much of the training for public service is provided within the ordinary educational system. This approach, particularly with regard to the higher levels of public service, explains why there are so few in-service training institutions designed to give a general training for a particular level or sector of the public service. But when it is a question of providing a more narrowly vocational and technical training after entry, the public service accepts responsibility for this. Thus agencies which have specialised tasks for which no outside body can provide the technical training, e.g. the Federal Revenue administration or the police services in each Land, organise their own training facilities and these are usually of a high professional standard. There is, therefore, in the Federal Republic a rather unusual combination of attitudes towards public service training: on the one hand the educational system is expected to turn out people qualified for different levels of public administration (a point to which we return below), whilst on the other there is extensive provision within the public services for the more specialised types of training required there.

The last feature of public service conditions to be underlined is the manner in which public service law confirms and guarantees the numerous rights and privileges of the different categories of public service. This is more marked in relation to officials as a professional group than to the others, but nevertheless there is throughout the system a tendency to enshrine in binding terms the conditions of service. Nor does this affect only the more obvious areas such as salaries, pensions, leave, and tenure. There are also elaborate arrangements intended to safeguard public employees against arbitrary decisions on the part of public authorities, and to allow them to make use of administrative courts as well as internal control bodies (such as the Federal Personnel Committee in the Federal Government) to ensure that their rights are respected. The outcome is a personnel structure which is unusually rigid in terms of contemporary management needs. There is currently some demand for more co-determination in the public sector. Yet there is little doubt that if measures were taken to meet such demands within the present framework of public service conditions of employment, the outcome might well be a form of public corporatism more rigid than even the present structure. It is clearly open to question whether this would be to the benefit of the public.

## OFFICIALS—BEAMTE

The part of the bureaucracy which has attracted most attention, both in the earlier history of Germany and more recently too, has been the professional civil service—officials or Beamte. The still considerable predilection for professional titles and rank in German society often expresses for the outsider the weight of this element in the evolution of the country. Structurally the official corps is divided into four levels: the basic service, the middle service, the executive service, and the higher service. These levels apply nationwide, regardless of the type of public authority with which the officials are serving. They still express essentially the levels of education on entry and, though less clearly, the type of tasks performed. The basic service comprises people with education to age 15 or 16, destined for manual office work and routine clerical jobs. The middle service calls for the same educational qualifications, but has a longer probationary period and offers possibilities of taking examinations which will lead to rather more responsible clerical work. The executive service consists of entrants aged at least 18 who have passed through a middle or technical school. The probationary period is three years, followed by an examination, after which a career in non-policy-making administration can be expected. Finally, there is the higher service for which the basic requirement is a university qualification and completion of a probationary period lasting as a rule three years. There is no specific subject requirement for this level. It depends upon which "career" within the higher service a candidate wishes to pursue: in general administration law is the most common (though no longer the exclusive) qualification demanded, but in the technical areas of administration a range of specialised qualifications is necessary, e.g. civil engineering.

The justification for describing these groups in some detail is that it is important to underline again the formality of the conditions governing the civil service and its professional structure. All this is embodied in law, supplemented by administrative regulation. Thus fundamental change has been difficult to achieve, though there has never been in either the Bundestag or in the Landtage any shortage of legislative work intended to improve this or that aspect of official service or to get round specific difficulties discovered in the complex body of civil service law. Obviously the relative rigidity of the structure has meant that German administration has not adapted easily or quickly to external change. Nevertheless it cannot be concluded that the bureaucracy had become an antiquated caste system, inefficient in operation and unresponsive to needs. It is notoriously difficult to make comparisons of bureaucratic performance. But there seems no obvious reason for concluding that the German civil service is less capable of performing its functions efficiently than the civil services elsewhere in Europe. Whilst it lacks the mystique attaching to the French "grand corps", its overall record of achievement in a period of sustained reconstruction is impressive: and there has been no serious protest from public opinion or politicians that the civil service has frustrated the achievement of desirable objectives and is in need of basic reform. Only in the years after 1969 has there been something like an official commitment to modernising civil service law and to bringing about a swifter adaptation of public administration to contemporary needs. In general, however, the Federal Republic has been successful in rapidly developing nearly all public services, and yet appears to have done this with a bureaucracy organised essentially on late nineteenth-century lines. How is this to be explained?

Part of the answer lies in the traditional virtues of the German official: integrity, a strong sense of duty, and a narrow but vigorous professionalism. What is more these virtues continue to enjoy approval in society, though much of the earlier deference towards the bureaucracy has vanished. Part of the answer is also to be found in the effects of the neo-Liberal economic policies pursued since 1948, which succeeded to some extent in restricting the public service to a more regulatory role and to the provision of public social services. In other words, very important areas of decision-making remained outside the governmental sphere: there was less scope for serious administrative policy failures and less likelihood of the public blaming the bureaucracy if the economic development of the country slowed down.

Indeed it would not in the sixties have occurred to many people to attribute such importance to the bureaucracy as to justify putting it into the forefront of reform considerations. With the rapidly rising levels of public spending in the late sixties this attitude seems to be changing and there are now signs that a greater operational significance for the progress of the society as a whole is being attached to the public service. This in turn has encouraged a more critical view of its characteristics and capabilities.

A more interesting explanatory hypothesis is, however, the suggestion that the growth of party political influence in and over the bureaucracy has at last guaranteed its responsiveness to political requirements in a manner which has both shielded it from criticism and most probably helped to improve its performance. We shall turn shortly to some aspects of political influence in the public service and how it is exerted. In the present connection it is only necessary to stress that it has in the Federal Republic become generally accepted that at those levels of the bureaucracy associated with political leadership and responsibility, it is reasonable to ensure that the officials sympathise with the political opinions of their masters. Not surprisingly this has sharpened responsiveness and given politicians certain motives for restraint in criticism of the administration. But equally the patronage system, by bringing in new blood and sometimes facilitating rapid promotion or transfers from one level of government to another, has on balance encouraged the release of initiative and energy, especially on the part of younger and more ambitious men. Though the majority of officials, once they have entered public service with a local authority, a Land administration, or the Federal Government, expect to pursue their careers at that level, there is movement between them, particularly from local to Land government, and from the latter to the federal level. Naturally this operates in reverse too. And it is political factors which often influence such movement. A high proportion of those who climb the ladder in federal politics emerge from party and governmental activity in the Länder: Brandt, Kiesinger, Schiller, Helmut Schmidt, to name only a few well-known examples. It is not uncommon for such people to bring to Bonn officials whom they have known in earlier stages of their careers, whilst in the Länder ambitious officials are well advised to establish links with political figures who may later acquire high office at the centre. In this way a network of connections is built up, partly based on shared party affiliations, but expressing also acceptance of the idea that individual leaders are entitled to establish a clientele of advisers and supporters committed to them on personal grounds. What marks a sharp break from the past is that it is party politicians who now enjoy the confidence of the bureaucracy and who are accepted as the legitimate makers of policy. The pretensions of the bureaucracy to a role above politics have, except for occasional echoes of the past from older officials, disappeared.

This links up with another aspect of the position of the public service which is worth underlining as a factor explaining why its rather old-fashioned structure and methods have survived with but muted criticism. This is simply that officials have lost most of the social prestige which they once had and have for this reason become less exposed to criticism. The upheaval of war and its aftermath shattered the position still held in many branches of the civil service and the armed forces by the Prussian aristocracy and the upper middle classes with easy access to the universities. Denazification had a marginal effect on the future character of the reconstructed public services. What shaped the outcome was essentially the need to start again after government had been virtually suspended for four years, and in a situation in which manpower losses had been heavy and the country was split in two. All this made it inevitable that the public service would recruit more widely, become socially more open and mixed at the higher levels, and begin to reflect the impact of a socially more mobile society dedicated to economic expansion. Though slow to build up, these trends became very marked in the late sixties, particularly when the older generation which dominated public service after 1949 came up to retirement age and, because of the generation gap attributable to the Second World War, began to be replaced by very much younger men recruited in the fifties. Added to these factors has been, until recently, the relatively modest salary levels of the public service compared with those obtainable in business, and the rapid growth in the prestige attached to a career in industry or commerce as compared with public employment.

The overall result has been that the German official no longer lays any claim to the high status which he enjoyed before 1933, has little or no sense of belonging to a prestigious and exclusive group in society, and recognises that in his official work he must come to terms with an environment in which the traditional values of the bureaucracy are discounted, or at any rate given relatively less weight. All this is not to deny that in the Federal

Republic there is still a fair amount of respect for bureaucratic norms, and even for the official as the representative of authority. But the situation is now very fluid and the older picture of the German bureaucracy as a socially exclusive corps dominating a deferential society has become merely an historical reminiscence. The public service remains important and influential for more instrumental reasons, because it possesses much of the knowledge and administrative skill which are required for managing the contemporary activities of government, and because it has become enmeshed in and subordinate to the politics of the Federal Republic.

## POLITICS, POLICY-MAKING AND PATRONAGE

We have already alluded several times to the manner in which the bureaucracy has become subject to party political influences. Clearly this is one way in which a bureaucracy may be made responsive to the needs of political leaders. Equally, the extension of the influence of politicians on bureaucratic appointments will usually strengthen their position, giving them scope for pressing their views or consolidating their power which otherwise would not be available. At the level of policy-making the relationship between bureaucracy and political leadership must always present difficulties and ambiguities, even when an attempt is made to keep the two spheres apart. But when no such attempt is made, the problem of assessing the role of the bureaucracy in the shaping of policy becomes peculiarly intractable. In this subsection it is intended to look rather more closely at the links in the Federal Republic between politics and public service, and then to consider how they affect the formation and execution of public policy at the federal level.

The formal regulations governing the public service are still written in terms which appear to suggest a neutral, non-political service. According to the Federal Civil Service Framework Law of 1965 the official "serves the whole people, not a party". He has to carry out his duties impartially and to maintain discretion in any political activity in which he engages personally.[5] In relation to appointments discrimination on grounds of religion and politics is illegal.[6] Undoubtedly there are many areas of public service

[5] *BRRG*, 1965, para. 35.
[6] *Ibid.*, para. 7.

where the idea of the official as an impartial servant of the state still holds its ground—in the financial administration, in the numerous technical services, and generally in the police. Nevertheless, prevailing practice and the relevant legal rules sanction the intervention of political interests in civil service personnel policies in a way which appears to be in sharp contradiction with the ideal of neutrality. Nor is this entirely an innovation, though more clearly recognised now. The current statutes accept that at the more sensitive levels of administration political leaders have a right to be served by officials who are "in continuing agreement with the basic political views and aims of the Government".[7] It follows from this that the holder of a post in the politically sensitive category can be transferred or retired without reason being stated.[8] Broadly speaking in the federal service all posts at the level of division head and above come into this category. *Mutatis mutandis* similar conventions apply in the Länder. In local government the situation is very complex owing to the different constitutional arrangements, some of which provide for the direct election of local officials (e.g. in Bavaria) and others for indirect election by the councils (e.g. in Hesse). But whatever the particular rules may be, it is generally recognised that party affiliations are decisive in local government, and that the "elected official", the Wahlbeamte, has a major part to play.

In the Federal Government service it is a relatively small number of senior officials, chiefly those of the rank of Ministerialdirektor (Division Head) and above, who come into the "political" class, amounting to about 200 in 1970. A fairly large proportion of these are in fact non-political career officials who may well serve in the same post for many years and under ministers of different parties. But at the same time this does leave a significant number of posts which are regarded as subject to the political preferences of ministers, and in the event of a change of party in office changes in the staffing of these posts can be expected. This may be brought about by transfer of the officials concerned to less sensitive posts, by sideways promotions or by early retirement on full pension.

Under the twenty years of CDU-dominated government (1949–69) the extent of politicisation of the civil service was hard to judge. There was a tendency for many officials to see themselves as mildly CDU just as British army recruits used to confess to being Church of England: in both cases the

[7]*BRRG*, 1965, para. 31 (1).
[8]*Ibid.*, para. 31 makes general provision for "political officials".

commitment was nominal. The sectors of very obvious politicisation were not numerous: the Chancellor's Office, the top levels of the Foreign and Defence Ministries, the former Ministries for Family Affairs and for Refugees, the Ministry of Agriculture, these were perhaps the most obvious areas where party influences were usually decisive. In the Ministry for Labour and Social Affairs the left-wing CDU and trade-union influence always coloured appointments (which explains in part why relatively few changes came after an SPD/FDP Government took office). In both the Finance and Economics ministries the FDP influence could be detected as well as the neo-liberal colouring imparted by Dr. Erhard. And in Interior and Justice (as in Finance) something of the old Prussian rectitude and neutrality *vis-à-vis* politics survived. The broad effect of these conditions was that the staffing of the federal administration at the senior level reflected many of the diversities within the CDU/CSU as well as in the main coalition partner, the FDP, but in a fairly discreet manner. The views and preferences of particular ministers were always important, especially if they stayed in office for long periods. This fact alone often gave stability to the official hierarchy.

The change of government in 1969 threw a sudden and rather harsh light on the extent of politicisation and its implications, though there had been a mild foretaste in 1966 when the Grand Coalition was formed. All the state secretaries (the highest civil service rank) who were not sympathetic to the SPD or the FDP were shunted out, and in many departments a substantial number of changes were made at the level of division heads. In the Chancellor's Office the requirement of political loyalty was extended downwards to embrace posts at section head level, which meant in practice that a political colouring was imparted to virtually the whole of the senior staff of the Office. The actions of the new Government were challenged in the Bundestag and a certain amount of information about the extent of political appointments became available. For example, a written question (*kleine Anfrage*) was put down towards the end of 1969 about postings which elicited the reply that eleven state secretaries and eight ministerial directors (heads of division) had been retired in October/November 1968 under the clause in federal civil service law which lists categories of "political officials". There were in addition over seventy repostings, though many of these were not made on political grounds.[9] In the Chancellor's Office seven

[9]Bundestag DS. VI/68 and VI/107.

changes at the division chief level and just below took place immediately after the election of 1969. Slightly later, further evidence emerged of personnel changes at senior levels involving at least eleven officials below the top ranks in the Chancellor's Office.[10] In these and similar cases it is difficult to measure the exact scale of political appointments. If a move is made on the authority of the appropriate statutory powers, the matter is clear. But it is equally possible to veil the process, moving officials about for reasons ostensibly arising from administrative needs, but in reality to suit political requirements. Probably it would be a fair estimate that in about 20% of the relevant "political" posts there is, on a change of government, likely to be a replacement of personnel, though at the highest levels the proportion would be far greater.

On this recent occasion the Opposition's demand for information was accompanied by somewhat unconvincing criticism of the SPD for having gone over to a spoils system and for having carried out "a purge". But such a description of what happened seems to exaggerate its scale as well as failing to recognise the extent to which political appointments in the bureaucracy had already become an established practice. What took place first in 1966 when the SPD entered the Grand Coalition, and then in 1969 when it assumed power with the FDP, merely made the conventions governing senior official appointments more obvious and gave the Opposition the chance of bringing them into public argument. Moreover, a higher rate of changeover in personnel had by the late sixties become inevitable simply in virtue of the current age structure of the federal civil service.

In reality all the parties are now too deeply implicated in the politicisation of key official appointments to be able to take an effective stand against the trend. The idea of a politically neutral official at the policy-formulating level, capable of advising impartially ministers of different political views, has virtually disappeared. Moreover, during the long years of CDU rule, many practices developed in the relationships between party and federal civil service which underlined the involvement of officials in party thinking and decisions. Indeed the CDU neglected to build up its own party organisation on a scale comparable with that of the SPD chiefly because it had such cosy links with the federal bureaucracy, and could plausibly regard it as being a good substitute for a party apparatus of

[10]Bundestag DS. VI/435 and VI/587.

its own. It was not, therefore, surprising that in 1969 the SPD/FDP coalition should seek to consolidate its position by making use of precedents which few politicians were disposed to question in principle.

It must be remembered too that the federal civil service is merely one level of the system of government. The parties have entrenched political interests in the control of official appointments which extend outwards and downwards. The prolonged wrangling in late 1971 about appointments by the Bundestag to four vacancies in the Federal Constitutional Court under-lined a rather undesirable and too blatant politicisation of such senior judicial appointments. The parties have too a major stake in the control of Länder and local administrations which makes them reluctant to resist politicisation at the centre.

The attitude of the public service, and in particular of the Association of German Civil Servants (the DBB), towards these developments has been ambivalent. Being somewhat conservative in outlook the DBB still sticks to the ideal of permanent, non-party public service, and in principle de-plores the growing political influence in the bureaucracy. But equally it is acknowledged in the public service that politicians are nowadays adamant in their demand for reliable political support at the key levels of the bureau-cracy, and that government is inescapably party government. It is recog-nised too that there are practical arguments in favour of a measure of political appointments: policy-making will often be more coherent and policies more actively pursued if the responsibility rests with politically committed officials rather than with people whose neutrality may be a mask for passivity or even discreet obstruction. And the law governing the political activity of officials and the terms on which some of them may be removed from "political" posts is generous in its treatment of officials' interests. Moreover, though serving officials are required to show restraint and discretion with regard to political activity, any official may stand for political office and does not need to resign before so doing. If elected he retains many of his rights as an official, including the right to a pension, to reinstatement at a later date should he leave political life, and to promotion with due regard to the expectations he would have had, had he remained in the public service. The detailed regulations are complex, but essentially they add up to arrangements which make the transition to politics relatively free from risks, and for that reason inevitably encourage such a transition. That nearly 40% of Bundestag members have some experience as officials (using this term in its broadest sense to include teachers) is not unconnected with the favourable terms on which officials can move into politics and back into administration.

In regard to the conditions just described it is doubtful whether officials generally and the DBB in particular will seek to reverse the trends now established. A resolute commitment to the old ideal of the neutral bureaucracy would nowadays require a reform of civil service law with the aim of making it harder to step across the line between politics and public administration, harder for the officials in that they would have to risk loss of material benefits, and harder for the politicians in that they would have fewer inducements to offer their clients. So far there are no signs that either side wishes to pay the price, and indeed constitutional objections would be raised against any attempt to limit the political rights of officials by denying them scope for active (as opposed to passive) party membership and activity.

There are, of course, some features of the situation just described which are disturbing. Given that there is now a quasi-two-party system, this is likely to encourage on a change of Government a degree of personnel turnover in the bureaucracy which may prove both inconvenient and inefficient. One way of moderating this is to establish within departments an understanding that a certain amount of internal rotation is accepted between politically sensitive posts and those which are less so. There are some signs that this may be occurring in some sectors. In effect this is an application of the "Proporz" idea, so long familiar in Austria. Moreover, with the growth of party bureaucracies, there is also scope for rotation between them and the federal administration. In addition, the federal system itself offers opportunities for moving personnel about in accordance with political needs which are absent in more centralised systems.

Another and more serious problem is the way in which officials enjoy the benefits of patronage and at the same time those of professional security derived from their rights under public service law. To give a simple example, a man who owes his rapid advancement to a combination of political patronage and administrative ability may nowadays reach the level of state secretary at the age of 40 or so. He thus secures at this early age a high salary and generous pension rights, both of which are safeguarded should there be a change of political control which leads to his replacement by an official of a different political colour.[11] It is hard to resist the conclusion that such officials get the best of both worlds: prospects of early career success and copper-bottomed protection against political risks at the same time.

Yet it is difficult to see a way round this problem. One development which is in prospect is a reform of public service law which would assimilate the conditions of service for officials and "employees", perhaps going as far as to put the former on a contractual basis in respect of salary, pensions, and other benefits. This does, however, throw up many problems, particularly that of the right to strike which might be held to be logically implied by a contractual status, and still encounters strong opposition from the officials themselves. Changes of this kind, even if eventually made, would not work against the practice of political appointment, but they might moderate some of the advantages to officials arising from it and make it easier to define a limited range of posts for which short-term contractual arrangements would be most suitable.

What is certain is that the future of the professional civil service, the "Berufsbeamtentum", is now more open to discussion than in the past. The outcome of the reappraisal now initiated is uncertain. Undoubtedly the traditional ethos no longer has its former attractions, but the interests involved are tenacious and will try to ensure that whatever changes are made will not lead to substantial reductions in the benefits which officials currently enjoy.

We must now turn to a brief discussion of some of the effects on policy-making in the Federal Republic of the foregoing trends, in particular at the level of the Federal Government. In broad terms three major factors are at work. Politicisation of key areas of the civil service has encouraged policy-making which is responsive to political demands, though at the same time this has worked in favour of a bureaucratisation of politics. The close links between politics and administration and the general acceptance of the right of the majority party's leaders to determine political objectives have removed any fear that the bureaucracy, or parts of it, might aspire to impose

[11]This example is modelled on a number of genuine recent cases. One example of a very different kind should, however, be mentioned: Helmut Schmidt was supported as Minister of Defence, 1969–72, by a state secretary brought in from industry who preferred to serve without salary until his return to private employment after the 1972 election. See also footnote 12.

policies on reluctant ministers. The relations between politicians and senior officials have undoubtedly become easier and more relaxed, and the majority of officials accept that in framing proposals they must aim at results which will be politically acceptable to ministers. But working in the other direction is the respect for official expertise and technical competence which is still strong in German political life. Thus we find that ministers are often prepared to defer to the advice of their officials and that the legislative process in both chambers is heavily influenced by the involvement in it of officials. Moreover, the preference for an administrative style of politics is buttressed by widespread acceptance of the idea that reasonable decisions can only be reached when the necessary knowledge and experience are brought to bear on issues, and bargains between interests are struck in a framework of private discussion. This helps to ensure that the bureaucracy plays a key part in the negotiation and consultation which are today indispensable in the formulation of politics.

The third factor arises from the particularism inherent in the formalised and decentralised structure of German government. Each agency tends to be very jealous of its rights and powers, and to develop its own particular set of policies and interests. Informal co-operation or co-ordination, though essential, is often difficult, and there is now barely any over-arching sense of belonging to a single public service which can bridge the institutional barriers which are necessarily present in a complex structure of government. A bureaucratic ethos survives, but it is segmented and often subordinated to party affiliations. The impact of this on policy-making is that particular branches of government tend to pursue independently their own policies, that political leaders all too often allow themselves to be captured by the officials of "their own houses", and collective decision-making, especially at Cabinet level, is made very difficult. The acrimonious disputes between ministers which are quite regularly revealed in press reports stem often enough from the fact that their officials have pursued narrow, agency-oriented policies and have been able to convince ministers that they must identify themselves with these.

The very importance of party political ties in the twilight zone where politics and administration converge has probably made it virtually impossible to maintain the degree of confidentiality and solidarity which some politicians and older-style officials would like to have. Despite a general preference for bargaining behind closed doors, leaks of information are common, and since many officials are so closely involved in political argument, there is no attempt made to pretend that on many issues the Government speaks with one voice. At any rate for the initiated, it is not difficult in relation to particular questions to discover what the main interests are, where the obstacles lie, what range of policy solutions are being envisaged, and who is arguing for a particular course of action.

As regards the professional qualities of the bureaucracy and their significance for policy-making, at first sight it might be thought that the continuing reliance on a legal training as the basic qualification for administration would have led to difficulties in the contemporary governmental context. Yet it is doubtful whether this is so. Undoubtedly the legal background of so many officials leads to a formalistic approach to administrative work, which then inhibits innovation and accessibility to techniques and modes of thought derived from other disciplines. At the same time the legal framework within which German administration has to work makes it imperative to have people familiar with juridical concepts and public law procedures: officials without these qualifications just could not operate in the language of the system. Moreover, it must not be forgotten that in the Federal Republic, as in a number of other European countries, a legal training is intended to produce a generalist suitable for the political and administrative environment which obtains rather than a specialised legal adviser of the kind familiar in Britain or the U.S.A. Thus the law-trained official expects in the course of his practical work to acquire skills and knowledge different from those with which he starts off. That the Germans have a preference for job-specialisation encourages this development of relevant expertise. However, the *Juristenmonopol* is weakening. For a decade now an academic training in social science (usually economics) has been recognised as a suitable qualification for entry into the higher service. At first the numbers taking advantage of this were very small. But gradually they are rising, to some extent reflecting changes in the pattern of university studies. As more agencies see the possibilities of using such people, it is to be expected that the role of the law-trained official will decline somewhat.

There are certain structural characteristics of the administrative system which buttress the officials' influence on policy, particularly in the federal sphere. One is the preference for deconcentrating purely executive work to subordinate agencies working within precise terms of reference. Thus in the Federal Government this has facilitated the retention of relatively small departments which still see legislation, rule-making, and the elaboration of ministerial policy as their main function. The more senior officials in these departments are relieved of much of the detailed casework which tends to arise in the day-to-day provision of services, and can thus concentrate more exclusively on policy questions, including, of course, their political implications. But equally, since so much executive administration unavoidably retains a policy element, the system of deconcentration means that many second-order questions of policy and political judgment are left to the discretion of the officials in the subordinate agencies.

Another aspect of working procedure which has been important in the past is the reluctance to rely extensively for policy proposals on committees of inquiry and similar external bodies. Naturally this meant that advice was expected to proceed from the bureaucracy rather than from independent experts. But in recent years the situation in this respect has begun to change with the growth of standing advisory bodies and the tendency to appoint *ad hoc* committees to report on difficult issues. The influence of the officials is, however, to some extent safeguarded as a result of the fact that it is not unusual to appoint former or even serving officials to such bodies, and in the case of standing advisory committees the departments, of course, provide the secretariat.

At the top levels, divisional heads and state secretaries can expect to have close contact with ministers and parliamentary state secretaries. Occasionally (and this too is a trend established only in recent years) an outsider who is not a career official is brought in at this level, though this may create difficulties in relationships within the hierarchy and run up against civil service law objections.[12] But generally ministers rely on their top-level permanent officials, and do not seek the support of "irregulars" from outside public service. There is no "cabinet" to come between senior departmental officials and their ministers. The former are accustomed to act in political matters on behalf of ministers and this is accepted as perfectly normal in German political life. Bundestag members, for example, would not challenge the major role of officials in piloting legislation

---

[12]An example of this was provided after 1969 by the action of the Defence minister, Helmut Schmidt, in bringing into his department at the highest level someone with business experience, though in this instance there do not appear to have been difficulties in his relations with the permanent officials. See also footnote 11.

through committees, nor when raising a specific issue would they necessarily expect to deal with a minister rather than one of his officials. Links between the Federal Government and the Bundesrat are also maintained chiefly by officials, with ministers only appearing on major occasions.

These structural aspects of the administrative system underline the fact that there is no sharp dividing-line between policy-making which belongs exclusively to ministers or elected representatives and policy advice as a function of the bureaucracy. The German official still sees himself as a source of professional policy advice, qualified by experience and training to offer authoritative opinions both on what should be done and how. He has come to appreciate very clearly the importance of political considerations and the need to respect the preferences of his political masters. He will similarly recognise the need to take account of organised interests and, even though he will probably think very much in agency or departmental terms, will accept the importance of trying to achieve consultation and co-ordination within what is a complex, multi-layered system of administration. He is aware too of the pitfalls and difficulties of legislative politics which call for skill in detecting where a bargain can be struck or a compromise agreed which will accommodate the pressures exerted by all the major groups within the parties. All this adds up to the conclusion that the official's influence on policy-making in the Federal Republic is substantial. To a large extent this mirrors the situation in many countries, and for the obvious and well-known reasons stemming from the vast expansion of public action and regulation.

But in assessing the bureaucracy's contribution to policy-making in the Federal Republic we must avoid the idea of neutral, subordinate advisers. Bureaucrats and politicians are both holders of public power, agents of the state. In this way traditional concepts live on. The authority of the politician is greater and his determination of basic questions now usually unchallenged. But his authority is hardly yet different in kind from that of the bureaucrat, who has in addition the advantages of longer tenure and greater specialised experience. It is this which confers a distinctive quality on the relationship between the German civil service and its political masters.

CHAPTER 7

# Controlling the Executive

THE problem of how to control the exercise of governmental powers presents itself in many ways. It is, of course, inherent in any system of representative government and in any society which attaches importance to the rule of law. The whole question of control has become more difficult in the Federal Republic as elsewhere as a result of the expansion of public activity and changes in the nature of the demands which many people expect the state to satisfy. Most techniques of control have their origins in a nineteenth-century preference for limiting the action of public authorities in the interests of individual rights and claims. To a significant extent this situation is now turned upside down: the demand for services has increased greatly and people tend to want more public action rather than less. Inevitably this puts a considerable strain on the control mechanisms. The Federal Republic is no exception to these trends.

There are three aspects of control which it is proposed to look at here. The first is concerned essentially with the maintenance of the rule of law, with the means by which public action is confined within legally enforceable standards. The second is much more internal to administration, the control of financial performance. The third will be described as political control: the manner in which public authorities are subject to political checks which help to keep them responsive to the demands of elected representatives.

## THE JUDICIAL MODES OF CONTROL

As pointed out earlier, the effort in Germany to subject governmental action to legally binding constraints antedates the achievement of representative government, and was indeed an important element in the development of the Rechtsstaat or German conception of the rule of law. In the last century there was a strong tendency to see administration as essentially the implementation of law, the putting into effect of formal rules. It followed from this that redress should be obtained by appeal to bodies competent to test specific acts against the relevant law. The influence of this view is still powerful, finding expression in the Basic Law's guarantee that the citizen shall always have access to the courts in order to contest the decisions of executive authorities which appear to encroach on his rights.[1] Underlying this is the assumption that every administrative act that has external effect is a specific exercise of sovereignty which can be defined and challenged in terms of its legal basis. Admittedly a great deal of contemporary administrative action escapes this net, but nevertheless this way of looking at the acts of public authorities does mean that a large part of what they do is subject to the possibility of challenge before a court.

The judicial control of administration through special administrative courts was already well established at the beginning of this century, particularly in Prussia, and was further developed before the advent of the Nazi régime. That experience strengthened the belief that public bodies should be confined within a strictly defined legal framework, as well as underlining the need to maintain an independent judiciary, firmly committed to the rule of law and the protection of citizens' rights. In addition, the collapse of the rule of law after 1933 and the subjection of the courts to political dictation encouraged a reaffirmation of faith in the idea that the citizen is likely to be better protected by judges than by politicians. The commitment to defining rights in legally binding and enforceable terms inevitably reinforced the preference for a judicial mode of resolving conflicts as compared with political conciliation or arbitration. And this happened despite the fact that the judiciary had been unable to offer much protection against the excesses of the Nazi régime, and that some judges had been all too willing to bend the law in the interests of those in power. But faith in politicians was far more shaken, and this to some extent explains the renewed emphasis on a firm legal basis for public action and the continuing faith in the efficacy of appeal to courts of law. Only gradually, as confidence in the new political system was established, has it

[1]Art. 19 (4), Basic Law.

become easier to take a more critical view of the reliance on judicial controls which has developed in the Federal Republic.

German government and administration operate within the limits imposed by both an extensive administrative law jurisdiction and the decisions of the constitutional courts. Of the latter the Federal Constitutional Court at Karlsruhe is politically by far the most important, though it has to be remembered that the Länder also have constitutional courts empowered to consider cases in which the decisions are challenged on grounds of incompatibility with their own constitutional provisions.

The system of administrative law jurisdiction is specialised and distinct from that of the civil courts.[2] Over a very wide field the general administrative courts (Verwaltungsgerichte) are competent. But for some sectors there are more specialised courts: the Finanzgerichte or Finance courts for questions arising out of the application of tax law, the Sozialgerichte or Social courts for the interpretation of social-security provisions, and then the Labour courts (Arbeitsgerichte) for the resolution of disputes arising under industrial relations law.[3] In addition there are a number of narrower and more specialised jurisdictions such as that for disciplinary cases in the civil and military services.

The structure of these jurisdictions varies somewhat. The general administrative courts have three tiers, one of first instance and one of appeal at the Land level, and then a final appeal court for the whole country (the Bundesverwaltungsgericht). The same goes for the Social courts, whilst the Finance courts have only two levels, i.e. courts of first instance and then a federal appeal court. The structure is complicated and not entirely consistent, but its coverage is impressive. All these courts are manned by professional judges, usually qualified in the particular areas of law most likely to concern the courts. Quite a number of these judges are former officials, a fact which is explicable in relation to the need to secure the right kind of knowledge and experience, but which sometimes invites criticism on the

---

[2]The general rule is that the law must specify when there is a right of appeal to an administrative court, and in the absence of this, the civil courts have jurisdiction (Art. 19 (4), Basic Law). In practice, whilst certain categories of cases involving private law rights do still come before the civil courts, the bulk of cases involving public authorities go to administrative courts.

[3]Labour courts deal, of course, primarily with disputes between individuals and organisations and are not, therefore, strictly analogous to other administrative courts. But they need to be included to complete the picture.

grounds that it reflects adversely on the independence of the various administrative courts. There is no single governmental body responsible for appointments to the administrative courts and for their general management: despite arguments that the federal Ministry of Justice (and *mutatis mutandis* the Länder Ministries of Justice) should be responsible, the different branches of public law jurisdiction have remained within the ambit of the related arms of government—for example, the Federal Administrative Court comes under the Ministry of the Interior in Bonn, whilst the Finance courts come under the federal and Länder Finance ministries.

In all there are about 3150 full-time judges occupied in the various branches of administrative jurisdiction in the Federal Republic,[4] and in addition they are assisted by a substantial number of judges and assessors sitting in an honorary capacity. Having regard to the fact that there are in the Federal Republic about 12,000 judges, this means that over a quarter are concerned mainly with public law matters, that is to say with disputes between individuals and organisations on the one hand and public authorities on the other. The case-load of these courts is heavy. Nearly 60,000 cases were settled in the general administrative courts in 1969. Inevitably the substantial flow of cases leads to delays and the procedural rules (now unified for the whole country) are not designed for facilitating speedy decisions. Access to the courts is not difficult and legal costs need not always be a substantial deterrent. Nevertheless, a strongly contested case which goes to two and possibly three instances can be a wearisome and expensive business, not lightly to be entered upon by the ordinary citizen.

It is important to be clear about what this kind of administrative court control can achieve, and what it cannot. Broadly speaking, it enables citizens to contest decisions already taken and which *prima facie* injure them in the enjoyment of rights afforded to them by the law. In many cases it is a question of asserting a claim against an authority's decision not to accept that claim, for example in social security or tax cases. There is no doubt that the system does impose upon all kinds of public authority a rigorous obligation to act within their powers, and what is more within a reasonable interpretation of powers. Moreover, they are subject to the procedural requirement of always justifying their actions by reference to the legal basis for them (Begründungszwang). Not infrequently public bodies find

[4]Source: *Statistisches Jahrbuch, 1971.* This estimate includes labour, tax, and social courts.

that they must change their policies and procedures because a court has reached a decision which invalidates what they are doing. In addition the system operates as a means of enforcing on public authorities certain procedural rules analogous to the principles of natural justice in the Anglo-Saxon common-law tradition.

On the other hand, there are limitations to what this highly formal mode of control can achieve. The courts cannot substitute their discretion for a discretion plainly granted to an administrative authority. They cannot for the most part deal with what is often called maladministration, a decision which stops short of misuse or outright misinterpretation of powers, but which may nevertheless be unfair and damaging to those affected by it. Nor can this system do very much to protect people against all the numerous side effects of contemporary public action which may often affect them adversely, but do not establish claims enforceable at law. In other words, the type of judicial control of public action so elaborately developed in the Federal Republic is effective when the citizen has a clearly justiciable complaint as a result of a specific administrative act. But, despite a widening of the concept of what is justiciable, this approach is less well adapted to some of the needs arising out of contemporary social and economic policies, for example in urban planning, highway development or the allocation of subsidies for economic purposes. Nor is it always adequate when the need is to forestall or modify public schemes: though injunctions in restraint of public bodies can be secured, judicial control normally begins to bite only after the stage at which, from the point of view of aggrieved parties, damage has been done. Nevertheless there is a fairly high degree of public confidence in these judicial procedures, and the plea made in recent years by some critics for the introduction of Ombudsman-type institutions to supplement the courts has not made much headway.[5]

Above, and separate from the administrative jurisdictions, lies that of the Federal Constitutional Court. Set up in 1951, the Court established its position only slowly. There has always been a political element in its composition and this has perhaps sometimes served to weaken its authority. Nevertheless its judgments have gained respect for their impartiality and

---

[5]In January 1973 the first steps were, however, taken in Rhineland-Pfalz to establish a "Citizens' Commissioner" or Ombudsman (referred to in German as "Bürgerbeauftragte"). This is the first case of effective political support for such an experiment. There is, however, a Military Ombudsman, for which see p. 179.

the quality of the reasoning in them, and there is no doubt that the Court is now an unchallenged element in the balance of powers within the Federal German political system. This is not the place to consider the procedures of the Court nor to outline in detail its competence. We are concerned more narrowly with its contribution to the control of powers. In this connection the impact of the Court has been felt chiefly in two directions: in the resolution of disputes between different levels of government, and in decisions ruling on the constitutionality of laws, administrative acts, or judicial decisions.

A major example of the former was the dispute in 1960–1 between the Federal Government and the Länder over plans for a second television service under federal control which was resolved when the Court decided (1961) that the proposal was in conflict with the distribution of powers between federation and Länder in the Basic Law. Another case affecting the distribution of powers, already referred to in another context, was that arising out of the Federal Government's conflict with Lower Saxony about the validity of the Concordat of 1933. This was decided in 1957, in part in favour of the Federal Government, though owing to the assignment of responsibility for education to the Länder under the Basic Law no action could be taken to constrain the Land Lower Saxony to abide by the terms of the Concordat.

In the broader sphere of constitutional appeal to test the validity of laws or to invoke the protection of the basic rights articles the Court has had an equally "political" task. Cases involving a challenge to the constitutionality of laws are handled generally by a process for the "control of norms", essentially a request to declare whether a rule is consistent with the Basic Law. This is a procedure which has to be set in motion by a constitutionally recognised institution, and it may be used either abstractly (i.e. the issue of constitutionality is posed because there is doubt about the validity of some measure) or concretely (i.e. the question is raised by a subordinate court which questions the validity of a particular legal rule). Pleas initiated by individuals or associations asserting infringement of basic rights as a result of public action must generally be tested first in the ordinary courts, after which they have to be referred to the Constitutional Court if it is held that there may be such an infringement. On the other hand, laws which appear to curtail basic rights may be appealed directly to Karlsruhe. The principle of equality of treatment has played a big part in the Court's interpretation of the Basic Law. For example, in a famous case decided in 1957[6] the Court invalidated certain federal tax provisions relating to the joint tax liabilities of married couples. In part this was because they appeared to disregard Article 6 of the Basic Law on protection of the family and marriage, and in part because they treated married women less fairly than those living in sin, and thus offended against the equal treatment principle. That the parties of the extreme Left and Right can claim a share in the public funds granted to political parties to enable them to fight elections is due directly to the Court's decision in 1968 that the requirement of a 2.5% share of the poll to qualify for a share was too high and offended against equal treatment and opportunity.[7]

The Constitutional Court has certainly made a major contribution to the development and awareness of constitutional law. This in turn has re-inforced the need for public authorities, including legislatures, to consider carefully the compatibility of what they are doing with the terms of the Basic Law. It has upheld the natural rights doctrines embodied in the Basic Law, and on the whole taken a strict view of the degree of protection of individual rights intended by the founding fathers. Yet notwithstanding these achievements the Court has had a narrow rather than a broad impact on the evolution of German politics and government. This is partly because the disposition on the part of public bodies to observe the constitutional norms has since 1949 been relatively high: much administrative action has been judicialised, and thus many conflicts have been avoided. There has been remarkably little serious political tension in the life of the Federal Republic and the Court has, therefore, been able to fulfil its role of "pro-tector of the constitution" in a measured way. In addition the Court is limited by the nature of the Basic Law itself. Whereas the American Supreme Court has had to apply a constitution drafted in broad terms to expound a theory of government of impressive simplicity, the Federal Constitutional Court has had to apply a constitution of a very different kind. Apart from the opening articles stating the basic rights, the Basic Law is not a bold statement of general political principles, nor does it present in grand outline the theory of government by the division of powers which underlies it. It is an exact and legalistic constitution, regu-

[6] *B Verf GE*, Vol. 6.
[7] *B Verf GE*, Vol. 24; 0.5% of the poll was deemed by the Court to satisfy the equality of treatment principle.

lating the allocation of powers in the system of government in considerable detail. This has tended to narrow the contentious areas within which judges exercise discretion. Moreover, except for certain entrenched clauses, constitutional amendment is relatively easy (provided there is a two-thirds majority in the Bundestag and Bundesrat), and thus it has usually been possible to forestall difficulties likely to arise out of appeal to the courts. This has been particularly so with regard to the provisions determining relations between institutions, for example the allocation of concurrent powers to the federation and Länder.[8] Another factor of some importance has been the reluctance of the Court's judges to encroach on the political discretion vested in governmental authorities both executive and legislative. That is to say, when required to do so it will apply the principles of the constitution to particular acts, but it would decline to pre-empt a decision which is properly a political one. And no doubt there is wisdom in this attitude, which is also reflected now in the growing reluctance of political leaders to try to force what are essentially political judgments into the framework of constitutional principles.[9] But despite these limitations the Court, together with similar bodies in the Länder, has made a major contribution to fixing the framework of principles within which government must work, and thus to establishing a dimension of protection of constitutional rights which is one of the most significant innovations of the past twenty years of German history.

The Federal German preference for judicial modes of control continues to reflect earlier experience, both in its negative and positive aspects. As long as this influence persists with its emphasis on the authoritative and objective interpretation of legal norms, then the procedures outlined here are likely to retain their vitality. But there are more and more areas of public activity which can only with difficulty be brought within this framework of control—the preservation of natural amenities, urban re-

[8]Most of the numerous amendments to the Basic Law have affected organic details rather than changed any of the basic conditions in it. Thus it is a much-amended constitution, but in its essential political components virtually unchanged since 1949.

[9]A recent example of this is the disinclination of many of the critics of the agreements concluded in 1972 with the DDR to test their validity before the Federal Constitutional Court. Apart from embarrassing the Court, this would have represented an attempt to subject a major political decision to very narrow questions of constitutional interpretation. In the end Bavaria did, however, decide to test the agreements before the Court.

development, the control of pollution or the application of financial incentives to industrial development, to quote a few examples. Here public
intervention often loses the precision which traditional forms of regulatory
action have. It becomes increasingly difficult to define public action in
terms of acts directly affecting individuals. It becomes a mode of social engineering and guidance, the results of which spread out to affect innumerable
aspects of life. Inevitably the question arises whether or not more flexible
methods of control than those provided by judicial bodies are needed.

In relation to judicial control one further comment is worth making.
This is that its prevalence obviously has effects on the style of administrative
action. Though it has major advantages in terms of the citizen's ability to
secure fair treatment from public bodies, it sustains a rather rigid and
legalistic approach to administrative activity. The panoply of judicial controls has reinforced a judicialisation of administration which many of
those in government have deplored. It slows down the processes of administration, often makes them unduly complicated for the citizen, and
induces over-caution in officials. The rapid expansion of government
functions and the changes in the character of many of them just alluded to
merely serve to underline some of the difficulties of the legalist tradition in
administration. Gradually changes are taking place. At the levels of policy-
making—and particularly in the federal administration—there is now less
emphasis on legal modes of thought and many of the younger officials see
themselves as having essentially a creative political role in the structuring of
society. But at the levels of executive action the older attitudes must retain
much of their influence, if only because the environment of control requires
it. Given the procedures discussed here one of the most interesting questions
for the future concerns the extent to which the Federal Republic may
develop two fairly distinct administrative styles, the one adapted to some
of the contemporary "planning" functions of government, the other to the
provision of those services to which the traditional standards of legal
rectitude can still be applied.

## THE INTERNAL CONTROL OF FINANCIAL
## PERFORMANCE

Like other highly developed administrative systems that of Western
Germany has evolved well-established procedures for the control of finan-

cial regularity. Historically such procedures have tended to serve two main purposes: the state's need of means of controlling the expenditure commitments undertaken by its own agents, and the desire of the legislature to be able to check that the funds it has appropriated have been used for the purposes it has approved. Generalising broadly, it can be said that in the U.S.A. and Britain the audit procedures have developed to serve both these ends, whilst on the whole the corresponding continental European procedures have been only loosely linked with parliamentary scrutiny (if at all) and have served rather more as control mechanisms internal to the structure of government. In practice the Federal Republic's financial control methods fit into the continental pattern, though in principle they are also directed to the possibility of some kind of parliamentary oversight.

For the federal administration the responsibility for carrying out a *post facto* scrutiny of spending rests with the Federal Court of Accounts. This is a collegial body, whose members are nominated by the Minister of Finance. It has in law an independent status similar to that of the courts, though its recommendations or decisions are not enforceable in the same way. The Federal Court of Accounts maintains a substantial organisation, the staff of which are engaged in the continuing examination of federal agencies. Annually a report is made to the Federal Finance minister who must then seek discharge, as it is called technically, from the Bundestag.

In keeping with the decentralised structure of German government the Federal Government has no responsibility for the financial control arrangements at lower levels of the system. Each of the Länder maintains its own court or chamber of accounts to check the spending of appropriations under the Länder budgets, and the local authorities too are generally responsible for their own audit arrangements. Where public bodies are running economic enterprises or have a substantial stake in them, commercial accounting methods are normally used and professional auditors employed.

For the most part the type of audit control applied in the Federal Republic has been of the formal kind. There is a check on legality: was there proper legal authority for each item of spending? There is a check on the objectives or purposes of expenditure: has it been conducted in conformity with the budgetary appropriation act? And finally, there is some attempt to consider efficiency and value for money. The first of these checks is highly formal, and even though in rare cases there might be some doubt about powers, it is hard to see what the Court of Accounts can do about it.[10] The same applies to the scrutiny of conformity with the appropriations, though in principle the appropriate legislative body could censure the Government for departing from the provisions which it had approved. But flouting the terms of budgetary law is rare: the German administrator's respect for the law works against this, and in addition German appropriations are still approved in a form which provides exhaustive detail of financial inputs and makes departure from their strict terms correspondingly difficult. This is particularly true of personnel costs which have to be tied rigidly to the numbers of posts approved in the relevant appropriations.

As to the control of efficiency, this aspect of performance checking has become of major importance in recent years. But it is doubtful whether the traditional audit methods used in the Federal Republic are well adapted to this task. The emphasis is still very much on specific inputs rather than on the appreciation of outputs or the relating of inputs to outputs.[11] Moreover, it is unlikely that the administrative services would take kindly to a more active and critical form of financial control: it would be argued that this would blur responsibilities as between the executive agents and the controllers as well as introducing considerations of opportunity which only the administration could properly assess. Nevertheless, the President of the Federal Court of Accounts has since 1957 normally held simultaneously the post of Commissioner for the Efficiency of Administration, which gives him a formal basis for a wide-ranging scrutiny of how services are provided. Though a certain amount has been achieved in this direction, the Court needs stronger backing by the political authorities if its work is to have full effect.

[10]A curious example of spending without legal authorisation was reported on by the Federal Court of Accounts at the time of the 1972 election. After the dissolution of the Bundestag in September the parliamentary state secretaries remained in office, continuing to draw their salaries. The Court took exception to this on the grounds that the relevant legislation stipulated that they must be members of the Bundestag, and that as this condition was no longer met there was no legal authority to pay them. The Government maintained the common-sense view that the legislation must have envisaged that those holding such appointments would after a dissolution stay in office until reappointed or replaced on the formation of a new Government. The parliamentary state secretaries stayed in office.

[11]For more information on audit control see E. L. Normanton, *The Accountability and Audit of Governments*, 1966, especially chap. IX. The present writer does, however, consider that the picture presented here rather overstates the role of the Bundesrechnungshof, especially in the control of efficiency.

The reports of the Court of Accounts, usually referring to the financial year two years back, are presented to the Bundestag and the Bundesrat, and to the Finance minister, who is legally responsible for the application of the federal budget. He has to seek discharge from the Bundestag from whatever criticisms are made. The same procedure applies in the Länder. In theory this means that the Bundestag could impose conditions and thus use the request for discharge as a means of inserting itself into the process of financial control. But it does not seriously try to do this. The reports are studied by a subcommittee of the Appropriations committee of the Bundestag, and in the light of its observations discharge is recommended. This is usually a formality. The subcommittee does not take public evidence (it discusses with officials in private), nor does it really try to use the Court of Accounts reports as a basis for drawing conclusions of its own about the performance of the federal services.[12] There is still a marked lack of interest on the floor of the Bundestag in the results of audit control, a fact which reflects the continuing preference for trying to influence commitments in advance through the exercise of the Bundestag's legislative and budgetary powers rather than getting involved in the politically less rewarding task of scrutinising past performance.

The Federal Republic has, of course, inherited a long experience of state enterprise, particularly in the field of public utilities, and here performance has been judged by more stringent commercial standards than could be applied to conventional state expenditure. Nevertheless, the concept of public benefit, or of satisfying a public need, has excluded the application of crude criteria of profitability even to services which are essentially of an economic character. Thus the control of financial performance has been directed far more to ensuring technical efficiency and sound management than to securing efficiency in the strict economic sense.[13] This approach has meant that there has been no sharp conflict between the older methods of ensuring regularity in the use of public funds and the use, where appropriate, of commercial methods of audit. Though there are signs of a growing

[12]For an extended treatment of these issues see S. Hoffman, *Die Kontrolle der Regierung durch parlamentarische Rechnungsprüfung im Deutschen Bundestag*, Göttingen, 1970.

[13]This can be illustrated rather flippantly by reference to the German Federal Railways. They are efficient in a technical sense: trains run to time, they are clean and comfortable, connections are good, etc. But the railways run at a substantial annual loss and can hardly be regarded as "efficient" in economic terms.

interest in the application to the public services of modern managerial techniques and cost–benefit analysis, it seems doubtful whether past and present political values would allow any serious attempt to push very far the analogy between many contemporary public services and private commercial enterprise. For this reason alone the methods of financial and efficiency audit are likely to evolve within the traditional framework which has laid so much emphasis on the observance of formal rules.

## POLITICAL CONTROLS OVER THE ACTIVITIES OF GOVERNMENT

A discussion of the political controls to which executive agencies are subject can easily widen into a consideration of how political influence is distributed in the society. In particular it can take us into an analysis of party structures and the manner in which particular interests and points of views expressed in them operate as constraints on those responsible for determining policies. But here it is intended to stick to a narrower view of political control as the opportunities open to legislative bodies to challenge what governments are doing and to ensure some responsiveness to parliamentary demands.[14]

There are three principal ways in which a legislature can influence executive action: it can try to impose its will on decisions which need parliamentary approval; it can make individual members of the executive dependent on its confidence; and it can seek to make a Government accountable by challenging particular actions, demanding justification or change. At the federal level in Western Germany the Bundestag tends to favour the first of these approaches. It has a clearly defined legislative authority and, within the limits imposed by a cohesive party system, it tries to use this authority to influence the proposals put to it by the Government. As will be clear already, it has next to no influence over individual members of the Government. Party considerations do affect the composition and behaviour of Governments, but the standing of ministers *vis-à-vis* the Bundestag as a whole is not a very significant factor. And the cohesion and simplification of the party system has put an end to the kind of controlling influence

---

[14]This chapter is restricted to controls exercised by the Bundestag which is technically the West German Parliament. For the role of the Bundesrat which embodies Länder rights in the legislative process, the reader is referred back to Chapter 5.

which groups in the legislature could previously exercise over ministers individually or collectively. There remains the scrutiny and challenge of Government actions. In this respect the Bundestag behaves ambiguously. It has opportunities for asserting the public accountability of ministers, but it uses them hesitantly. The temptation to seek instead a share in the executive power—what is called in German "mitregieren"—remains strong, and despite the trend towards a quasi-two-party system. Thus political success in the Bundestag tends to go to those who have skill in influencing what Governments want to do rather than to those who are anxious to make them justify what they have done.

The control of the day-to-day actions of public authorities in the sense of securing redress of grievances has never in Germany depended substantially on the intervention of political representatives, whether parliamentarians or local councillors. This continues to be true in the Federal Republic, though in a variety of ways elected representatives are more active on behalf of their constituents than was the case in earlier times. The reasons for the relatively modest role of members of the Bundestag in asserting a control over specific executive actions are complex. A major factor is simply the federal system and the decentralised structure of administration. This means that the responsibilities of the Federal Government for decisions which directly affect the public are limited: there is just no point in constituents taking up their grievances in planning or education matters with members of the Bundestag, because the Federal Government has no executive rights or duties in these fields. Another decisive reason is the extent of more formal modes of control as discussed in the first part of this chapter: many complaints would be seen as more suitable for reference to some kind of administrative tribunal or to the competent administrative agency itself. Yet another factor is the procedural framework of the Bundestag (reproduced with variations in the Länder parliaments too) which places most emphasis on the legislative functions of committees and correspondingly less on procedures directed to asserting the public accountability of the Government before the Bundestag. (And of course the fact that many parliamentarians are elected on a list rather than for a constituency also affects their attitudes towards handling individual complaints.)

Nevertheless the Bundestag has means of exerting a political control over actions of the executive which deserve some attention. Foremost amongst these is the institution of parliamentary questions. The device was intro-

G

duced early in the life of the Bundestag[15] and has struck root. On average about 3500 oral questions are put to ministers annually, though a significant proportion of these are answered in writing. As for oral answers, each plenary session (and there are sixty or so of these per year) includes a question hour and up to twenty questions are usually dealt with. Many of them are detailed and specific, eliciting thorough and painstaking replies. In the interchanges which take place through supplementary questions there is not much cut and thrust of argument: the proceedings often resemble an exchange of statements rather than the sharp interplay of critical question and defensive answer. Though Governments have gradually become more conscious of the need to navigate the question hours successfully, it is doubtful whether the institution contributes as much as some had hoped it would to maintaining an atmosphere of accountability, or whether many Bundestag members regard it as a major instrument for calling the Government to account. Occasionally questions have had a dramatic effect, as for example in 1962 on the fate of Herr Strauss, then Defence minister. But they tend still to lack the character of a continuous inquisition. Since 1965 question hour has been supplemented by the device of the "aktuelle Stunde", an opportunity for the Bundestag to hold debates not exceeding an hour on motions of topical interest. This is potentially a means of holding the Government to account for specific decisions, though as with oral questions there has been some reluctance on the part of members to exploit the technique.

Another method of extracting information from the Government which has been employed with marked success is the so-called "minor interpellation", the "kleine Anfrage". Essentially this is a series of written questions presented by a minimum of twenty-six members,[16] to which in principle reply should be made within fourteen days. It is usual for the Government to provide very extensive answers which can then be used by the party or group of members which put the question. The aim here is not to initiate debate in the Bundestag, but to secure information which may be used in committee or in the course of continuing political arguments about particular issues. Though this device does not make a big public impact, it is

[15]See N. Johnson, Questions in the Bundestag, *Parliamentary Affairs* XVI (1), 1962/3, and P. Schindler, Die Fragestunde des Deutschen Bundestages, *PVS*, Jg 7, 1966.

[16]Twenty-six members represent the current minimum size of a Fraktion in the Bundestag.

an effective means of getting information which is then available in the public record of the Bundestag. It has become an increasingly popular Opposition technique since 1969.[17]

Another control device which has proved difficult to operate is the committee of investigation (Untersuchungsausschuss). On a motion of one-quarter of the members of the Bundestag such a body can be established and charged with the investigation of executive misdemeanours. Between 1949 and 1972 seventeen such investigatory committees have been set up by the Bundestag, but relatively few of them have brought their inquiries to a successful conclusion. The main reason for this is that the institution was intended to protect the rights of the Opposition, or at any rate of minorities in the Bundestag, and this has inevitably meant that many of the investigations proposed have been opposed by the Government. Since such committees are manned on a basis which reflects party strengths, disagreement within them was usually unavoidable and their proceedings have lacked the kind of impartiality which would have given authority to the findings. Indeed the record of committees of investigation bears out the continuing difficulty of establishing confidence in the ability of politicians to behave objectively. This stands in sharp contrast with the willingness to trust the impartiality of judges which has already been referred to.

In one particular field of public service the Bundestag has set up its own agent of scrutiny and control. This is in the armed forces which, since their re-establishment after the entry of the Federal Republic into NATO in 1955, have been subject to the supervision of the Wehrbeauftragte or Military Ombudsman. This official, first appointed in 1959, reports to the Bundestag and is responsible for dealing with complaints put to him by military personnel. Though not all the holders of the office have come up to expectations, it has proved a useful means of bringing to the attention of the Bundestag both individual complaints and more general information about morale and conduct in the armed forces. Given the earlier history of the army the Military Ombudsman has been a useful innovation. It has helped to open up conditions in the armed forces to public discussion and

---

[17]The number of "kleine Anfragen" has steadily risen, viz.
>1961–5: 308
>1965–9: 487
>1969–72: 569

Simultaneously the number of interpellations ("grosse Anfragen") has declined.

established a link with the Bundestag which is no longer seriously challenged. This is not to say that the Bundestag devotes a great deal of public attention to the reports of its agent: occasionally they have excited debate and controversy,[18] but more often than not have been dealt with quietly by the Defence committee of the Bundestag.

There is one other method of *post facto* control which merits a brief mention. This is the use of petitions, an inheritance of parliamentary development in the last century. The right of individuals to petition the Bundestag is guaranteed, and in fact a surprisingly large number of such petitions are presented, currently about 7500 per year.[19] The flow of petitions is referred to the Petitions committee of the Bundestag, the staff of which sort them out and refer them to the appropriate authorities for information. If they contain complaints which fall within the competence of a Land, they are sent on to the corresponding committee of the appropriate Landtag. Occasionally the Bundestag Petitions committee may discuss cases at length and question officials along with the petitioner. To some extent the receipt of petitions is a substitute for an Ombudsman-type institution.

As has been shown, there are several ways in which the Bundestag can and does challenge the actions of the executive. Yet this activity is not central to the conception of what is the role of Parliament. It remains a basic principle of the German system of government that public action must take place within a framework of law. The Bundestag sees itself as having a vital part to play in determining that framework, but when it comes to the control of what is done within it, the Bundestag sees itself as stopping up certain gaps or supplementing other means of control rather than as being a central point to which citizens may turn when they object to executive actions. Compared with previous parliamentary institutions in Germany the Bundestag (to some extent the same goes for the Landtage too) has been more energetic in making use of its control powers: but the

[18] A controversial case arose in 1964 when v. Heye, then Wehrbeauftragte, made sharp criticisms of the way in which the military leadership approached the question of how best to maintain sound morale, and was then unwise enough to add to his strictures in an article in the magazine *Quick*. He had to resign. For further comments on the Military Ombudsman, see F. Ridley, The Parliamentary Commissioner for Military Affairs in the Federal Republic of Germany, *Political Studies* XII (1), 1964.

[19] This is a total figure and includes many items which are strictly "requests" rather than "complaints".

theory of a separation of powers between executive and legislature remains influential. Though it strengthens the claims of the Bundestag to a legislative role, it inhibits the development of a more critical response to the sins of omission and commission of Governments. Nor must it be forgotten that the Opposition has gradually become the crucial counterweight to the Government. This means that political control in the broadest sense becomes a function of the Opposition. A major consequence of this is that most of the control mechanisms just outlined become subject to the influence of Government–Opposition rivalry. Government supporters become inhibited in the use of them and Opposition members tempted to exploit them for party purposes. Thus they run the risk of losing some of their importance as control mechanisms for Parliament as a whole *vis-à-vis* the executive.

Control over future policies is seen by the Bundestag very much in terms of examination of legislative proposals and budgetary demands. We have already in Chapter 4 said something about the relations between the federal ministries and the committees of Parliament in the handling of legislation. In the present context it is necessary only to underline some of the ways in which the specialised committees of the Bundestag do see their role as one of control. The process of law-making in the Bundestag is essentially a committee process. Bills generally go straight into committee after a formal first reading, so that subsequent plenary debate takes place on the basis of the expert scrutiny which proposals have already received. Indeed, though the rules provide for general debate on all three readings, they have now been modified to allow this only on demand, i.e. it does not take place as a matter of course. Committees have in practice considerable autonomy both in relation to the Bundestag as a whole and in relation to the Government: they are not managed by ministers and they determine their own proceedings. Moreover, the committees reflect not only the subject specialisation which takes place as a matter of routine amongst members, but the specialisation and mobilisation of interests within the political parties. Though an increasing number of public hearings have been held since 1966, the committees do most of their business in private, maintaining close contacts with the federal departments and the major organised interests. It is significant too that a high proportion of Bundestag members have civil service experience. They are thus well equipped to carry out a painstaking examination of Government proposals and capable of drafting alternative formulations to meet the demands presented by the diverse interests which exist both inside the political parties and in the world outside.

The outcome is a legislative process which is thorough and relatively slow. In recent years the average time required for dealing with bills from introduction to finish has been about nine months, though this is misleading and disguises the fact that on many complex and controversial measures the time needed is far longer. The bulk of legislation is nowadays proposed by the Federal Government, and if it is determined, the Government can usually count on securing a substantial part of what it wants. But it has to be prepared to make concessions to secure agreement in the committees and to allow to them a considerable influence on detail and presentation. As a highly qualified legislating chamber, backed up by substantial supporting staff, the Bundestag has few, if any, rivals in Western Europe. This is a type of control which it understands and which imposes both technical and political limitations on the freedom of Governments to go their own way.

Though legislative control is the main preoccupation of the committees of the Bundestag, they have in the course of time acquired in a somewhat haphazard way something like powers of administrative oversight. This is the result of the fact that they are the recipients of a very large number of reports, for the most part submitted to them by the Federal Government. Thus, for example, the Economics committee will receive both the annual report of the Committee of Experts for the Appreciation of the General Development of the Economy and the annual economic report of the Federal Government which follows it. Since all committees are entitled to deal with matters in their own "area of business", even if not before them as legislative drafts, the committee is then entitled to report on these items to the Bundestag. In practice it may not do so, preferring to ensure that its views on them are made known less formally to the Government, which appreciates that they may influence the committee in its consideration of legislative measures submitted to it. Or again, the Education committee has in recent years received an increasing amount of statistical and other material about educational matters which has enabled it to reinforce the growing concern at the federal level with the development of the education system. The general effect of this continuing flow of information to committees, some of it stemming from binding obligations laid on the Federal Government, is that they are put in a better position both to raise and report on particular issues within their area of concern, and to react critically to legislative proposals brought before them. So far the committees have not tried to develop anything closely resembling the kind of select committee examination of departmental action familiar in the House of Commons, but in many respects they are well equipped to do so.

In one committee, the Appropriations committee, a species of administrative control is well established. This is one of the most prestigious of Bundestag committees, and is charged with reporting on the annual budgetary proposals. Technically this is legislative scrutiny because the estimates are embodied finally in the Budgetary Law or Appropriation Act. What the committee does is to carry out a careful scrutiny of expenditure proposals which brings it into close contact with the details of administrative operations. It works through specialised subcommittees and in association with the relevant subject committees, and over the years has built up a very close relationship with the Ministry of Finance. Both party relationships and the character of contemporary spending programmes prevent the committee from making major changes in Government plans, but it has some influence over details and sometimes over the timing of commitments. It is not uncommon for the Appropriations committee to tie particular expenditures to the need to secure its approval at the time of commitment, a practice which more old-fashioned constitutional theorists criticise as legislative interference with the prerogatives of the executive. The main significance of the work of the Appropriations committee undoubtedly lies in the discipline which it imposes on the Government to set out clearly and in detail its expenditure plans. Though this results in a financial framework which is in some respects uncomfortably rigid for contemporary needs and on too short a time-scale, the price may be worth paying if it helps to maintain a critical awareness in the Bundestag of the range and complexity of federal financial commitments.

Critics of the Bundestag often deplore its dedicated thoroughness, the monotony of many of its proceedings, and its relative neglect of public controversy and confrontation. Yet it is these characteristics which go far to explain why it has maintained substantial influence over what Governments propose to do, particularly in internal policy. To some extent all legislatures in the West face a dilemma: either they try to equip themselves in terms of knowledge and organisation in an attempt to keep pace with the growth of the executive, and thus run the risk of losing political colour and popular interest, or they stick to more traditional ideas of Parliament as a debating arena and place of challenge to the executive, with the concomitant risk of becoming hopelessly ill informed and ill equipped to understand or impede what the executive proposes. The Bundestag has so far preferred the first course, and in so doing has remained faithful to major elements in the German parliamentary tradition. Whether the rhythm of a Government–Opposition confrontation will allow it to stick to this course is a question for the future.

# CHAPTER 8

# The Challenge of Expanding Government

In Western Germany as elsewhere the growth in government functions has had the effect of bringing into sharper focus a number of important problems. Some of these concern the capacity of the system of government to perform effectively, to plan and provide the many services which are now expected of it. Since the pattern of government in the Federal Republic has expressed a commitment to structural diversity and the decentralisation of responsibilities, the problem of effective performance has often to be seen in terms of achieving closer integration and co-ordination within the network of federalism. A crucial factor working in the direction of more closely co-ordinated relationships is the pressure for better planning and control of public expenditure programmes. Taken all together they currently claim annually about 30% of the gross national product.[1] The scale of public spending is such that it is no longer possible to avoid taking a national view of the overall rate of increase and of the distribution of priorities within the total. At the same time this development suggests some reassessment of the role of government, and in particular of the Federal Government, in the management of the economy as a whole, and thus inevitably calls into question at least some elements in the social market economy doctrines which have hitherto shaped economic policy-making both in the private sector and in government.

[1]Estimate based on figures in *Finanzbericht 1972*, Bundesfinanzministerium, Bonn. It should, however, be stressed that the proportion of GNP devoted to public expenditure varies very much according to the definitions used and the way in which statistics are compiled. This is a crude estimate expressing total public spending of all kinds, including transfers, as a proportion of GNP at current prices.

We shall offer some remarks both on the question of closer co-ordination within the system of government and on the implications of this new awareness of the need for more centralised planning of expenditure programmes. As these will indicate, though there is a perception of some of the difficulties which are encountered within the present complex structure, this has not so far led to any radical reappraisal of it nor of the habits consolidated over the past twenty years or so. Indeed there is still considerable confidence in the adaptability of the system and in the capacity of those who work in it to achieve a gradual and piecemeal modification of relationships to meet some of the current needs.

Another aspect of the changing environment of government in the Federal Republic which it is important to mention in any appreciation of current trends is the impact of involvement in the process of European economic integration. The Federal Republic has been firmly committed to the success of the European Economic Community and by now many of the tasks of government have to be seen within their European dimension: they are no longer matters for purely domestic treatment. Though Community membership has so far had less impact on the character and operations of German government than on the general environment in which the economy functions, the further development of the Community may present a serious challenge to Germany policy conceptions, and to a lesser extent to the Federal Republic's complex institutional arrangements.

Finally, it has to be remembered that the expansion of government presents problems which go beyond operational effectiveness and the adaptability of institutions to new demands. It also affects the political responsiveness of the system, its ability to absorb and interpret competing claims and to embody them in acceptable policies. This brings us back to some reflections on the constitutional order of the Federal Republic and the political values which it has embodied.

## CO-OPERATION AND CO-ORDINATION

It is essentially the pressure for better and more uniform services, combined with the high degree of party cohesion and the commitment of all parties to programmes of economic and social action, which has sharpened the demand in the Federal Republic for closer co-ordination of the various layers of government both in the making of public policy and in its implementation. As already indicated in Chapter 5 this problem presents itself to a large extent in terms of adapting the federal system to the need for a higher degree of central guidance and direction. But before discussing further how far changes in this sense are taking place, it should be emphasised that, though the division of powers between the centre and the Länder constitutes the major element in the dispersion of responsibilities found in the structure of government, this is not the only aspect of diffusion inhibiting more centralised forms of direction. Already we have had occasion to refer to the autonomy and self-confidence of local authorities, whose position is protected both by their influence within their respective Länder, and by the fact that local ties and influence constitute the basis on which many national political careers are built. Consequently, in many sectors where services prescribed by federal legislation are actually provided by local agencies, the claims and interests of the local level of government cannot be discounted in framing the policies for them. The diffusion of powers in the public sector does, however, extend still further. In the regulation of industry and commerce, for example, the public law status of chambers of trade and chambers of agriculture gives them a stake in the carrying out of public policies which reinforces their influence as interests which must be consulted by the relevant departments in Bonn and in the provincial capitals. There are too many other "public law corporations" which play a big part in social regulation and in the provision of many public services, and which have, in virtue of status and functions, a degree of autonomy that is resistant to centralised discretionary political management and control. And even within the central area of government the preference for delegating executive functions to organisations separate from the central ministerial structure encourages autonomy and specialisation of interest.

It is, however, the question of the relationships between the Länder and the Federal Government which is most sharply posed by the demand for more comprehensive national policies, for the more uniform provision of services and for the more centralised supervision of how they are provided. This suggests a transition from reliance on the harmonisation of objectives between the different levels of government (for which the German term *Abstimmung*, suggesting negotiation leading to consensus, is so often used) to a more positive view of co-ordination in which the right of the leading component, the Federal Government, to shape

the processes of decision and execution is more extensively acknowledged.

In principle it might be held that in the sphere of relations between the
federation and the Länder there is little difficulty in finding a solution under
the existing rules. The federal authorities have wide powers of legislation
which enable them to determine policies in most sectors nationally and to
prescribe at least some of the conditions for their implementation. Yet in
fact if we consider a few recent examples of new powers conferred on all
levels of government, it has to be recognised that the shift towards a more
centralised view of co-ordination is hesitant and ambiguous. They tend to
show that whilst broad objectives can be laid down centrally, the present
way in which powers are conferred and exercised does not allow the Federal
Government a decisive role in the determination of priorities and of the
rate of progress aimed at. This underlines some of the limitations which are
inherent in the Federal Government being confined substantially to a
legislative definition of policy objectives: this generally means that objectives are set in broad terms without binding all the executive agencies to
specific programmes and without giving the central authority the right to
direct them in their day-to-day activities. Moreover, there may be a
fundamental difficulty in relying so much on traditional concepts of law
and legislation for defining the conditions for so much contemporary
public activity. Often public policy now seems to require a high degree of
flexibility and a discretionary framework allowing constant adaptation. To
this the legal mould offers obstacles. There is also the fact that policy and
administration is often a continuum in which the problems and special
needs of the actual provision of services have to be taken into account in the
further development of policy, and this is made difficult by the way in
which the German approach to conferring powers maintains an institutional and conceptual separation between policy and administration.

Yet some changes in the co-ordinating role of the Federal Government
are emerging. This will be illustrated from three fields of domestic policy.
In two cases, urban redevelopment and financial guarantees for new investment in hospitals, the federation has concurrent powers and can, therefore,
regulate on a national basis. In the third case, education, the federal powers
are still very limited on paper, though, as will be seen, they may allow a
more interventionist view of federal co-ordination than is possible within
the more traditional framework.

In the course of 1971 legislation was passed conferring new powers on the appropriate authorities, principally the Länder and local authorities, to effect schemes of slum clearance and town redevelopment.[2] The measure strengthened local planning powers and required local authorities to set the use of its provisions within the broad context of a local "social plan". The Federal Government becomes involved in the process of urban renewal chiefly as a result of provisions allowing it to make financial contributions to those costs not covered by the return on particular redevelopment schemes, though more indirectly it is acquiring a very wide interest in urban land use planning, partly as a result of the growing preoccupation with the environment, and partly in the wake of the rapid rise in land values. Provisionally a programme of financial aid for town redevelopment schemes was included in the 1971 budget and the aim is to have a continuing programme in the future. The legislation limits the federal share of costs to one-third of the total, the balance being borne by the Länder and local authorities. As for the drawing up and agreeing of programmes, the process prescribed leaves most of the initiative with the local and Länder authorities, and without giving the federal ministry any clear right of detailed approval.[3]

In a limited way the measure marks an accretion of federal influence. The Federal Government gets a financial stake in an area from which it was previously absent, it secures rights of continuing consultation with the Länder on the progress of programmes, it is guaranteed a regular flow of information (though not in very much detail), and in some sectors such as experimental schemes or those which are undertaken for special economic reasons it is enabled to influence priorities by discriminating in favour of particular schemes. Nevertheless, the formal framework carefully preserves the principle of collaboration between independent authorities. Much of the financial responsibility remains with the lower tiers of government, thus strengthening them in the selection of schemes for support, they possess virtually all the administrative resources for actually drawing up programmes and putting them through (the relevant federal ministry, now

[2]The legislation in question is the Städtebauförderungsgesetz, *BGBl*, July 1971.

[3]The constitutional basis for federal aid was provided by the new Art. 104 (a), added to the Basic Law in 1969. In particular it legitimises federal aid to the Länder for projects deemed desirable to maintain economic stability or to even out differences in economic resources.

entitled Planning, Town Development and Building, is still small), and the general rules covering the conditions applicable to federal aid have to be agreed with the Länder. The rate of progress does, therefore, depend very much on how the lower tiers use the provisions. The federal minister may seek to encourage and persuade if he thinks this necessary, but his means of exerting direct pressure are still slender.

In the case of hospital development the Federal Government has also recently assumed powers which enable it to make contributions to capital expenditure on new developments and to regulate charges.[4] Here we are concerned only with new developments because it is this aspect which involves finance and some degree of direct federal intervention. Legislation was introduced at the end of 1970 and passed eventually in March 1972.[5] It imposed on the Länder the duty of preparing medium-term programmes of hospital development and gave the Federal Government the right to contribute up to one-third of what the Länder spend on particular kinds of scheme. As with the previous example, the responsibility for drawing up programmes and for selecting annually projects for support rests with the Länder. Machinery is provided representing the two main levels of government to examine plans (with the chairmanship rotating rather than remaining with the federal Health minister), and there is also provision for a body representing the hospital interests and other qualified groups to advise on the standards required for satisfactory hospital services and on charges. (Hospitals are by no means a state service in the Federal Republic: a large contribution is made by private agencies, social insurance bodies, charitable associations, etc. The Länder, and to a larger extent local authorities, also run hospitals.) Except in relation to teaching hospitals attached to universities, the Federal Government cannot pay grants to specific institutions nor insist on a centralised determination of investment priorities. Again, what has happened in the first place is that the federal financial obligation has been extended. For the moment the rate of progress in this field still depends mainly on Länder initiatives, and the federal Government could not start talking realistically of "its hospital programme". Nevertheless, having once established a policy responsibility of this kind and entered into a financial commitment, it is unlikely that the federal ministry will retreat. The ground has been marked out for an increase in

[4]By the addition in 1969 of item 19(a) to Article 74 of the Basic Law.
[5]*Krankenhaussicherungsgesetz, BGBl*, June 1972.

federal knowledge of this field—which means an increasing capacity to respond to demands relevant to it—and the federal ministry and Länder are from now on associated in institutions which have a broad oversight of progress.

The education sector has been entirely managed by the Länder until recently. The conferment on the federation in 1969 of powers to contribute to the cost of new university development, along with the duty of collaborating with the Länder in working out a general plan for educational development, represented a major break with past experience.[6] What is of particular significance here is that because these items of development came into the new category of "joint tasks" the opportunities for federal involvement in the planning stage become greater than in the more traditional examples just quoted where the federation is making use of its ordinary concurrent powers. Though it is true that the federal Ministry of Education and Science remains strictly excluded from direct involvement in the educational services of the country, its right to sit down with the Länder in order to work out plans has been recognised. The planning machinery, which was described earlier in Chapter 5, works slowly, and this has been particularly so on the broader issue of agreeing an education plan (Bildungsplan). This was under consideration from 1970 to 1973, and has appeared only with reservations from Länder doubtful about some of the objectives in it. For example, Länder with CDU/CSU majorities are on the whole reluctant to accept the principle of comprehensive school organisation which the present government in Bonn appears to favour. However, an "education plan" is something so broad in character that it is doubtful how effective an instrument it can be for actually determining education policy and the levels of spending throughout the country. In contrast, federal participation in the financing of university development went through the new machinery much more rapidly. A federal contribution rising from 1100 million DM in 1971 to 2000 million DM in 1975 was agreed.

The effects of federal involvement in planning some aspects of education and in making a financial contribution have not yet been dramatic: on some issues there is sharp political controversy and prudence requires that the federal Ministry of Education and Science should proceed cautiously. But because the planning machinery brings the Federal Government in as

[6]See Chapter 5.

an equal partner of the Länder collectively,[7] the scope for federal initiative is wider than in the majority of other sectors, where at best the federation is dependent on giving support to programmes over the content of which it has only severely limited influence.

One feature is common to all these examples. This is the growth of federal financial aid. In the first two cases the amounts are relatively modest, contributions of about 150 million DM per year for urban renewal and rather less to service interest charges on hospital investment. In the higher education field the federal contribution, excluding the financing of research, is already running at over 1000 million DM per year and is intended to cover half of the total capital cost involved. Yet the scale may not be decisive. What really matters is that this represents a rather open departure from the traditional principle which has governed financial relations between the centre and the provinces, namely that the Länder (and local authorities) should receive a share of total revenues adequate to meet their obligations. The shift to something much nearer a grant-in-aid carries with it the prospect of growing federal influence over the terms on which the grant is made. Of course federal aid to the Länder is not an innovation: it has been practised haphazardly for a long time. The difference now is that the technique is being used more widely, and that wherever federal aid is being offered roughly similar conditions are being applied to its provision. Significant amongst these is the requirement that all participants must relate their schemes to a medium-term public expenditure programme. Federal interest in the rate of growth of commitments is thus underlined.

It is hard to see the ultimate effects of these and similar developments on the system of government. For those who think in traditional legal categories they express a blurring of powers and duties which will make the system both more difficult to operate and probably less efficient. For the defenders of federalism, usually found in CDU/CSU-ruled Länder or in richer Länder ruled by the SPD/FDP such as Hamburg or North Rhine Westphalia, they are bound to represent an erosion of the autonomy which the Länder have to a large extent enjoyed so far. But those who support stronger central initiatives welcome them as a step in the right direction and as a means of bringing greater coherence into the application of national policies.

[7]The distribution of votes with eleven to the Länder and eleven to the Federal Government ensures this.

What has been happening in respect of co-ordination through federal influence and support in recent years represents rather the beginnings of a transition to something more centrally controlled than a definite change of relationships. So far the emphasis remains on providing a national legislative framework within which initiatives must be taken at the executive levels, with the Federal Government brought in chiefly as a source of supplementary finance and with limited opportunities to influence priorities and the rate of progress. But the power of the purse is vital, and as knowledge of the services supported grows within the federal bureaucracy, so the potential capacity of the federal ministries to reach down into administrative operations is likely to grow. In this way the door has been opened to an increasingly active federal co-ordinating role.

## PLANNING THE USE OF RESOURCES

The planning of public expenditure over a longer time span than that of traditional annual budgets is to a large extent but another aspect of the co-ordination of policies and the determination of priorities. But the planning of public spending in the Federal Republic raises issues which go beyond changes in political and administrative procedure: it affects firmly held views about the role of the state in the economy and the powers of government. The post-war reconstruction of the German economy took place on terms which rejected planning notions and did not see state spending as a desirable and decisive instrument of economic steering. One sign of change was recognition in the early sixties of the need for some means of forecasting economic growth and prospects. This already involved some reassessment of the role of government, if only because it confirmed that the provision of data about economic trends was a public responsibility. Then within a few years came official recognition that the scale and content of public expenditure has a major impact on the economy and that this inevitably requires a more interventionist role by governments. Thus the shift towards conscious medium-term expenditure planning in 1967 and after called into question at least some elements in the social market economy ideology.

This ideology allowed in principle only a minimal role to the state. Its more strictly economic components emphasised market competition and stability of the currency as key factors in economic growth and the main-

H

tenance of equilibrium, whilst the social components, rather uneasily grafted on to neo-Liberal stock, underlined the autonomy of all the "social partners" within the framework of the competitive order. True, there was no explicit rejection of the legitimacy of public regulation of the framework or ground rules within which the economy had to operate, nor of specific acts of public support for economic developments (often by provision of fiscal incentives and subsidies). But there was wholehearted rejection of the *dirigisme* associated with planning conceptions and far more faith in the ability of the banking system to steer the economy than in a beneficent supervision by the Government.[8] In keeping with this outlook the regulation of the money supply, a vital factor in post-war economic policy, has rested with the Federal Bank, whilst until the later sixties deficit spending by the state was firmly prohibited by both budgetary law and the powers of the Bank itself.[9] The decentralised structure of political institutions also reduced the role of the central Government.

During the years of rapid economic reconstruction and growth it was possible to finance a rising level of public services through relatively stable (though high) rates of taxation. The obstacles to using public spending as an economic regulator did not constitute a serious embarrassment in a society in which the cardinal economic problems appeared to have been solved—how to secure full employment with stable prices, high growth rates and a favourable balance of payments.

By the mid-sixties this situation was showing signs of change. The economy continued to expand at a rate of between 4% and 5% per year and inflationary pressures were generally contained. But the demand for public services was beginning to rise steeply and budgets at all levels of government were increasing at a rate which threatened to outstrip the rate of growth of available resources. The economic recession of 1966–7 administered a shock which persuaded many people that the automatic nature of the economy's march to prosperity could no longer be taken for granted, and that the Federal Government needed wider powers if it were to be enabled to act to

[8]See A. Shonfield, *Modern Capitalism*, chaps. XI and XII, OUP, 1965, for reflections on German attitudes to planning and the use of state powers. Mr Shonfield's main concern is with planning concepts, and perhaps as a result of this he tends to underestimate the *laissez-faire* component in post-war German economic thinking.

[9]Revision of budgetary procedure took place in 1969 and the restrictions on credit financing were loosened, though not so far as to encourage it. Meeting expenditure from revenue is still important.

keep the economy on course. This meant, *inter alia*, that there had to be a new approach to public expenditure planning. It was recognised that the time-scale of much spending had changed, and that the scale and content of the programmes could no longer be virtually ignored in the context of the overall management of the economy.

The outcome, already alluded to in another context, was the Law on Stability and Growth of 1967 and the introduction of medium-term financial planning. These developments had far-reaching implications. They committed the Federal Government to an active counter-cyclical policy in which the Länder were to be joined through membership of the Trade Cycle Council set up in 1967. It became accepted doctrine that expenditure commitments should be planned in a way which would take account of their impact on the development of the economy as a whole. In other words, public expenditure control was raised to the status of a tool of macro-economic management. These changes took account of the fact that Federal expenditure is only part of the total demand of the public sector on resources by bringing the Länder into the new system by the establishment in 1968 of the Financial Planning Council. Thus the capacity of the Federal Government to shape overall financial and economic policy was substantially increased. This was to be done on the one hand by joining the Länder with the federal authorities in agreements to medium-term projections of expenditure (i.e. a five-year period) and on the other by enabling the Federal Government (with the agreement of the Bundesrat) to require the other levels of government to co-operate in a variety of counter-cyclical financial measures.

On paper the development of medium-term financial planning since 1967–8 looks persuasive. There has been a significant strengthening of the federal Finance ministry, the Government has steadily gained a clearer picture of forward commitments both within its own sphere and at other levels, and a substantial amount of information about expenditure plans and their economic significance and relationship to resource assessments is now published. Yet the record of continued increases in federal spending above forecast levels suggests that the system is not proof against particular ministerial demands, whilst in the Länder and local government the rates of increase in spending have generally exceeded those in the federal Budget, in part as a result of new responsibilities laid on the Länder by federal provisions. This suggests that as a system for keeping public expenditure within projected limits it is still somewhat fragmentary. Indeed there is no doubt that interest is still heavily concentrated on annual budgetary appropriations and that the methods used for forecasting medium-term expenditure trends are not yet highly sophisticated. Some of the difficulties are institutional. The Federal Government does not "control" spending outside its own field. At best it can agree guidelines and use some of the means at its disposal to influence the subordinate bodies in the right direction. In essentials, therefore, medium-term financial planning for the public sector remains a co-operative venture, and one in which those involved are often willing to act in a pre-emptive fashion to strengthen their own claims on resources.

Given favourable conditions this rather moderate reception of Keynesian demand management doctrine may prove adequate. But whether this turns out to be so will depend on political and economic factors. If there were shifts of opinion in favour of much more unified national services in certain sensitive sectors such as education, this would imply stronger federal control. Likewise a preference for raising the share of the national product devoted to public programmes, as expressed by the Left wing of the SPD for example, would also be likely to strengthen the federal role. Another crucial aspect is the development of the economy. Were the rate of growth to flatten out significantly—and there are signs that this may happen—the gap between the rate of growth of available resources and the rate of growth in the demand for public services would widen. In this situation the determination of priorities becomes a more difficult political problem and it is likely that it could be dealt with only by increasing the powers at the centre to control commitments lower down in the system.

The current style of co-ordinated medium-term expenditure planning represents a compromise between recognition of the inadequacies of the previous absence of public sector financial planning and respect for the separate interests institutionalised in the system of government. But it has not yet been put to the test in really difficult conditions, and there is some reason to doubt whether it could respond with sufficient speed to the need for radical changes either in levels of spending or in the distribution of priorities if this became necessary.

Let us now turn to some further effects of these changes. From a view of public expenditure as economically neutral, which went along with acceptance of the old ideal of balanced budgets, there has been a transition to acceptance of the importance of public spending as a tool of government economic policy. This has to be seen alongside the increase in support for the Social Democrats with their preference for more public services and "planning where necessary".[10] There is now a political basis for a more active view of the state's role in the economy. Yet rather surprisingly the changes in economic thinking underlying the policies of the Federal Government have remained within narrow limits. There is continued support for maintaining a competitive market economy, an emphasis on re-establishing price stability in the face of the present inflationary trends, a commitment in principle to containing inflationary increases in public spending, and a strong preference still for relying more on monetary policy than on other forms of intervention to maintain internal economic equilibrium. In international trade and monetary policy too the Federal Republic continues to oppose dirigiste measures in a situation in which its liberal stand leaves it increasingly isolated. All this owes something to the influence of Professor Schiller, Economics minister from 1966 and joint Economics and Finance minister from mid-1971 until his resignation in the middle of 1972. His support for neo-Liberal economic doctrine appeared to grow in intensity the longer he stayed in office. His dislike of state interference with market forces, his hostility to tax increases which in turn forced him to oppose too rapid a rise in public spending, and his hostility to exchange controls eventually led to his break with the SPD. Yet his departure alone made any marked shift in economic policy impossible in the run-up to the election of 1972. Moreover, there is plenty of evidence that the leadership of the SPD, sensitive both to public opinion and to the views of its Free Democrat coalition partner, remains for the most part favourable to reliance on the traditional approach to economic management, and in particular to using monetary policy in the interests of price stabilisation. This brings us back to organisational questions and the dispersion of powers.

Except for just over a year between 1971 and 1972 the Federal Republic has always had a division of responsibilities between a powerful Economics ministry and the Finance ministry. Until the development of financial planning outlined above the Finance ministry was primarily a traditional ministry for establishing the budget (i.e. putting together financial demands) and for taxation. Macro-economic policy, trade policy, com-

[10]This is the famous formula used in the Godesberg Programme of 1959: "as much competition as possible—as much planning as necessary!"

mercial regulation and responsibility for currency and credit rested with Economics, though effectively the Federal Bank looked after monetary policy. The changes after 1967 tended to increase the influence and economic policy interests of Finance, a development masked for a while after 1969 by the ascendancy of Professor Schiller and then by his control of both departments. The reshaping of the Government at the end of 1972 has led to a marked strengthening of Finance, to which monetary problems have been transferred from Economics. Though the latter remains responsible for trade cycle policy (*Konjunkturpolitik*), and is headed by a member of the FDP, its means of making its influence felt have been diminished and it is now more like a ministry for trade and industry. However, these changes do not mean that Finance becomes the unchallenged arbiter of economic policy, and one of the principal reasons for this lies in the position and functions of the Federal Bank.

The Federal Bank is unusual in enjoying both extensive powers and a high degree of autonomy under the Federal Bank Act of 1957. Its responsibility is primarily to ensure the stability of the currency, and to this end it has wide powers over the whole credit and banking system. The determination of interest rates is within its competence and it plays a decisive part in managing the foreign exchange market. Though the council of the Bank is appointed by the Federal Government, it operates independently and is not subject to instructions. It has not hesitated on occasion to make its views known publicly. Nor is it uncommon for the Bank's President to attend Cabinet meetings in order to advise ministers on measures he deems desirable in the management of the economy.[11]

There is little doubt that over the years the Bank has used its considerable powers with great skill and a high degree of success. In this it has nearly always had the support of Governments and usually of public opinion too. Indeed the acceptability of such an autonomous regulator of monetary policy can only be explained against the background of strong public commitment to price stability and firm control of the monetary supply to that end. The position of the Federal Bank goes a long way towards explaining why the Finance ministry cannot claim (and probably does not

[11]The Federal Bank demonstrated its independence shortly after Professor Schiller's resignation in July 1972 by issuing a public statement underlining its responsibilities and defending the line it had taken in recommending measures to control the inflow of foreign exchange, to which Schiller had been opposed.

wish to) an overall responsibility for assessing and influencing all the major variables in the economy. Its powers are balanced not only by those of the Economics department, but by those of the Bank, which in turn is largely free from political tutelage. There are, of course, some clouds on the horizon which might disturb what has so far been a successful partnership. Acute difficulties in international monetary relations are forcing the Government to identify itself more publicly with decisions of the Bank. For social and political reasons the resort to restrictive internal monetary policies may at some stage be challenged. The growing volume of public expenditure has already made the Government's role in economic management more prominent. And there is an undercurrent of hostility towards the Bank as a symbol of the capitalist economic order. Circumstances could, therefore, arise in which a Government might be compelled to undermine the Bank's independence. The price it would have to pay, however, would be to assume responsibility itself and there is so far no decisive evidence of a desire to take on such a burden.

Moreover, there might be many intangible losses if the dispersion of responsibilities for economic and financial questions were replaced by the dominance of a single Treasury or Finance ministry wisdom. From 1949 on there has been competition between Finance and Economics; the central bank was powerful and independent; during the sixties bodies such as the Experts for the Appreciation of the General Development of the Economy and the Trade Cycle Council began to make a contribution to economic policy-making; there was too the "concerted action", a consultative device established by Professor Schiller to bring industry, trade unions and public authorities into the discussion of economic trends and policies; then after 1968 there was the Financial Planning Council to co-ordinate public expenditure programmes. In these different ways a relatively loose texture of economic management and policy-making has been maintained in which opinions have had to some extent to prove themselves in competition with each other. This has its weaknesses, but equally has also made a contribution to the wider public understanding of economic issues, to a wider sense of responsibility on the part of public and private interests involved in economic decisions, and thus in an indirect way to maintaining an environment conducive to continued economic growth.

## THE EUROPEAN COMMUNITY
### DIMENSION

It has been suggested tentatively and with many qualifications that the trends so far discussed are working towards some reinforcement of the position of the central political authority. Yet this is happening at a time when the Federal Republic is deeply committed to the process of integration within the European Economic Community, and when its national Government is, therefore, losing some powers. Thus there is not only a problem of how to adapt relationships internally to the need for more closely co-ordinated management of public policies: there is equally the challenge of working within a framework in which both methods and objectives must express a consensus acceptable to other European states with different habits and expectations.

The Federal Republic identified itself with the cause of European integration for two main reasons. One was the political conviction that this was essential in order to re-establish good relations with her partners in Western Europe, and in particular with France. This was the consideration which weighed most heavily with Adenauer in 1950–1 and again in 1955–7 when the Treaty of Rome was being drawn up. The other was economic. It was clear that the creation of a customs union and the disappearance of trade barriers within it would bring great advantages to German industry. Nor is there any doubt that, with the achievement of a common market in Western Europe, German exports and foreign investment have surged ahead.

The first decade or so of the process of economic integration did not present serious problems for the Federal Republic, though the relationship with France became increasingly difficult after 1963. This was the result of the conflict between the French desire to make economic integration in the Community dependent on acceptance of French views about internal structure and attitudes towards the rest of the world, and the German commitment to close relations with Washington and preference for liberal trade policies. But during this period the Federal Republic was able to absorb fairly easily the domestic changes required by Community membership. There was broad political acceptance of the course which had been followed. The gradual adaptation of the German economy to Community regulations establishing the customs union and harmonising the conditions of competition in it did not provoke serious problems, and as for the common agricultural policy which painfully took shape by 1966, though this involved considerable German indirect support for French and Italian agriculture, it also embodied a structure of price support and modernisation subsidies which were not unwelcome to German agriculture. Moreover, German Governments were already giving extensive support to the agricultural industry: the effect of Community policies has been chiefly to shift responsibility for some of this from Bonn to Brussels.

It is probably impossible to distinguish the impact of Community membership on the structure and methods of government from the influence of so many other domestic changes which have taken place. In dealing with Community affairs there has been both diffusion and concentration. Much of the responsibility for the handling of business coming from Brussels has rested with the European division of the Economics ministry, thus underlining the extent to which the Community has been seen as an economic undertaking. But other ministries, notably Foreign Affairs, Agriculture, Finance and more recently Transport, have also been closely involved in Community business. A variety of co-ordinating devices have been set up to give greater cohesion to German policy-making in the Community, but on the whole these have not been so successful as the more tightly organised control of Community matters achieved in Paris. This has been one factor contributing to the relatively modest impact which the Federal Republic has had on the political development of the Community and on the manner in which the Brussels administrative system has developed.

In some areas Community membership has modified policy responsibilities considerably. A very substantial part of the policy-making formerly in the hands of the Agriculture ministry has shifted to Brussels or become a matter for negotiation with the Commission of the Community. The Economics and Finance ministries have felt the impact of the limits laid down by Community policies, though this has not so far affected crucial core sectors such as budgetary policy. An increasing number of senior federal officials have to work within the European dimension as the boundaries of "harmonisation" are pushed further outwards. There have been big changes in the activities of organised interests, many of which must maintain as close contacts in Brussels as they do in Bonn. There have been consequences too for the Bundestag, which so far has been the only Parlia-

H*

ment in the Community to establish a comprehensive method of scrutinising European legislation. Admittedly this depends on the usual private scrutiny in specialised committees and has of necessity little public effect. Nevertheless, it has been a sign of the seriousness with which parliamentarians regard the growing bulk of Community regulation which both supplements and replaces domestic legislation. Even the Länder have been drawn into the affairs of the Community and maintain a listening post in Brussels. Their involvement has been inescapable (and often productive of cumbersome administrative machinery) in questions affecting education and vocational training, but has often been necessary on economic questions too, for example in late 1972 in the adaptation of internal agricultural support measures to Community participation in them. Moreover, with the prospect of a Community regional policy the Länder will be affected even more directly.

Nevertheless, though the effects of Community membership have been pervasive, they have not so far had very decisive effects either on the policy discretion of Governments and legislatures in many important areas, or on the working style and relationships within German administration. To a large extent this is simply because the Community has so far not advanced a long way along the road to full economic union. What has been achieved up to now has been compatible with the preservation of a high degree of national autonomy. Furthermore, along with the growth of the Community and the pursuit of integration at the European level, there has been a growing preoccupation with new problems which so far, despite the fact that some of them transcend frontiers, are still primarily matters of domestic responsibility: improving the environment, traffic control and road development, restructuring the education system, reforming the penal code, to mention a few examples. That Community membership has also not inhibited the German Government from pursuing new initiatives on major political problems is demonstrated by the changes in relationships with the Soviet Union and Eastern European states which have taken place since 1970. Indeed the Ostpolitik has done more to identify the Federal Republic as an independent actor in international affairs than any action ever taken within the Western European framework.

But if we underline the extent to which Community membership has not yet become a dominant element in any analysis of the German system of government, we must also indicate briefly some of the ways in which it may in the future throw up awkward political choices. Further progress towards economic union has serious implications for budgetary and monetary autonomy of the member states of the Community. Though welcoming such progress in principle, German Governments have been hostile to moving forward by the application of policies which might be both dirigiste and restrictive. This has generally meant opposition to measures which would weaken the discipline provided by orthodox management of the monetary supply and to interventionist controls over exchange rates and the movement of funds. Underlying this stand is a dislike of policies which might force the Federal Republic to import the inflationary pressures which other Community members may, for political and social reasons, be unwilling to contain, though with the recent rapid rise in domestic inflation this objection appears less convincing.

So far, therefore, German Governments have been somewhat ambivalent about pushing too vigorously the cause of economic union, doubting their capacity to convince their partners in the Community of the validity of the economic policies which they have pursued and fearing that progress might be achieved only on terms which would weaken the German economy and thrust new responsibilities on a Government which is not keen to assume them. For undoubtedly major steps in the direction of economic and monetary union could have disturbing effects on relationships within the German system of government. Depending on how it were achieved, monetary union might upset the balance between the banking system and the departments of government concerned with economic affairs, whilst a move towards harmonisation of budgetary policies, presumably entailed by effective economic union, would require more centralised control of the position internally in order to meet the requirements of harmonising budgetary policies at the Community level.

There is some irony in such prospects. If the European Community is to evolve into a closer union, it is hard to see how it can have anything other than a confederal structure. Of the member states (before and after January 1973) only the Federal Republic can offer the experience of working a decentralised, federal system of government. Looked at in theoretical terms it seems reasonable to argue that the Federal Republic has far more to offer to the future evolution of the Community in the shape of an administrative and political model than has any of the more centralised states in it. Yet there are signs that in the slow development of Community policies directed towards closer economic integration, the Federal Republic may find it hard to convince its neighbours of the soundness of its approach to economic policy and to the role of government in its application, whilst in the search for institutional models appropriate to the gradual merging of national sovereignties the influence of the experience of the centralised state may, paradoxically, continue to fascinate the European policy-makers. Perhaps in this sphere, as in others, the Federal Republic suffers from a lack of political *rayonnement* which is part of the penalty still being paid for the aberrations of the Third Reich.

## POLITICAL CHANGE AND THE RULE OF LAW

In the conditions of contemporary Western societies the stability of the system of government depends very considerably on its responsiveness to needs. This has two aspects. One is the ability of institutional structures to perform the tasks set by public policy and to show efficiency and adaptability in so doing. Thus, a system of government is likely to run into difficulties if it fails to provide benefits and service at least roughly commensurate with the level of expectations in the society. The other aspect of responsiveness is more strictly political: the capacity of the system to respond positively to demands and aspirations, to interpret and reconcile these, and to maintain a continuing stream of political consent.

The German system of government can so far show up a favourable record in both respects. Enough has been said already to indicate that in the provision of services and the maintenance of an acceptable framework for private action the complex institutional pattern has not proved as serious an impediment to efficient performance as might have been expected on *a priori* grounds. Undoubtedly critical questions are now being put more frequently about the adequacy of the institutions as now structured to handle some of the more pressing of contemporary problems. But the prevailing preference is still for working through well-tried and familiar structures rather than for radical experiment.

Turning to political responsiveness in the broader sense, success here is largely attributable to the manner in which political parties have developed and behaved in the past twenty years. The emergence of two major parties and the survival of a minor one has ensured that the institutional safeguards designed in 1949 to reconcile stable executive leadership with effective political representation have worked successfully. The parties have become deeply embedded in state and society. Though embracing as members only a small proportion of the electorate,[12] they are well organised throughout the country, providing a vital network of personal ties and group loyalties. In public affairs their influence is decisive at every level, from the parish pump right up to the central government. Like any other party system, the German one has its imperfections, the most serious perhaps being a too eager professionalism and a lingering tendency to sectarianism: the former leads members to absorb too easily the style and values of the public service, the latter keeps alive a kind of dogmatic irresponsibility, especially at the lower levels of party organisation. But the experience of the Federal Republic suggests that on the whole the parties have been able to provide responsible leadership at all levels and that they have understood how to define needs and to respond to demands in a constructive fashion.

In all this they have been assisted by the active pluralism of post-war German society which has permitted a vigorous and tenacious expression of competing interests. Naturally this has not excluded situations in which particular interests have been able to manipulate parties for their own purposes. But the dependence of the parties on sinister interests has nearly always been exaggerated: they are themselves too open to a wide range of interests to be the tool of any single interest, and for many years now the growing competition between the two major parties has forced both to show themselves responsive to all the major organised groups.[13]

Another factor which has favoured a serious view of the duty of parties to articulate interests and opinions in the society is the attitude towards the constitutional norms according to which the society has been governed. There are few European countries in which the language of constitutional law plays such a prominent part in political argument. It is easy to dismiss this as German legalism and formalism, a hangover from the past. But this

---

[12]Currently not more than 4% of the electorate of about 40 million are party members. The proportion of activists is, of course, far smaller.

[13]This view would be rejected by radical critics of the Federal Republic's political system, most of whom tend to see parties, and in particular the CDU/CSU and the FDP, as the trusty lieutenants of a few major business interests engaged in comprehensive manipulation of the society. Such arguments would command more respect if supported by serious empirical evidence, and if the terms used in them were more clearly defined. An example of such a critique is to be found in *Der CDU Staat* (2 vols.), edited by G. Schäfer and C. Nedelmann, Suhrkamp, 1969.

must be seen in relation to the situation from which the Federal Republic emerged. The reaffirmation of constitutional norms underpinned the process of political reconstruction, and had positive and beneficial effects in many directions, not least in giving legitimacy to the role of parties and influencing them to see that role in broader and more comprehensive terms than was ever possible before.

These remarks are not intended to suggest that the question of responsiveness can be regarded complacently as settled. In the Federal Republic, as elsewhere, the pattern of government has become more dense, public regulation weighs heavily, and the range of public activity widens continually. The very fact that the parties are so deeply involved in the direction of public affairs increases the risk that they become too closely identified with the executive apparatus and for this reason less sensitive to their representative functions. It is anxieties of this kind which have helped to stimulate discussion in the Federal Republic of the issue of participation. Originally the argument was fairly narrowly confined to industrial relations and to the case for co-determination in industry. At the beginning of the fifties progress was made with the introduction of worker co-determination in the management of the coal and steel industries, whilst throughout the rest of industry the rights of workers' representatives to participate through works councils in the supervision of social and personnel matters were recognised.[14] But the case for more participation is now put on a much broader front—in industry, in education, in local affairs, and in public administration—and with the aim of widening the area of decision-making to which it would apply. Whilst the demand is voiced by many as a serious plea for increasing direct individual involvement in the running of social and political institutions, it is, of course, for a section of the radical Left an element in a crusade against the whole social and political order. The more extreme versions of the participation case have little public backing, but the more moderate presentation of it seems to be gaining support, at any rate judging by the amount of discussion and the number of schemes which are put forward for different sectors of social life and public service organisation.

[14]There is a highly developed legal framework for the "Betriebsverfassung", the internal "constitution" of businesses. This was most recently added to by the Betriebsverfassungsgesetz of January 1972, which widened the rights of the works councils in industry considerably.

The difficulties in trying to widen participation are great and perhaps the whole case for it as currently presented has a Utopian quality. Meanwhile it is worth noting that in the discussion of how to increase opportunities for participation in the "self-management" of all kinds of institution, a number of problems suggested by the present character of German government are often overlooked. As previously indicated, some factors are now working towards stronger central direction in the governmental relations of the Federal Republic. Yet the extension of participation threatens to reinforce separation and particularism in public affairs. This underlines a dilemma: satisfaction of the demand for better and more uniform services suggests more centralisation, the case for participation, if pursued seriously, implies an even looser system, more difficult to co-ordinate and steer. Further, a more participatory society seems to require a high degree of confidence and informality in social relations as well as in relations between public bodies and citizens. Yet the continuing preference for the formal regulation of public powers and of the relationships between individuals and public authorities, this being closely linked with the prevalence of a judicial mode of resolving conflicts, indicates that these conditions of confidence are not yet met in the Federal Republic—or at any rate not fully. Unless the attitudes which sustain a certain rigidity of outlook on the part of both the citizen and public authority towards each other change, it is hard to see how wider participation can work satisfactorily or prove acceptable. And ironically, as is shown by the recent experience of many universities, when participation is extended without the right basis in individual and group relationships, it may simply institutionalise mistrust and actually reinforce the disposition to try to resolve disputes by invoking formal controls.[15]

If the interest in participation suggests that there is a critical awareness of some of the problems of political responsiveness, it cannot be said that the gradual extension of the role of the Federal Government at the expense of the lower levels, and in particular of the Länder, has yet become a major political issue. This is in part because public opinion supports more active government and improved public services, and accepts that much of the

---

[15]I refer here to numerous instances in the past five years in which individuals and groups in universities have had resort to the courts in the pursuit of intra-university disputes or in conflicts with the supervisory authorities. Inevitably such action makes relationships of mutual trust even more difficult to attain.

initiative must now come from the centre. It is also a result of the fact that only a small part of the population feels any strong provincial loyalties. Public opinion surveys indicate no strong dissatisfaction with the existing Länder, but equally relatively little commitment to them. The interests most closely associated with them are mainly within the public sector, including in particular politicians and public servants. These constitute strong and articulate groups in favour of maintaining the present pattern of executive action by consensus and co-operation. And so long as this system continues to perform adequately it is unlikely to be exposed to really powerful popular demands for greater centralisation. For this reason a gradual drift towards more centralised co-ordination rather than a drastic transference of powers to Bonn seems to be the most likely pattern for future development. A negotiated reduction in the number of Länder would find its place in such an evolution.

Let us come back finally to the stability of the legal and constitutional framework within which political life unfolds and governments operate. Though in this chapter we have deliberately highlighted some question-marks, they do not add up to a serious challenge to the Basic Law in its present form. The conviction is widely held that it has provided a satis-factory foundation for the new state: of the Basic Law it can fairly be said, "ce n'est que le provisoire qui dure". Its major conditions have survived intact and the political parties, except for a minority in the SPD, are still firmly committed to the values embodied in it. But the Basic Law has done more than provide a stronger framework than ever existed before for the development of democratic politics. One of its most significant effects has been to reinforce the legal mode of public action, the casting of govern-mental and administrative action, in the mould of formal and binding instruments. This followed naturally from the reaffirmation of law as the foundation of the policy. The nature of much contemporary public action and the tendency to see the responsibilities of government as all-embracing may suggest that this outlook is out of touch with reality, an obstacle to the kind of progress which some wish to see. But here one comes up against that aspect of the German system of government which has the deepest roots in the past, and which for this reason may be most resistant to change. The preference for a legal mode of public action expresses a particular view of how best to gain protection against the abuse of powers: it requires that powers should be defined in some detail and that their misuse be open to challenge before an authoritative body. But it is also an expression of the belief that public powers constitute some kind of unity—indeed this is the way in which the state is defined. It is these two complementary beliefs which explain why a system of government as internally differentiated as the German holds together, and even functions harmoniously. Of course, party affiliations and loyalties have come to play a major part in securing cohesion and resolving conflict between the various parts of the system. Yet this alone does not explain how it coheres. There is another equally important factor, German public law. Strengthened by the way in which the Basic Law has been applied and interpreted, public law in the broadest sense is still a vital ingredient in the cement which binds the system together. It ties all the separate institutions into a hierarchy of powers and provides a unifying framework for the operations of government. To an unusual extent the languages of law and politics overlap in the Federal Republic. Up to the present they have generally sustained and complemented each other. The character of West German government in the future will depend a great deal on whether it continues to be possible to maintain a fruitful relationship between the public law tradition and the style and aims of contemporary politics.

# Bibliography

This list contains only a small number of works which may be of value to the reader who wishes to pursue further some of the topics dealt with in this study. Many of the works footnoted are not listed here.

AMPHOUX, J. *Le Chancelier fédéral dans le régime constitutionnel de la République fédérale d'Allemagne.* Paris, 1962.

ARNDT, H. J. *West Germany: Politics of Non-planning.* Syracuse, 1966.

BARING, A. *Aussenpolitik in Adenauers Kanzlerdemokratie.* München/Wien, 1969.

BÖCKENFÖRDE, E-W. *Die Organisationsgewalt in Bereich der Regierung.* Duncker and Humblot, 1964.

BRECHT, A. *Federalism and Regionalism in Germany.* OUP, 1945.

BRECHT, A. and GLASER, C. *The Art and Technique of Administration in German Ministries.* Harvard, 1940.

CHAPUT DE SAINTONGE, R. A. *Public Administration in Germany.* London, 1961.

EBSWORTH, R. *Restoring Democracy in Germany: The British Contribution.* Stevens, 1960.

EDINGER, L. J. *Politics in Germany.* Little, Brown, 1968.

ELLWEIN, T. *Das Erbe der Monarchie in der deutschen Staatskrise. Zur Geschichte des Verfassungsstaates in Deutschland.* München, 1954.

ELLWEIN, T. *Das Regierungssystem der Bundesrepublik Deutschland.* Köln/Opladen, 1965.

ELLWEIN, T. and GÖRLITZ, A. *Parlament und Verwaltung. I. Teil: Gesetzgebung und politische Kontrolle.* Kohlhammer, 1967.

FRIEDRICH, C. J. and SPIRO, H. J. The Constitution of the German Federal Republic, in Litchfield, E. H. (Editor), *Governing Post-War Germany.* Ithaca, 1953.

GOLAY, J. F. *The Founding of the Federal Republic of Germany.* Chicago, 1958.

GROSSER, A. *Deutschlandbilanz.* München, 1970.

HENNIS, W. *Richtlinienkompetenz und Regierungstechnik.* Tübingen, 1964.

HENNIS, W. *Verfassung und Verfassungswirklichkeit.* Tübingen, 1968.

HERZ, J. H. Political views of the West German Civil Service, in Speier, H. and Phillips Davison, W., *West German Leadership and Foreign Policy.* Row, Peterson & Co., 1957.

HESSE, K. *Grundzüge des Verfassungsrechtes der Bundesrepublik Deutschland.* 3rd ed. Karlsruhe, 1969.

HIRSCH, J. *Parlament und Verwaltung, II. Teil: Haushaltsplan und Haushaltskontrolle in der Bundesrepublik.* Kohlhammer, 1968.

JACOB, H. *German Administration Since Bismarck: Central Authority versus Local Autonomy.* New Haven, 1963.

KAACK, H. *Geschichte und Struktur des deutschen Parteiensystems.* Köln/Opladen, 1971.

LOEWENBERG, G. *Parliament in the German Political System.* Ithaca, 1966.

McWINNEY, E. *Constitutionalism in Germany and the Federal Constitutional Court.* Leyden, 1962.

McWINNEY, E. Judicial restraint and the West German Constitutional Court, *Harvard Law Review,* **75,** 1961–2.

MERKL, P. H. Executive–Legislative federalism in West Germany. *APSR* **LIII,** 1959.

MERKL, P. H. *The Origin of the West German Republic.* OUP, New York, 1968.

NEUNREITHER, K-H. Federalism and the West German bureaucracy, *Political Studies* **VII,** 1959.

OPPEN, BEATE RUHM VON. *Documents on Germany under Occupation 1945–54.* OUP, 1955.

PINNEY, E. L. *Federalism, Bureaucracy and Party Politics in Western Germany. The Role of the Bundesrat.* Chapel Hill, 1963.

SCHATZ, H. *Der parlamentarische Entscheidungsprozess.* Meisenheim, 1970.

VERBA, S. Germany: The remaking of political culture, in Pye, L. and Verba, S. (Editors), *Political Culture and Political Development.* Princeton, 1965.

WELLS, R. H. *The States in West German Federalism.* New York, 1961.

WIESE, W. *Der Staatsdienst in der Bundesrepublik Deutschland.* Luchterhand, 1972.

ZUNKER, A. *Finanzplanung und Bundeshaushalt.* Metzner Verlag, 1972.

# Index

ADENAUER, KONRAD 6n, 32, 33, 38,
47, 48, 49, 51, 52, 53, 54, 56, 57,
59, 64, 71, 72, 75, 93, 115, 133
Administrative courts 14, 166–8
Agriculture, decline in numbers
employed in 39
Angestellter (employee) 145–6; see
also Public service
Aristocracy, effects of war on 40,
152
Austria, in Germany 2–4

Baden 3
Baden-Württemberg 33, 39, 99, 106,
136
BÄHR, OTTO 14
BAHR, EGON 57n
Basic Law 9, 15, 26, 27–9, 30, 44, 45,
46, 50, 84, 94, 100, 101, 102, 104,
105, 106, 107, 120, 123, 125, 127,
132, 142, 165, 166n, 169, 170,
189n, 190n, 208, 209
Basic rights 8–9, 15, 27
Bavaria 2, 99, 100, 106, 132, 136,
154
Beamter see Public service
Berlin, West 99, 100, 106
BISMARCK, OTTO VON 3, 4
BRANDT, WILLI 28n, 32, 34, 36n, 47,
52, 53, 54, 55, 57n, 58, 60, 65, 69,
115, 119, 133n, 151
BRAUER, MAX 119

Bremen 99, 10, 106, 136
BRENTANO, HEINRICH VON 70
Britain, post-war policy of, in Germany
23, 25
Budget, federal 95, 195, 197
Bundesrat 28, 62, 99, 105, 116, 120,
121, 122, 123, 125, 136, 137, 163,
171, 176n, 195
and legislation 106–10
Bundestag 11, 12, 28, 30, 31, 33, 36,
45, 47, 49, 50, 51, 53, 58, 61, 62,
64, 72, 79, 80, 82, 83, 85, 93, 96,
99, 106, 107, 108, 109, 120, 130,
133, 155, 157, 171, 173, 175,
176–84
committees of 52, 66, 67, 72, 78,
83, 84, 85, 86, 116, 162, 175, 179,
180, 181, 182–3, 201–2
Bureaucracy see Public service

Cabinet see Federal Government
Cabinet Committees see Federal
Government
Chambers of Agriculture 87
Chambers of Trade 87
Chancellor democracy 52
Chancellor, Federal 9, 11, 28, 45,
46–8, 71–2, 75
of the Reich 4, 5n
powers of 49–59
Chancellor's Office 49, 54, 56, 57–9,
65, 92, 93, 96, 155–6

213

Christian Democratic Union (CDU)
6, 31, 32, 33, 36, 37–8, 47, 50, 51,
52, 59, 70, 72, 83, 85, 119, 154,
155, 156, 191, 192
Christian Social Union 31, 37, 50, 51,
72, 83, 119, 155
Coalition agreement, 1961 48
Coalition politics 35, 36, 48, 51, 61, 64
Co-determination *see* Participation
Commissioner for the Efficiency of
Administration 174
Communist Party (KPD/DKP) 34
Concordat 1933 101, 169
Constitutionalism in nineteenth
century 7–12
Consultative committees 89–90, 162
Czechoslovakia 39

Defence Council 63
Deutsche Angestelltengewerkschaft
(DAG) 146
Deutscher Bauernverband 87
Deutscher Beamtenbund (DBB) 146,
157, 158
Deutscher Städtetag 87, 124
DICKENS, CHARLES xiii

Economic "miracle" 41–2
Economic policy 41–2, 150, 194, 199,
203–4
Education
policy 69, 134–5, 191
responsibilities for 118, 135, 191
EHMKE, HORST 58, 59
Elections 30–1, 32, 35
in Länder 33, 133
Electoral law 33, 33*n*
ERHARD, LUDWIG 33, 41, 47, 52, 53,
55, 58, 61, 72, 155
European Economic Community
186, 200–3
Experts for the Appreciation of the
General Development of the
Economy 90, 182, 199

Federal administration
dependent agencies of 78–80, 102
links with Länder 115–16
number of personnel in 76–7
relations within 91–6
structure of 74–80
Federal Archives 79
Federal Bank 198–9
Federal Constitutional Court 15, 16,
19, 26, 29, 33, 101, 104, 106, 157,
166, 168–71
Federal Court of Accounts 95, 173–5
Federal Government
committees of 55, 63–4
size of 55, 75
social character of 69–71
structure of 45–9, 56, 60, 62, 63–4,
68
Federal Office for Crime Detection 79
Federal Office for the Protection of the
Constitution 79
Federal Press Office 59
Federal Statistical Office 79, 80
Federalism
and absence of unitary tradition 2–7
and particularism 4, 5, 29
co-operative 102, 118, 124, 132, 134
financial basis of 120–6
principles of, in Federal Republic
100–5
revival of, in 1949 6–7, 28
structure and operation of 96,
98–131
trends in 114, 131–7, 185
Federation of German Industry (BDI)
87
Finance courts 166, 167
Financial planning 63, 94, 118, 129,
133, 193–9
Financial (Planning) Council 90, 94,
118, 129, 195
Foreign policy, conduct of 53–4
"Framework" laws 103–5, 135
France, policy of, in Germany 1945–9
23, 24

Franco-Prussian War 3
FREDERICK II, KING OF PRUSSIA 138
FREDERICK WILLIAM IV, KING OF
   PRUSSIA 8
Free Democratic Party (FDP) 31, 32,
   35, 36, 38, 47, 52, 54, 59, 72, 83,
   124, 155, 156, 192, 198

Gemeinden 127, 129
German Democratic Republic (DDR)
   ix, 39, 171*n*
German Empire 1871–1918 3–5, 10,
   11, 14, 46, 142
German Party (DP) 31
GLOBKE, HANS 57, 59
GNEIST, RUDOLF VON 13
GOPPEL, A. 134*n*
Grand Coalition 1966–9 32, 34, 36, 47,
   52, 60, 72, 77, 85, 90, 122, 155, 156

Hamburg 99, 100, 106, 123, 137, 192
HEGEL, G. W. F. 13, 16–17, 18
HEINEMANN, GUSTAV 60, 73
Hesse 99, 104, 106, 137, 154
Hesse-Darmstadt 3
HEUSS, THEODOR 73
HITLER, ADOLF 23, 142
Hospitals, expenditure on 190
Housing policy 41
HUMBOLDT, WILHELM VON 139

JELLINEK, GEORG 14
Judges in Federal Republic 165–7
Judicial controls 164–72
Juristenmonopol 141, 161

KAISEN, WILHELM 119
KANT, IMMANUEL 12–13
KIESINGER, KURT-GEORG 34, 47, 53,
   58, 72, 134*n*, 151
Königstein agreement 116
KOSCHNIK, H. 134*n*
KRONE, HEINRICH 55
KÜHN, HEINZ 134*n*

LABAND, PAUL 14
Labour courts 166
Länder
   administrative powers of 101–2,
      110–19, 136, 187–9
   as agents of the federation 102, 112
   constitutions of 100
   delegations of, in Bonn 116–17
   exclusive legislative powers of 105,
      112
   expenditure of 111, 113, 124–5, 193
   general characteristics of 4, 99–100
   impact on political parties 36, 151–2
   and local government 127, 128, 129
   personnel employed by 111
   revision of boundaries of 136–7, 208
Landtage 133, 177, 180
LEBER, GEORG 61
Legal formalism 13–14, 16
Legislative powers, division between
   federation and Länder 101, 102–5,
   135, 188–9
LEUSSINCK, HANS 69, 82
Liberals
   in Federal Republic *see* Free
      Democratic Party (FDP)
   in nineteenth century 8, 9, 13, 46
Local authorities 122, 123, 126–30,
   154, 187, 189
Lower Saxony 37, 99, 101, 106, 132,
   137, 169
LÜBKE, HEINRICH 72, 73
LÜCKE, PAUL 60, 77

Market economy doctrines 41–2, 197
Marshall Aid 42
Mediation Committee 108
Minister for the Affairs of the Defence
   Council 55, 63
Minister of Economics 61, 90
Minister of Education and Science 134
Minister of Finance 63, 93, 173, 175,
   183
Minister of Interior 63, 65

Minister of Justice   63
Minister of Transport   61
Minister without Portfolio   55, 57*n*
Ministerial responsibility   9, 46, 60, 82, 177
Ministers, federal   9, Chapters 3 and 4 *passim*
Ministries
    federal   65–71, 74–97
    relations between   91–6
    relations with the Bundestag   81–6
    relations with organised interests   86–9
    relations with other public bodies   81–91
Ministry of Agriculture   65, 75, 76, 87, 155, 201
Ministry for the Bundesrat and the Affairs of the Länder   65, 114
Ministry of Defence   63, 65, 66, 75, 76, 155
Ministry of Economic Co-operation   65, 75, 76
Ministry of Economics   60, 63, 65, 75, 76, 90, 94, 155, 197, 198, 201
Ministry of Education and Science   65, 69, 75, 76, 191
Ministry of Famliy Affairs   75, 155
Ministry of Federal Property   65, 75
Ministry of Finance   58, 60, 65, 75, 76, 78, 90, 92, 93, 94, 95, 155, 195, 197, 198, 199, 201
Ministry of Foreign Affairs   65, 66, 74, 75, 76, 155, 201
Ministry of Health   65, 75, 190
Ministry of Housing and Planning   65, 75, 76
Ministry of Inner German Relations   65, 75, 76
Ministry of Interior   65, 75, 76, 77, 77–80, 147*n*, 155
Ministry of Justice   65, 75, 76, 77, 155, 167
Ministry of Labour and Social Affairs   65, 75, 76, 77, 87, 148, 155

Ministry of Posts   65, 76
Ministry for Refugees   65, 75, 155
Ministry for Research and Technology   65, 66, 76
Ministry of Transport   65, 75, 76, 77, 112, 201
Mittelinstanz   127, 128, 130
Möhl, Robert von   13
Möller, Alex   61

Napoleon I   139
National Democratic Party (NPD)   33, 34
National Socialists, regime of   6, 15, 19, 22–3, 26, 27, 29, 40, 142, 165
Neo-Nazism   33
North Atlantic Treaty Organisation (NATO)   75
North German Confederation   3, 10
North Rhine Westphalia   99, 106, 136, 192

Officials   *see* Public service
Ombudsman, Military (Wehrbeauftragter)   179–80
Opposition, role of   32, 34, 51, 64, 82, 83, 109, 156, 179, 181
Organised interests   86–9, 205
Ostpolitik   110*n*, 202
ÖTV (Public Service and Transport union)   147

Papen, Franz von   5
Parliamentary State Secretaries   55, 60, 67–8, 77, 162, 174*n*
Participation   206–7
Petitions   180
Planning staff in Chancellor's Office   57, 58, 96
Plato   17
Poland   39

Political parties
   changes in, since 1949   30–1, 32–3,
      36, 38, 204–5
   minor   30–1
   structure of, and federalism   119
Polizeistaat   12
President, Federal   28, 44, 49, 50, 51,
   72–3, 106, 147
Proporz politics   36, 158
Prussia   2–4, 14, 19, 46, 99, 138, 139,
   140, 165
   dissolution of   6
   preponderance of   6
Public expenditure   123–5, 151, 185,
   193–7
Public law   14, 111, 131, 148, 161,
   208–9
Public service   20, 41, 138–63
   duties of   142–3, 149–53
   lawyers in   81, 139, 141, 161
   organisation of   144–9
   politics and   66–7, 141–2, 151,
      153–9, 163
   role of officials (Beamte) in   149–53
   size of   145
   training of   138–40, 148, 149


Questions in Bundestag   178


Radicalism
   of the Left   33, 34, 43, 170
   of the Right   33, 170
Rechtsstaat   8–16, 141, 165
Referat   78, 80
Refugee Party (GB-BHE)   31
Reichstag   11
REUTHER, ERNST   119
Revenue-sharing   120–6
Rhineland-Pfalz   99, 106, 137
Richtlinienkompetenz   45, 52
Rome, Treaty of   201
ROUSSEAU, J.-J.   17
Ruhrsiedlungsverband   130

Saarland   99, 100, 106, 123, 137
Saxony   2, 5
Schaumburg-Lippe   2
SCHEEL, WALTER   54
SCHILLER, KARL   60, 61, 62, 151, 197, 198
Schleswig-Holstein   37, 99, 106, 132,
   137
SCHMIDT, HELMUT   61, 151, 159n, 162n
SEEBOHM, HANS CHRISTIAN   61
Social change in Federal Republic   39,
   40–1
Social courts   166
Social Democratic Party (SPD)   6, 31,
   32, 34, 35, 36, 47, 48, 49, 51, 52,
   54, 59, 70, 72, 83, 85, 119, 124,
   127, 155, 156, 192, 196, 197, 208
Socialist Reich Party   33
Soviet Union   23, 24, 25, 39, 202
Sozialer Rechtsstaat   27–8
Stability and Growth, Law on   129,
   195
Stadtratsverfassung   26
Standing Conference of Education
   Ministers   115
State
   ideas of   1, 16, 17, 18–19, 209
   separation of, from society   16–20
State secretaries   67, 80, 155, 158, 159
STEIN, FREIHERR VOM   126
STOLTENBERG, GERHARD   61, 134n
STRAUSS, FRANZ-JOSEF   61, 178


Taxes, distribution of   120–5
Third Reich   see National Socialists
Thuringia   5
Trade Cycle Council   90, 118, 195, 199
Trade unions (DGB)   37, 87, 146, 147
Troeger Report   122, 134, 135


United States of America   24
   policy of, in Germany 1945–9   23,
      25, 26
United States Supreme Court   170

Universities and public service training
138–40
Urban redevelopment   188–9

Vogel Bernhard   134*n*

Waldeck   2

Wehner, Herbert   36*n*, 61
Weimar Republic   5–6, 11, 28, 30,
44, 46, 142
Westrick, Ludger   55, 59
Wissenschaftsrat   116
Württemberg   3

Zinn, August   119